LOOKING IN. ⌐ᴧ⌐ᴇᴿ LIFE

Tavistock Clinic Series

Margot Waddell (Series Editor)
Published and distributed by Karnac Books

Other titles in the Tavistock Clinic Series

Orders
Tel: +44 (0)20 7431 1075; Fax: +44 (0)20 7435 9076
Email: shop@karnacbooks.com
www.karnacbooks.com

LOOKING INTO LATER LIFE

A Psychoanalytic Approach
to Depression and Dementia in Old Age

Edited by

Rachael Davenhill

KARNAC

Extract (p. 24) from *The God of Small Things* by Arundhati Roy (1997) courtesy of Flamingo. Extract (pp. 26–27) from *Germs: A Memoir of Childhood* by Richard Wollheim (2004) reprinted by permission of the Waywiser Press, London. "Fathoms" (pp. 62–63) and "Geriatric"(pp. 201–202) reprinted by permission from R. S. Thomas, *Collected Later Poems: 1988–2000* (Bloodaxe Books, 2004). Extract (pp. 68–69) from *The Emigrants* by W. G. Sebald (1996) reprinted by permission of Vintage. Extract (pp. 77–78) from *The Heather Blazing* by Colm Toibin (Picador, 1992) reprinted by permission. Extract (pp. 90–92) from *The Prince of West End Avenue* by Alan Isler (1996), published by Jonathan Cape, reprinted by permission of the Random House Group Ltd. "The Pink Ribbon" (pp. 248–268) reproduced from *The Little Black Book of Short Stories* by A. S. Byatt, published by Chatto & Windus; reprinted by permission of The Random House Group Ltd. "Conveying the Experience of Alzheimer's Disease through Art" (pp. 298–330) reproduced by permission of Galerie Beckel-Odille-Boïcos, Paris.

First published in 2007 by
Karnac Books
118 Finchley Road
London NW3 5HT

British Library Cataloguing in Publication Data

A C.I.P. for this book is available from the British Library

ISBN: 978–1–85575–447–8

Edited, designed, and produced by Communication Crafts

Printed in Great Britain

www.karnacbooks.com

For my parents and grandparents

CONTENTS

SERIES EDITOR'S PREFACE

Margot Waddell

Since it was founded in 1920, the Tavistock Clinic has developed a wide range of developmental approaches to mental health which have been strongly influenced by the ideas of psychoanalysis. It has also adopted systemic family therapy as a theoretical model and a clinical approach to family problems. The Clinic is now the largest training institution in Britain for mental health, providing postgraduate and qualifying courses in social work, psychology, psychiatry, and child, adolescent, and adult psychotherapy, as well as in nursing and primary care. It trains about 1,700 students each year in over 60 courses.

The Clinic's philosophy aims at promoting therapeutic methods in mental health. Its work is based on the clinical expertise that is also the basis of its consultancy and research activities. The aim of this Series is to make available to the reading public the clinical, theoretical, and research work that is most influential at the Tavistock Clinic. The Series sets out new approaches in the understanding and treatment of psychological disturbance in children, adolescents, and adults, both as individuals and in families.

Looking into Later Life is a powerful volume. Its contents have been gestating in the mind of the Editor for over twenty years. The book belongs to a long tradition at the Tavistock of work focused on the mental and emotional well-being of the elderly. It draws on the Old Age Workshop at present running from the Adult Department as well as on the multidisciplinary experiences of those attending the course on Psychodynamic Approaches to Old Age.

The book applies psychoanalytic thinking to areas that have generally attracted very little sustained attention over the years. In two parts of the book—"Mainly Depression" and "Mainly Dementia"—accounts are offered of clinical, consultative, and supervisory work, whether with individuals, couples, groups, or institutions. Each part brings sensitivity and psychoanalytic expertise to bear on areas of mental functioning that are considered to be among the most opaque and refractory and are certainly outside the compass of psychodynamic thinking as normally conceived.

The range and depth of the work represented in this volume are impressive. Politically, it is hard hitting in terms of addressing the woeful inadequacy of any proper provision of psychological care for this age group. Psychoanalytically it is informative and accessible in its descriptions both of some of the centrally relevant psychological mechanisms, but also of the reflective observational method that is so clearly crucial in this kind of practice. All authors display enormous insight and responsiveness to the clinicians, professionals, and carers about whom they are writing.

Unusually, other kinds of account of mental deterioration are also included: one fictional (a short story by A. S. Byatt), one through a series of paintings by the artist himself, and two first-person descriptions of, respectively, the impact of serious physical illness and that of Alzheimer's.

The other chapters, all but one written by staff members at the Tavistock, explore a variety of different ways in which the later years of life may be weathered, mentally and emotionally. There is a general emphasis on the delicate relationship between internal resources and external provision and on the different powerful emotions—rage, despair, fear, abandonment—that are inevitably stirred in workers and sufferers alike. Ultimately, however, the book is realistic, compassionate, and encouragingly hopeful.

ABOUT THE EDITOR AND CONTRIBUTORS

ANNE AMOS is a Fellow of the Institute of Psychoanalysis. She has been a member of staff of the Tavistock Centre for Couple Relationships and currectly works full time as a psychoanalyst in private practice.

DAVID ARMSTRONG is a Principal Consultant at the Tavistock Consultancy Service, the Tavistock & Portman NHS Trust.

ANDREW BALFOUR studied English Literature before going on to train as a Clinical Psychologist at University College London and then as an Adult Psychotherapist at the Tavistock Clinic. He currently works as a Consultant Clinical Psychologist at the Tavistock Clinic, where he teaches in the area of old age. He is also Head of Clinical Services at the Tavistock Centre for Couple Relationships.

A. S. BYATT is the author of several novels, books of short stories, and criticism. Her works have been translated into at least 28 languages. Her most recent novels are *A Whistling Novel* (2002) and *The Little Black Book of Stories* (2003).

CYRIL COUVE is a Psychoanalyst, a member of the British Psychoanalytical Society, and a Consultant Clinical Psychologist and Unit Head in the Adult Department at the Tavistock & Portman Foundation Trust.

ANNA DARTINGTON [1945–2007] was Senior Clinical Lecturer in Social Work and a Psychoanalytic Psychotherapist at the Tavistock Clinic until her retirement in 2001.

RACHAEL DAVENHILL is Head of the Old Age Development Unit; Course Organizer for "Psychodynamic Approaches to Old Age"; and Consultant Clinical Psychologist in the Adult Department of the Tavistock Clinic. She is a psychoanalyst and a Fellow of the British Psychoanalytical Society.

MAXINE DENNIS is a Consultant Clinical Psychologist and Adult Psychoanalytic Psychotherapist. She leads a Psychosocial Therapies in Primary Care service in London and clinically works with individual groups and couples.

CAROLINE GARLAND, whose first degree was in English Literature at Cambridge University, went on the study psychology and eventually to train as a psychoanalyst with the British Psychoanalytical Society, where she in now a Fellow. She works in private practice as well as in the Adult Department of the Tavistock Clinic, where she is a teacher, clinician, and writer. At the Tavistock her primary interests have been in understanding the long-term impact of trauma on the personality, and in understanding the dynamics of group functioning. She has written, taught, and lectured both nationally and internationally on both topics. She has consulted to many organizations in trouble and situations of conflict at home and abroad. Her books include *Understanding Trauma*, the second edition of which was published by Karnac in 2002.

RONALD MARKILLIE is a psychiatrist and a retired member of the British Psychoanalytical Society.

PATRICE POLINI is a psychiatrist and psychoanalyst working in Paris.

REBEKAH PRATT, a community psychologist and researcher at University College London, is now based at the University of Edinburgh working in the area of primary mental health.

MARGARET RUSTIN is Consultant Child Psychotherapist at the Tavistock Clinic, Organizing Tutor of the Tavistock Child Psychotherapy Training, and Head of Child Psychotherapy. She is also a qualified adult psychotherapist and worked with Rachael Davenhill on the adaptation of infant-observation methodology to the observation of later life. She has co-authored, with Michael Rustin, *Narratives of Love and Loss* (Verso, 1987) and *Mirror to Nature* (Tavistock/Karnac, 2002) and co-edited *Closely Observed Children* (Duckworth, 1989) and *Psychotic States in Children* (1997) and *Assessment in Child Psychotherapy* (2000), both published in the Tavistock/Karnac series.

MARGOT WADDELL is a Member of the British Psychoanalytical Society. She works in private practice and is a Consultant Child Psychotherapist in the Adolescent Department of the Tavistock Clinic. She teaches and lectures widely both in Britain and abroad. The second edition of her most recent book, *Inside Lives: Psychoanalysis and the Development of the Personality*, was published by Karnac in 2002.

HEATHER WOOD is a clinical psychologist and psychoanalytic psychotherapist. A member of the BAP, she works as a Consultant Adult Psychotherapist at the Portman Clinic, Tavistock & Portman NHS Foundation Trust, and in private practice. She is joint editor (with J. Hiller and W. Bolton) of *Sex. Mind and Emotion: Innovation in Psychological Theory and Practice*, published by Karnac in 2006.

PREFACE

Twenty years ago, prior to training as a psychoanalyst, I was fortunate enough to work as a clinical psychologist in the only Community Psychology Department based within a social services department in Newham, East London. The head of department, Mike Bender, significantly prioritized the provision of services to older people at a time when there was a dearth of clinical psychologists working with people who were older, and there were many unfilled vacancies in old age. Bender ensured that all psychologists in the department were involved in providing psychological input to old age residential and day-care facilities. Rate capping was at its peak, and all the day centres for older people were under threat of closure. I also ran a counselling service with a team of counsellors offering short-term counselling to adults. In examining data on referrals to this service over a twelve-month period, I found that of the 268 people referred, only one was over the age of 65. At the same time I started to attend a fortnightly old age workshop at the Tavistock Clinic run by the psychoanalyst Peter Hildebrand. This workshop was influenced by the work of David Malan, who had also worked at the Tavistock Clinic, developing and refining his model of Brief Individual Psychotherapy. The workshop consistently provided examples, through case presentations and video material, of the psychotherapeutic work that many clinicians were successfully undertaking, at both an individual and group-work level, with older people. It helped to contain and support me in role and taught me an enormous amount about the possibilities and very real limits regarding the work I was undertaking—particularly when all the services for old age were saved from closure but the Community Psychology Department was shut down! What did not shut down was an abiding interest in the opportunities and challenges of working with old age services. In 1993, I came to work in the Adult Department of the Tavistock Clinic and have been fortunate enough to be able to continue and to build on the tradition of specialist thinking in old age.

I want to thank all my colleagues both from within and outside the Tavistock who have taught on or attended the two-year post-qualification course Psychodynamic Approaches to Old Age, in terms of the work and observational material that they have brought for discussion and for their generosity in allowing me to refer to their work in this book. I am grateful to Martin Blanchard in the early days of the course for taking the old age psychodynamic observational method formally through ethics procedures and supporting the initiative externally. Anton Obholzer, Margot Waddell, and Margaret Rustin all provided encouragement from the very beginning of the old age project at the Tavistock, contributing to the old age course while in its infancy and to the annual old age conferences. Linda Clare, Martin Rosser, Julienne Meyer, Mark Ardern, and Jane Garner from the worlds of, respectively, neuropsychology, neurology, nursing, and psychiatry are much appreciated for their flexibility and interest in crossover work. My main thanks, however, have to go to my colleague, Andrew Balfour. He has never wavered in his enthusiastic support for the old age training endeavour and has worked unstintingly in the service of its development.

Margot Waddell has guided this book with patience and generosity into becoming a reality as part of the Tavistock Series. I am grateful to Pat Utermohlen and Francis Cape for their help with the final chapter. Jean Matheson provided intense and thoughtful secretarial support in the final stages of preparing the book for publication and Helen Oliver was of great help with the references. Klara King compiled the index, and, last but not least, Eric King edited and produced the book with great patience, commitment, and dedication.

Jenny Sharman and Raymond Salter provided encouragement at different points early and late on in the writing. In the final stages,

Chris and Sue Mawson allowed me to use their peaceful retreat, whose surrounding landscape enabled the task of writing to become a joy.

At heart my gratitude goes to Hanna Segal, Anne Amos, Betty Joseph, Ruth Malcolm, Michael Feldman, Ines Sodre, Martha Papadakis, and John Steiner, all of whom have contributed in different ways to the development of my thinking over time. But of course the final acknowledgement must go to my family, John, Lauren, and Ella, who have had to tolerate my preoccupation with this book for far too many years—thank you.

LOOKING INTO LATER LIFE

"There is only one solution . . . and that is to go on pursuing ends that give our existence meaning—devotion to individuals, to groups or to causes, social, political, intellectual or creative work.

In old age we should wish still to have passions strong enough to prevent us turning in upon ourselves. One's life has value so long as one attributes value to the life of others, by means of love, friendship, indignation, compassion.

It is better to live a committed life even when all illusions have vanished."

Simone de Beauvoir, 1972

Introduction

Psychoanalysis provides a powerful conceptual framework for understanding the equally powerful loves, hates, and passions evoked in both the person who is older and those involved in his or her care. This book aims to bring alive the relevance and value of psychoanalytic concepts in supporting the core role of colleagues working directly in services for people who are older. It will also be of interest to analysts and psychotherapists interested in old age and the application of psychoanalytic thinking in the public sector. I do not aim to provide a comprehensive overview of the whole field of either old age or psychoanalysis but wish, rather, to share an enthusiasm, commitment, interest, and curiosity that has developed over time, in terms of an approach to thinking that has been helpful to me as a clinical psychologist working within the NHS and as a psychoanalyst working with people coming for consultation and intensive psychoanalytic treatment in the latter part of the lifespan.

It will become evident to the reader that while each chapter is different and stands in its own right, there are certain psychoanalytic concepts that appear and reappear again and again. Specifically these are the concepts of transference, countertransference, projective identification, and containment, which are the theoretical and clinical bedrock on which psychoanalytic psychotherapy rests. I hope that each chapter will offer a different lens to the reader that will broaden and

1

deepen understanding of such core concepts and their straightforward applicability in strengthening the quality of treatment offered within both old age services and psychological therapy services for people who are older in the public sector.

PART I.   OVERVIEW: PAST AND PRESENT

Chapter 1: "Developments in Psychoanalytic Thinking and Therapeutic Attitudes." The introductory chapter describes the development of Freud's thought and contemporary developments in psychoanalytic thinking that are used directly in clinical work with older people. An introduction to the current context for the delivery of old age and psychological therapy services in old age in Britain is given, and the example of Falls is used to highlight the difficulty in current service provision in taking account of the psychological as well as the physical needs of people who are older.

PART II.   MAINLY DEPRESSION

Part II covers the process of psychoanalytic assessment and treatment interventions offered within the Adult Department of the Tavistock Clinic. As the section progresses, the relevance of the "talking cure" in understanding the refractory depressions of old age are explored in depth, offering readers who may not necessarily be familiar with psychoanalytic approaches an alternative way of addressing depression in their own particular clinical setting. The final chapter in this section is a moving account of a retired psychoanalyst's recovery from a serious physical illness.

Chapter 2: "The Metapsychology of Depression." In this chapter, Cyril Couve provides a metapsychological account of psychoanalytic theory which can be used as a framework for understanding the tenacious and challenging quality of chronic depression presenting in many of the referrals to old age services. He differentiates the normal process of mourning from abnormal or failed mourning and gives a detailed clinical illustration of the efficacy of psychotherapeutic work in the treatment of depression.

Chapter 3: "Assessment." This chapter introduces a basic framework for undertaking a psychodynamic assessment. It also illustrates the usefulness of "second-opinion" assessment. Here, psychoanalytic thinking enables the assessor to work with the referrer and patient in planning an appropriate treatment intervention when formal psychotherapy is contraindicated.

Chapter 4: "Individual Psychotherapy." The importance of establishing a secure setting for both patient and clinician within which a psychoanalytic psychotherapy can be undertaken is discussed. A detailed clinical description is then given of the process of formal individual psychoanalytic psychotherapy with an 80-year-old man as practised on a once-weekly basis within the NHS.

Chapter 5: "Couples Psychotherapy." Anne Amos and Andrew Balfour describe the principles underlying couples work and give an account of their work with a couple married for over forty years. They explore the way in which longstanding partnerships can sustain a particular balance for long periods of time. Like a see-saw, this balance is determined by a number of factors, and it can tilt one way or another when the psychic equilibrium is disturbed through, for example, illness or retirement. The authors outline a model for working with couples in their description of "marital fit" which involves a shared defence and a shared unconscious phantasy.

Chapter 6: "Tragical–Comical–Historical–Pastoral: Groups and Group Therapy in the Third Age." Group psychotherapy is an extremely effective treatment modality in the treatment of depression in later life. In her chapter, Caroline Garland describes the importance of time, task, and territory in determining the appropriate boundaries for any group. She gives working examples from her extensive experience of running and supervising groups in the Adult Department both in mixed-generation groups and in groups run specifically for people over the age of 65. (In Part IV, "Mainly Dementia", Heather Wood describes her experience of running a group for people caring for a partner with dementia.)

Chapter 7: "The Experience of an Illness." In the final chapter in this section, Dr Ronald Markillie, a retired psychoanalyst, describes the working-through of an associated depression making use of his personal analysis from fifty years previously. In detailing the way that a severe physical illness at the age of 85 led to an equally serious emotional collapse, Dr Markillie describes how memories surfaced and were reworked in a way that made meaningful the experience he was undergoing and how this affected his recovery. He gives a moving account of the impact that illness, surgery, and the eventual move into a nursing home had when experienced in the eighth decade, with important reflections on dignity and the staff–resident relationship. He concludes by detailing the greater capacity he subsequently enjoys in facing the further trials of ageing. Dr Markillie worked at the Tavistock Clinic between 1949 and 1956.

PART III.   OBSERVATION AND CONSULTATION

Chapter 8: "Psychodynamic Observation and Old Age." In this chapter a rigorous and effective method of psychodynamic observation is described. Its importance as a means of learning about the lived experience of old age with the resultant strengthening of a capacity for effective intervention is advocated as a core component in the education and training of health and social-care professionals working with people who are older.

Chapter 9: "Consultation at Work." Maxine Dennis and David Armstrong present a detailed description of a psychodynamic approach to consultancy. They give an account of the fine-grain detail of a consultant's work with a staff group as it developed over the course of a year. The authors highlight how this approach to staff consultation provides a setting in which the emotional demands of the work can be thought about and understood, providing an opportunity for development of a greater understanding of both the challenges and the opportunities facing such staff in the front line of health and social care for older adults.

Chapter 10: "Where Angels Fear to Tread", by Anna Dartington, was originally published in the *Journal of the Squiggle Foundation (Winnicott Studies)*. While not addressing old age specifically, it has been included in this section as an important paper in exploring fundamental aspects of nursing care. Dartington highlights the dichotomy between what is theorized regarding the philosophy of person-centred care and what is often enacted with the emphasis on action- and, at times, panic-centred care. She emphasizes the way in which there is little chance of person-centred care for patients when there is no person-centred care for staff in terms of what is needed to sustain their everyday work.

PART IV.   MAINLY DEMENTIA

In 1901, Dr Alois Alzheimer was in charge of diagnosing the mentally disturbed inhabitants of Frankfurt. He described in detail his contact with a 50-year-old German woman who told Dr Alzheimer that she was known as Mrs Auguste and had forgotten her other names and so was remembered only as Auguste. When asked who she was, she repeated again and again, "I have lost myself".

A recent report on the prevalence and cost of dementia (*Dementia UK*: Alzheimer's Society, 2007) estimated that there are currently 700,000 people with dementia in the United Kingdom (1 person in every 88). This is set to increase by 38% to 940,110 by 2021 and by 154% to 1,735,087 by 2051. Current estimates include 11,392 people from black and minority ethnic groups with dementia. The area of younger people with dementia has received increasing attention in recent years, and it is currently estimated that 15,034 people have young-onset dementia (onset before the age of 65). However, according to the *Dementia UK* report, it is likely that these numbers are far higher, as data on the number of young-onset cases are based on referrals to services only. Within this cohort, 6.1% of black and minority ethnic groups have young-onset dementia, in contrast with just 2.2% for the whole population of the United Kingdom. Despite increased awareness of dementia and the disproportionate impact it has on the capacity for living independently, as well as its impact in terms of life quality for the main carer, it is still a neglected area. According to the 2003 World Health Report Global Burden of Disease estimates,

> dementia contributed 11.2% of all years lived with disability among people aged 60 and over; more than stroke (9.5%), musculoskeletal disorders (8.9%), cardiovascular disease (5.0%) and all forms of cancer (2.4%). . . . Public funding for dementia research lags far behind that of other serious medical conditions. The proportion of research papers (since 2002) devoted to these chronic disorders reveals a starkly different ordering of priorities: cancer 23.5%, cardiovascular disease 17.6%, musculoskeletal disorders 6.9%, stroke 3.1% and dementia 1.4%. [Alzheimer's Society, 2007, p. 16]

In this section, different aspects of dementia are explored through clinical, research, and observational material—art, literature, and subjective accounts of the experience of the person with the dementia, as well as those in close contact with him or her, whether family member or professional carer.

Chapter 11: "Only Connect." Margot Waddell bridges the worlds of the very young and the very old in a sensitive delineation of a central concept linking early life with old age: the psychoanalyst Wilfred Bion's concept of "containment". In her detailed observation of Mr and Mrs Brown, she illustrates the earliest anxieties of infancy, and the way in which these can re-emerge in old age, along with the relevance of the oedipal conflict for understanding some of the communications made by the person with dementia.

Chapter 12: "No Truce with the Furies." The issue of containment and dementia is explored further in relationship to unconscious factors involved in the silencing of debate regarding the provision of long-term care for people in later life suffering from dementia. Particular attention is paid to factors internal and external that led to the decimation of local authority and NHS provision in this area from the late 1980s onwards.

Chapter 13: "Facts, Phenomenology, and Psychoanalytic Contributions to Dementia Care." Andrew Balfour reviews the extensive literature examining the phenomenology of dementia, focusing specifically on the family of research looking at self, identity, and self-awareness in the person with dementia. He highlights the growing body of literature indicating the role of individual, couples, and group psychotherapy in the early stages of dementia. He then brings a psychoanalytic view to bear on the different "units of care" involved in the care of the person with dementia. These can include the dyad of a lifelong partnership where one partner receives the diagnosis of dementia; the larger family setting; and, finally, the community and institutional settings for continuing care, in which the relationship between the paid carer and the person with dementia is discussed.

Chapter 14: "The Pink Ribbon" is a short story from A. S. Byatt's *Little Black Book of Stories*. It is a privilege to have received permission to reprint this short story of such depth, which explores the importance of memory, trauma, and loss within a marriage. It reaches the affective core experienced in reality by so many couples in which one partner may have a degenerative disease. It is a powerful exploration of feelings evoked in the "carer" relationship—of the difficulties for the carer and for the person being cared for, including the intense emotions of love, hate, compassion, and disgust. The linkage of present and past through myth and the linkage of lived experience, past and present, in terms of the dementing process and its impact, is evocatively conveyed through, among many things, Antonia Byatt's inclusion of the "fetch". According to the dictionary a Fetch is "A wraith—the ghost of a living person. . . . Fetches most commonly appear to distant friends and relations at the very instant preceding the death of those they represent" (*OED*).

Chapter 15: "Caring for a Relative with Dementia—Who Is the Sufferer?" Heather Wood describes her experience of running a group for people looking after a spouse with dementia. She highlights the strengths a group can have in cutting through isolation and providing a setting in which some of the intense pressures and pains that the carer is having to bear, often on a full-time basis, can be shared and understood.

Chapter 16: "My Unfaithful Brain." This chapter gives a subjective account by the psychotherapist Anna Dartington, in discussion with Rebekah Pratt, of the experience of receiving the diagnosis of Alzheimer's Disease at the age of 54 and of its aftermath. Whilst there is often much activity leading up to and immediately after diagnosis in terms of formal scans and neuropsychological testing, Anna Dartington and Rebekah Pratt highlight the importance of having a place to process the experience of receiving a diagnosis of dementia. In talking about this experience, Anna Dartington also refers to her therapeutic contact with a psychoanalyst.

Chapter 17: "Conveying the Experience of Alzheimer's Disease through Art: The Later Paintings of William Utermohlen." Patrice Polini introduces the work of William Utermohlen, a figurative artist diagnosed with Alzheimer's Disease in 1995 who continued to convey his internal experience post-diagnosis through his painting. The result is a stunning, disturbing, and revealing documentation of the determination to hold on to self-identity for as long as possible. The capacity to draw on a long-established craft embedded in the artist's heart and mind continues to elicit in the viewer—as the formal structure of true art should do—the full gamut of emotions experienced by the artist and enables us to come closer to understanding the experience of progressive loss of self over a number of years.

PART I

OVERVIEW: PAST AND PRESENT

CHAPTER 1

Developments in psychoanalytic thinking and in therapeutic attitudes and services

Rachael Davenhill

In the beginning

In 1896, Freud wrote of his father in his final illness "He is . . . steadily shrinking towards . . . a fateful date". In 1939 the last book Freud read before his own death, according to his personal physician Max Schur, was Balzac's short story *The Incredible Shrinking Skin* [*La peau de chagrin*]. The irony of his choice was not lost on Freud. According to Schur (1972), "When he finished reading it, he told me, as if by chance: 'It was the right book for me to read, it talks about shrivelling and starvation'." The skin is the boundary between the inside and the outside of the body, and at the beginning of life and toward the end of the lifespan the skin holds special significance as a repository for both internal and external reality. Early on, when all goes well, the skin of the baby is given privileged significance. It is touched, treasured, smelt, cooed over. Even the baby's filled nappy can be experienced as a sweet rather than repugnant smell. From the beginning "we inhabit the body and are inhabited by it at all times" (Britton, 1989). The way in which the mother can respond to and contain the pains and pleasures of her infants' bodily needs will transform how these are experienced in terms of their emotional significance, and it will lead to the integration of the body itself as an internal object in the psyche (Laufer, 2003). However, this response does not often extend to the

11

latter part of the lifespan. What is noticeable again and again in the care of older people is the lack of significance given to the body other than in a purely functional way—it is there to be washed, fed, toileted—but the emotional meaning of each of these tasks is often denuded. The fragility of the older person's skin can evoke anxiety in the caretaker (for example, a doctor recently expressed his anxieties about resuscitation following repeated traumatic experience of rupturing the older person's skin and breaking the rib cage in the process). The care of older people is often criticized for only focusing on physical care and not communication, but, of course, physical care is a nonverbal form of communication.

According to Freud, none of us is alone internally. Instead, he suggested, we are inhabited by a company of others—not without, in terms of external reality, but within, in terms of what he called *psychic reality*. Crudely put, the concept of psychic reality is a little like gathering together the ingredients for a cake and mixing them together—the ingredients start off separate but, once mixed, cannot then be undone in terms of reverting back to the original component parts. He thought there were certain core ingredients that make us who we are. In 1923 he introduced what is referred to as the structural model of the mind, based on psychological forms of internal-object relatedness. This had three main elements. First the id, which Freud thought was completely beyond the access of the conscious mind and formed the basis of the instinctual drives; second the ego, which is the reality sense; and third the superego. The superego is based on an internalized early relationship to the parents and forms the basis of conscience. It can both be benign, in enabling the individual to develop a capacity for making decent judgements in life, or be experienced at times as a harsh, cruel presence, constantly judging the individual in an unremitting and critical way. These structures in the mind develop very early on, and the form they take will vary depending on the infant's perceptions of his or her relationship with his or her parents, partly real and partly based on unconscious phantasy. Conscious and unconscious perception can vary and change within the individual depending on the prevailing internal state in interaction with the external environment, and providing a basic template for the mapping of future relationships.

Psychic reality does not predetermine what is internal and external, but in working with the person who is older it does give us the freedom to think in our own minds and with them about not just the external event in itself, but also the individual's subjective experience of the event. It allows in and recognizes the emotional significance of human experience and its qualities, and it underlines the importance of looking at the emotional significance of the event rather than the "facts of the event" alone. Later on in life, memory will be influenced both by the actual event and by the way in which it may have been distorted by the internal meaning bestowed upon it by the individual. Here the cognitive associations and the emotional associations of the event come together and form the *unconscious phantasy*, the ether that permeates the internal world of every individual. Once the notion of unconscious phantasy is allowed into the picture, a much richer and deeper colour and texturing of understanding can come to the fore for both patient and clinician. According to Caper (1988), it was from "this shifting from the raw, literal event toward the melding of external and internal instincts, that Freud became a psychoanalyst". Freud's last paper was *Outline of Psycho-Analysis*. He wrote sixty-three pages at the age of 82 (immediately after arriving in London following his escape from Nazi-occupied Austria) between July and September 1938, and it was published in 1940. In his editorial comment to the paper, Strachey wrote that "at the age of 82 Freud still possessed an astonishing gift for making a fresh approach to what might have seemed well-worn topics. Nowhere else, perhaps, does his style reach a higher level of succinctness and lucidity. The whole work gives us a sense of freedom in its presentation which is perhaps to be expected in a master's last account of the ideas of which he was the creator" (Strachey, in Freud, 1940 [1938], p. 143).

The colouring of any external event is influenced by the psychological processes of *projection* and *introjection*, processes that operate continuously throughout the lifespan and help to make us who we are. From the beginning the baby needs to feed and defecate in order to survive, and these basic instincts are the template for introjection—the capacity to feed or take in—and for projection—the capacity to expel, push out, or get rid of. The tiny baby instinctively moves towards the breast and feeds when hunger is felt, and fills his or her nappy when discomfort is felt, and these physical processes are imbued with psychological resonance for the baby and his or her carer. The way in which the baby learns to navigate, and is helped to navigate, his or her way through complex emotional states such as hate and frustration can powerfully influence the course that psychic development and the capacity for love and reparation can take at future points in life. (Figure 1 is a representation of this process, and in finishing this drawing it struck me that it has a resemblance to an eye—perhaps a psychic eyeball that can, on a good day, perceive

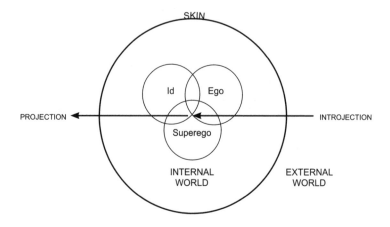

Figure 1.   Illustration of ongoing oscillation between the internal and external worlds

the psychic truth of the matter in terms of the capacity to perceive internal and external reality more accurately—one of the key aims of psychoanalytic treatment.)

In his 1917 paper on "Mourning and Melancholia" Freud introduced the notion of "identification" and the incorporation of the lost object into the ego in cases of melancholia or what would now be referred to as an abnormal grief reaction. If the relationship with the dead person has been very ambivalent, the work of mourning is much more difficult in that more loving feelings have been overtaken by hatred. Anger is a normal part of mourning, but if this predominates in the long term then forgiveness and more reparative drives are squeezed out while fury and resentment predominate, which can then lead to severe depression. Throughout life we have constant experiences of loss that have to be mourned in order for new developments to take place. Freud pointed out that losses can include loss of, for example, the mother country or loss of an ideal, as well as loss through death. Karl Abraham, a friend and colleague of Freud, disagreed with Freud's earlier pessimism and in 1919 described the successful analyses of older patients, commenting that "The prognosis in cases even at an advanced age is favourable . . . the unfavourable cases are those which already have a pronounced obsessional neurosis, etc in childhood and who have never attained a state approaching the normal. These . . . are . . . the kind of cases in which psychoanalytic theory can fail even if the patient is young." Like Freud, he thought that the work of mourning involved establishing in the internal world the person who had been lost externally. Melanie Klein had been analysed by Abraham, and in the development of her thinking she agreed with him that age-specific factors were not central, but that an understanding of the patient's level of mental functioning was. Klein thought that the foundations for dealing with loss were established very early on in life, with the earliest loss taking place during the weaning period when the baby has to negotiate the transition from a two–person relationship—usually the feeding relationship with the mother as main caretaker—to a three-person relationship incorporating the father as representing the outside world. She thought that two things interacted constantly when the baby was faced by primitive anxieties at points of transition which inevitably stirred anxiety. One was the capacity of the baby to tolerate frustration, which she thought had a constitutional basis; the other was the way in which loss was responded to by the mother or main caretaker, which could support—or not—the way in which the baby traversed feelings of frustration, loss, guilt, and persecution.

Hanna Segal was the first psychoanalyst to give a detailed published account of the analysis of a 74-year-old man, in her vivid description of working with a man who was referred to her following a psychotic breakdown (Segal, 1958). The paper conveys the importance of holding to the analytic framework as a container for understanding the patient's unconscious anxieties and phantasies with regard to his fear of death and feelings of persecution in relation to his internal objects, which over the course of the treatment dissipated. Segal regarded this case as one of her most successful in that she heard later that her patient was able to die a "good death". In a recent Preface (in Junkers, 2006), writing in her late eighties, she further commented on this 1958 treatment as follows:

> I learned a tremendous amount from this analysis, particularly about the importance of the fear of death. It made me understand the importance of coming to terms with the finiteness of things at any age. It was poignantly put to me by another patient, who suffered from severe mania, and who told me one day that there was nothing more tragic than getting old when you have not matured. I also learned that old people, though they face particular problems having to do with their age, particularly in analysis the humiliation of being dependent on somebody much younger than themselves, are in fact no different from other patients—each has his or her own individual history and problems which become more acute in old age.

At any age—child, adult, or older adult—there can be complications in really accepting some of the basic facts of life. In popular discourse, being taught the "facts of life" usually refers to sex and sex education. However, on a profound and deeper level, as well as sex (including the differences between the sexes and across generations) there is "the recognition of the inevitability of time and ultimately death" (Money-Kyrle, 1971). While the fact of death—or, perhaps more pertinently, the fear of death and the fact of its reality and the finiteness of life—is of universal relevance whatever age or stage of life, it holds a particular poignancy, strength, and urgency as a motivational force for people in the latter part of the lifespan. For many people it may be that, for the very first time, there is a new-found opportunity through psychotherapy or analysis to deal with an aspect of reality that Money-Kyrle thought was extremely difficult to come to terms with and yet remains crucially important—that of the fact of death, the reality of loss, and the need to mourn if the psyche is to live on creatively and as fully as possible in the latter part of each of our individual lives.

Two riddles

Riddle 1

> This thing, all things devours;
> Birds, beasts, trees, flowers;
> Gnaws iron, bites steel;
> Grinds hard stones to meal;
> Slays king, ruins town;
> And beats high mountain down.

Although this is a book on later life, the riddle is from a children's book, *The Hobbit* by Tolkien. In the story, the little hobbit, Bilbo, is being set increasingly difficult riddles to answer by the menacing character of Gollum, culminating in the one above. As Gollum strides towards Bilbo, demanding an answer to the above riddle, Bilbo wanted to shout "Give me more time, give me time!", but in his panic all that came out was "Time! Time". To his amazement and relief he discovers that he has indeed come up with the right answer—for "Time" is the correct solution to the riddle. Many of the depressions presenting in old age are precipitated by panic in the face of time, which, like the figure of Gollum, if not recognized and understood can take on an increasingly frightening and persecutory persona. Time is a direct challenge to the "high mountain" in Tolkien's riddle, in that it challenges the common feeling that life can carry on forever, highlighting the narcissistic traumas inherent in aspects of the ageing process, and the difficulties this can give rise to. In his pioneering work using brief psychodynamic psychotherapy with older patients at the Tavistock clinic in the 1970s and 1980s, Peter Hildebrand emphasized the reality of time as a strong motivating factor for people seeking out and making use of psychotherapeutic treatment in later life, where there are particular tensions surrounding the reality of time passing and of ageing. Whilst these are not problems specific to later life, nonetheless the facts of life brought in through increased age—of increased physical demands on the body, falls, or actual physical illnesses or disability developing; of retirement; of the death of partner, husband, wife, or friends as time goes by—certainly present a challenge as to how the later phase of life may be weathered emotionally.

Dylan Thomas wrote to his dying father, "Do not go gently into that good night, / old age should burn and rave at close of day; / Rage, rage against the dying of the light." In much of the writing on old age there is an emphasis on integration and acceptance of one's lot as an outcome of any decent therapy. Increasingly I am not so sure about this. It may be the case that some individuals are constitutionally more at peace with themselves and with life (and, if so, it is unlikely that they would be seeking out treatment) or that the many older people who do not suffer depression are those who have been able to face earlier experiences with a capacity to mourn rather than become depressed. One of the central tasks of therapeutic treatment is to enable the individual to reclaim areas of themselves that in fact they may have done their very best to get rid of, such as the capacity to become aware of and to feel love, hate, pain, grief, rage—and psychoanalytic psychotherapy in old age involves as much a fight as at any other point in the lifespan. Thomas's poem illustrates the way in which individuals have the opportunity of becoming more fully alive to who they really are and who they are in relationship to others, at both an external and an internal level. In terms of normal ageing, we do not see the bulk of people. This is where, with sufficient internal resources and a supportive external environment, the challenges of later life can be weathered and worn. But it is often where there may be areas unresolved at an internal level from much earlier in life or pressures externally, or usually a combination of the two, that depression may present itself in old age. If things have not gone so well early on in terms of dealing with the first loss—that of the two-person relationship and the exclusive tie to the main caretaker—then inevitably the losses and pressures of old age will leave the individual more vulnerable. In "Do Not Go Gentle", Dylan Thomas is writing from the perspective of the one about to be left behind—please don't go, hang on to life, do not leave me for then I will have to work through the painful process of mourning you. And this equally well applies to the person who is older, who actively remains aware of the need to struggle and work through the transitions and losses of old age, where there is no age bar to internal conflict and it cannot be retired from.

Clinical illustration: Mrs A

Mrs A came into her session saying that she was going to bring her camera to take a photograph of me so that she could frame it and pin it to the wall. Following this she went on to say that she wanted to spend the rest of the session discussing an episode she'd written about in her autobiography, even giving the exact page reference on which it was written down. Although the taking of the photograph and the writing seem different, the underlying problem was the same—depression—which she said was due to writer's block. It transpired that she had been trying to complete the autobiography since her son's death, finding herself unable to proceed in writing about her life beyond the age she had been when her son had died. She explained that she had started to write her autobiography as she sat next to her teenage son's bedside thirty-five years previously when he was dying of cancer. I thought the wish to frame me was in part a way of wanting to control me in time, and we were able to explore the way in which she felt pinned in time, unable to move forwards or backwards, something that the perseveration in going over and over one page in the autobiography also seemed to indicate. Mrs A needed to fully mourn her son in order to move onto a new chapter, not of her writing, but of her life. Over the course of the consultation it became more possible to think with her about the way in which both her problem with writing and her wish to frame me in a static way was an unconscious repetition of her difficulty in moving on.

Riddle 2

"What being, with only one voice, has sometimes two feet, sometimes three, sometimes four, and is weakest when it has the most?"

Traversing the lifespan challenges the individual over and again with the oedipal dilemma, which continues to appear and reappear alive and kicking whether 5, 55, or 95 years old. In the myth of Oedipus, Oedipus, fresh from killing (unbeknown to him) his father, Laius, on the road to Thebes, is confronted by the Sphinx, who throttles and devours anyone unable to answer the above riddle which she sets. Oedipus responds with the correct answer: "Man, because he crawls on all fours as an infant, stands firmly on his two feet in his youth, and leans upon a staff in his old age". At this, the Sphinx hurls herself from the mountain and dashes herself to bits. Oedipus is pronounced king by the grateful subjects of Thebes and goes on to marry his mother. When he realizes what he has done, he puts his eyes out and wanders as a blind beggar until he arrives at Colonus, where the Furies hound him to his death. According to Graves (1955), the Furies "were personifications of conscience, but conscience in a very limited sense: aroused only by the breach of a maternal taboo".

While it is true that according to the answer to the Sphinx's riddle there may be an eventual weakening of the body in old age, it is also clear that age does not diminish the strength of the oedipal conflict. Graves pointed out that, while Oedipus should have died as a baby, having been abandoned on the mountainside, in fact the Fates have determined that he will live to a "green old age". In the latter part of the lifespan, although the individual is still on the green side of the sod, there really is less time to try to sort things out, internally and externally. In the face of loss and separation it is normal to protest. Old age can involve both a celebration and an acknowledgement of the paths that have been taken and, where things have gone for better rather than for worse, an awareness of paths not taken, with some understanding and acceptance of why and why not, respectively. It also involves a true mourning of aspects of life that have not been, or may have to be, given up if, for example, ill health sets in, a point at which the individual may have to tolerate his or her increasing awareness of becoming more dependent on other people. How the balance of dependence and independence is approached for the individual and those who care for him or her is a theme that will recur throughout this book, raising important and fundamental issues with regard to dignity and personhood that are breached almost as a matter of course in many interactions with older people. For example:

> An old lady with diabetes was visiting her son and his children for the day. At teatime, the family sat down and the grandmother

asked for her glasses and teeth (which she had taken out when she had an afternoon nap and then mislaid). Her son said that she didn't need them as the bread was soft "and you don't need your glasses to eat your toast".

Here we can see the way in which the older woman has become a mouth and a stomach, with the reducing of the adult to an infant. The entitlement to engage with the outside world—that which can be seen and taken in—is taken away with the refusal to acknowledge the importance of the woman's glasses and teeth as integral to her identity. In the next section I look at some of the factors that contribute to the "invisibling" of people in later life in terms of the marginalization and splitting that occurs in providing decent psychological as well as physical care.

Contemporary overview

Early life is a precious time, and so too are the years of later life, which contain within them pressure points in which things can break through and can either be worked through or break down. Since the Second World War, life expectancy has increased dramatically with the development of the welfare state, which allowed in the possibility, for the first time, of universal quality health and social service provision for all at the point of need. In 1951, there were only 300 recorded centenarians. By 1991 this figure had increased to 4,500, and the expectation in terms of the increase in numbers of people over the age of 100 by the year 2031 is 45,000.

The prevalence of depression in older patients is twice that of the older population in general (i.e. 20% rather than 10%: Mann, Graham, & Ashby, 1984), and for older people in residential and nursing homes it runs as twice as much again (i.e. 30–40%: Ames, Dolan, & Mann, 1990). Depression is the commonest cause of suicide in older people (Cattell & Jolley, 1995). In 1996, a major review of the psychological therapies offered within the NHS was undertaken by the Department of Health, summarized in a key reference for those involved in providing services for older people, *What Works for Whom: A Critical Review of Psychotherapy Research* (Roth & Fonagy, 1996). Here, Woods's review chapter on old age highlighted the fact that older people do not receive equitable access to psychological treatment (Woods, 1996). As a crude index, he found that less than 10% of initial contacts with British clinical psychologists were aged 65 or over, even though older people form

16% of the total population. Addressing the research literature on old age, Woods provided a thorough review of the effectiveness of various psychological interventions with research from randomized controlled trials (RCTs), with evidence that brief psychodynamic psychotherapy with an experienced practitioner is effective in the treatment of depression. He also highlighted efforts made "to identify characteristics of older patients not responding to any form of intervention for depression. Those still depressed at 2 years tended to be those who hadn't responded initially to treatment and their depression remained intractable . . . there is a need to develop more effective treatment strategies for 'hard to treat' patients." At the Tavistock Clinic, a major RCT research programme on the outcome of psychoanalytic psychotherapy on refractory depression is currently underway (Richardson et al., in press). This includes people over the age of 60, and over time it will provide further detailed clinical information in terms of widening the current knowledge base on "hard-to-treat" patients.

Looking at the figures regarding the higher incidence of depression in older people, and the evidence regarding the effectiveness of psychological treatment, along with an increasing number of reports calling for increased access to psychological therapy services for older people, (DOH, 2001b, 2004a, 2004b, 2005a, 2005b; Hill & Brettle, 2004) it would seem reasonable to anticipate that there would have been a marked increase of referrals for people aged 60 and over for psychological therapies. And yet it is still the case that patients do not get referred, by and large, for any kind of "talking treatment"—never mind psychoanalytic psychotherapy—as a treatment of choice.

One reason for this links to referral practice. Older patients' views on help for psychological problems indicate that while the prevalence of psychological problems in older people is no different from that in other adult age groups and, as we have seen, is much higher in terms of depression, older people are less likely to present psychological problems directly in primary care. They are also less likely to have their psychological problems identified by GPs and other primary healthcare workers and are less likely to be referred for counselling or psychotherapy. Often the patient may approach the GP with a seemingly somatic complaint, and of course it is absolutely necessary and appropriate to deal with the presenting complaint. But if the psyche within the soma remains unnoticed, then the danger is that dealing with the presenting physical complaint alone becomes a defensive solution to really making contact with the underlying psychological difficulties that the patient may be having but at the point of presentation may be unable to put into words. Innovative work on enabling primary care practitioners to recognize depression in older people and feel confident in referring on may, over time, impact on this (Blanchard, Waterreus, & Mann, 1995). It is transparently clear that if older people in general are routinely not referred for "talking treatments", then black and minority ethnic elders specifically are even less likely to be referred for any form of mainstream psychological therapy provision. A number of initiatives are being undertaken to address this (Crisp, 2004; DOH, 2005a, 2005b; National Institute for Mental Health, 2003; Cabinet Office, 2006), but there remains a major gulf in the need for and the provision of appropriate services for older people from minority ethnic groups.

At the Tavistock Clinic, the Adult Department provides a tertiary specialist psychoanalytic psychotherapy assessment and treatment service and has a longstanding commitment to the provision of the "talking cure" to adults across the lifespan; currently about 5% of patients are aged 60 or over. Regular audit of the service indicates that the bulk of these referrals was from GPs and, in particular, from one or two practices that had a particularly strong profile on providing a good primary care service locally for their older patients. Many older people attending their GP practice may ask to see the practice nurse as they feel uncomfortable about "bothering the doctor". Here Blanchard's work in developing continuing professional development courses for practice nurses, sensitizing them to depression in older people, can instil clinical confidence in practitioners talking to the person who is older about his or her experience and can feel that part of their role can be to refer on for more specialist "talking treatment", if appropriate. A second factor relates to anxieties aroused in the clinician to whom the older person may be referred. Walker (1999) undertook a survey of clinical psychologists and psychotherapists in Scotland and found that very few psychoanalytically informed practitioners had experience of working with older patients, and they expressed anxiety about doing so. Conversely in the NHS there are many clinicians working with people who are older but relatively few trained to Level 2 or Level 3 in psychoanalytic psychotherapy, leading to a skills gap in the provision of specialist psychotherapy for older people.

We have approached this in the multidisciplinary training of psychologists, psychiatrists, nurses, and social workers undertaking the four-year NHS training in psychoanalytic psychotherapy in the Adult Department by ensuring that patients over the age of 60 are accepted as mainstream referrals within the department. When an older person is referred to the department, she or her comes into the ordinary distribution of referrals in the clinical team meetings held on a weekly basis and is taken on for assessment by whoever has a vacancy available. This ensures that both trainees and supervisors have the experience of working with and supervising the treatment of older people and means that this area of work remains integrated within the ordinary everyday life of the department. While as a tertiary service we have not been forced to operate any form of age apartheid, many adult psychology and psychotherapy services are still reluctant to take patients over the age of 65, and many old age services have limited access to specialist psychotherapy services. The framework put forward by national policy documents—including the NHS Psychotherapy Review (NHS Executive, 1996), *Treatment Choice in Psychological Therapies and Counselling* (DOH, 2001b) and the *National Service Framework for Older People* (DOH, 2001a)—is extremely important to use in terms of arguing the case for innovative crossover services between the traditionally separate areas of old age services and psychotherapy.

Within the NSFOP, Standard 7 on mental health with regard to depression and dementia is of direct relevance to this book. What is of interest in reading the NSFOP beyond this, however, is the stark demarcation between the physical and the mental, particularly with regard to Falls (Standard 5), which has direct consequences for psychological therapy provision. The recommendation for both of these areas is for highly funded specialist teams to be formed to work specifically with older people who have suffered a fall. However, in looking in detail at the make-up of these teams, what stands out by its absence is any psychological dimension—not a glimmer or a sliver of a psychiatrist, psychologist, psychotherapist, or counsellor is mentioned in terms of the core staff of these proposed specialist teams. Does it matter? The concerted effort by colleagues in the British Psychological Society and the Royal College of Psychiatrists, and listening carefully to feedback given by old people who have fallen, would suggest that it does.

Body and mind—falling into depression

At a local hospital, the first thing I saw when rounding a corner was a large sign (Figure 2): at the top it read "Neonatal Unit"; underneath was an arrow pointing in the opposite direction to the "Day Hospital" for older people; directly below this was an arrow pointing towards the "Oncology Unit"—from pre-birth to death, with the day hospital somewhere in the middle. The day hospital was specifically for older

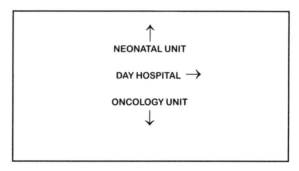

Figure 2

people with physical problems, many of whom were attending because they had had a serious fall.

Many of them were in their sixties and early seventies—far from the beginning of life, which the neonatal unit might represent, and most still a long way from the very end, which the oncology unit brought to mind, but somewhere in the middle, where an end was a bit more in sight and the severity of a fall had the capacity to bring that horizon into even sharper relief. The writer Arundhati Roy, in her novel *The God of Small Things*, conveyed this when writing of her central characters that "They are no longer what they were . . . their lives have a size and a shape now. . . . Edges, Borders, Boundaries, Brinks and Limits have appeared like a team of trolls on their separate horizons. Short creatures with long shadows, patrolling the blurry end. . . . Not old. Not young. But a viable die-able age" (1977, p. 161).

In reviewing the area of falling in people who are older as an example of the relationship between body and mind, I shall now explore why attention to the psychological as well as physical experience of older people who have experienced a fall deserves serious consideration. In this country, 30% of people over 65 experience a fall each year (Gillespie et al., 2003), and falls are the highest contributing factor of accidental death for women over 65 and of unplanned admissions into nursing and residential homes. There are profound economic costs associated with falls and fractures, with unintentional falls accounting for an estimated £1 billion of NHS and social service costings. There are also profound emotional costs attached to falling. Research evidence identifies depression as a possible factor in increasing the chance of falling (Lawlor, Patel & Ebrahim, 2003) and increasing the incidence of subsequent falling (Whooley et al., 1999).

Many hospitals now offer short-term Falls Groups, in which older people who have experienced a fall can learn strategies by which future falls may be avoided. The groups are usually run along cognitive behavioural lines and can be extremely effective in reducing anxiety and rebuilding confidence in terms of physical functioning. However, they are often run by young members of staff who may find it difficult to deviate from what are often highly structured interventions. Too rigid an adherence to the formal structure may be used defensively in restricting the way in which group members can really talk with each other.

> In one particular group, for example, about a third of the group members had experienced a bereavement in the year preceding their fall. One group member, Mr J, repeatedly said to the staff member running the group, "I can't seem to get back on my feet, can I come back again till I get back on my feet?" He mentioned in passing that his wife had died six months previously. The physiotherapist responded by going back to the flash card on "Hazards", which she had just gone through with the group, which listed all the ways in which falls could occur (tripping on flagstones, not attending to stairs, etc.). She breezily reassured Mr J that if he remembered everything on the card, then it would be unlikely he would fall again.

By attending only to the body, an important opportunity was lost in terms of attending to the emotional meaning of Mr J's communication, in which he seemed to be indicating how knocked off-balance he had felt since the death of his wife. The use of the flash cards—more usually provided for preschool children learning their first words—seemed to be more for the therapist's security than the patient's and indicates the dangerously fine line there is in terms of catering for failing sight or hearing on the one hand, and infantilizing the person who is older on the other. Closer contact between Falls Services and Psychotherapy or Psychological Therapy Services in identifying older people with residual depressions who need longer-term psychological help following the specific help offered on a short-term basis by a Falls Group can often lead to fruitful and creative service developments.

Figure 3 is by the Scottish artist Michael Andrews and was part of an exhibition some years ago at the Barbican, London, appropriately called "Transitions". It is a powerful piece of work and hits us,

Figure 3: Michael Andrews, "A Man Who Suddenly Fell Over", 1952.

the viewer, in terms of our being able to see the impact that falling has. From the individual's point of view there is the shocking loss, temporarily, of adult capacities. There is also the shock on the face of the observer, the woman standing behind. In infancy we can observe babies and toddlers trying to pull themselves up, before toppling over again. Little children love playing "Ring a ring of roses, a pocket full of posies, Atishoo, atishoo, we all fall down . . . ". There is a springiness, a development in the tipsy-turvy movements from instability to stability, with the robust confidence of growing bones and body, so that they all happily jump up again "With a one, two, three!". Even so, the issue of what enables development to take place in an unimpeded way is complex, and for the tiny child, the recovery from a fall can be determined by the receptivity of the carer in conjunction with the internal resilience of the infant.

In the opening pages of his autobiography, the philosopher Richard Wollheim writes evocatively of his first remembered experience of falling:

It is early. The hall is dark. Light rims the front door. The panes of violet glass sparkle. The front door has been left open. Now I am standing outside in the sun. . . . Lifting my eyes, I see that the garden, and everything in it, moves. . . . I am standing in the sun, my body is tipped forward, and I am walking. Walking I shall trip, and, if I trip, trip without a helping hand, I shall fall. I look above me, and I feel behind me, searching for the hand that is always there. There is no hand, and therefore, if I trip, or when I trip, and now at long last, the waiting is over, and I have tripped, and I am, am I not? I am falling, falling—and was it then, in that very moment when magically I was suspended in the early light, when the soft smells and sounds seeping out of the flowers and the insects and the birds appeared to be doing for me for a moment what the hand that was not there could not do, or was it not then, but in the next moment, by which time the magic had failed, and the path was racing towards me, that I did what I was to do on many later occasions, on the occasion of many many later falls, and I stretched out my hands rigid in front of me so that my fingers formed a fan, not so much to break my fall, or to make things better for me when I hit the ground, but rather to pretend, to pretend also to myself, that things were not so bad as they seemed, or disaster so imminent, and that this was not a fall but a facile descent through the air, which would leave me in the same physical state, clean, ungrazed, uninjured, that I was in before I tripped, and that the urine would not, out of sheer nervousness, pour out of me?

When I landed, a large rose-thorn, which had been lying in wait on the gravel path, most probably since the early hours of the morning when it had fallen from its stalk, confronted me, and met no resistance as it slid itself under my thumb-nail, and then, like a cold chisel, worked its way up into me, making its own channel as it went, until it came to rest on the pad of pink, quivering flesh that forms a cushion underneath a nail.

Cries of surprise, cries of pain, cries of outrage, resounded through the garden and tore apart the morning serenity.

Within seconds, someone, alerted to my absence, has run out of the house, and brusquely collected me up into her arms. Held with what was to be memorable pressure against the surface of a starched apron, I was hurried back, breast-height, along those few yards of path which my feet had just traversed in an outward direction. But now the sounds and smells that had lured me onwards were blotted out by the protective breast. [Wollheim, 2004, pp. 11–12]

Everyday conversation is littered with falling phrases: people fall in and out of love, fall for each other, fall pregnant, burdens fall onto shoulders, fall into a depression, we fall from grace. This latter is a good starting point in bringing us back to the first fall and all that that represents—the fall from the Garden of Eden, where all is provided, to the world of the ego, including the body ego, which has to face reality, including the uncertainties of life with its shames, embarrassments, loves, and hates. The body is the boundary between inside and out-side. In later life, falling can impact equally powerfully not just on the individual's physical state but also on his or her psychic equilibrium. Whether there is the equivalent of the "protective breast" at an internal or external level is an important component to consider in terms of recovery from a fall or series of falls.

> Mrs G, a woman in her early sixties and an avid cyclist, described sitting shaking on the edge of the road after she fell off her bike. She started to cry and said that she realized that she was crying not because she had been physically hurt, but because she had remembered her capacity following a fall thirty years earlier in just being able to bounce up and back onto her bike without if affecting her in any way. Her cryful rage was suddenly realizing that her body was no longer as resilient as it had been and that the fall had had a major impact on her at an emotional level in challenging her internal conviction that she was still 30.

It is this area of narcissism and narcissistic injury that Freud starts to address toward the end of "Mourning and Melancholia" (1917e [1915]).

In the following examples, the way in which the physical and psychological understanding of falling can enter into the therapeutic work are shown.

Clinical illustration 1: Mrs B and the walking stick

Mrs B had been referred for psychotherapy by her local Falls Serv-ice following an episode of clinical depression precipitated by an operation on her ankle the previous year following a fall. She came into her session and told her therapist that she had used a walking stick for the first time that day—something she had resisted doing, although her therapist had become increasingly alarmed at how shaky she seemed to be when she persisted in walking unaided. Mrs B went onto interpret this negatively, saying that she thought the walking stick was like her therapy, just a crutch. Her therapist was able to take up with her the attack on treatment and to differ-entiate between an ordinary dependency on her treatment—which seemed to have been helpful the previous day in allowing in an exploration of the patient's underlying and, in part, more narcissistic reasons for refusing to use a stick, which she thought would mark her out as an old person—and the reality of finding she could make use of the therapeutic work by allowing in the walking stick and a realistic dependence on her therapist. Paradoxically, this increased Mrs B's capacity to function independently, in terms of decreasing the risk of a fall, and symbolized the way in which allowing in and acknowledging an ordinary dependency on her treatment enabled Mrs B to feel she had a strengthened internal resource to lean on within herself.

Clinical illustration 2: Mr C and the crevasse

Mr C was an active and attractive-looking 68-year-old man who came for psychotherapy because, according to him, it was required for an introduction to a counselling course he had decided to do; according to his GP, however, it was because Mr C was repeatedly requesting antidepressant medication. Mr C had never had any major illness and prided himself on keeping fit and continuing to work for various organizations on a freelance basis. He seemed full to bursting with areas of external need that he would be helping out with, and real contact with his close family or me in the therapy seemed to be squeezed out by his constant movement. In terms of the motif of falling, Mr C told me of a recurrent nightmare in which *he found himself on the edge of a crevasse that he was unable to stop himself falling into, and he found himself exhausted in the effort to scramble out of it.* Early on in the treatment, a number of Mr C's close family members died in an accident. Mr C was unable to mourn, telling me that he had so many other urgent commitments he found himself unable to take a day off to go to any of the funerals. One day he came into the room and fell as he walked towards the chair. He said that this was the fourth time he had fallen, but he had not wanted to say anything to me as he prided himself on being so fit. His lifelong mantra to himself was that he felt he would be able to go on for ever.

The mourning process can be arrested because of a number of defences, which can include the paranoid and the manic defence against guilt. It was predominantly the latter that seemed to strengthen its vice-like grip on my patient following all the deaths, with an alarming escalation in the number of activities he became involved in. In this example it is possible to see the narcissistic blow to Mr C's view of himself that the family deaths and his falls brought in. His phantasy in connection to the fall in my room was that it brought to the surface his unvoiced unconscious fear in relationship to the final fall—namely, that into the grave. For the first time he was able to talk about his terrors not so much of death, but in relationship to dying and finding that his body was no longer under his control.

One of the most stark areas presenting to both the person who is older and those who care for him or her in terms of falling is how quickly life can fall out of one's control in terms of self, identity, and relationship. To start with the current situation first and work backwards, let us take a phrase that any reader browsing through current policy documents and papers on old age will come across again and again—the notion of "person-centred care". But what does this mean in practice? When close observation takes place in old age settings, it becomes clear that while the idea of person-centred care cannot be anything other than a sensible policy, it often shifts, under a certain constellation of pressures, into panic-centred care. In walking into many acute wards, whiteboards can often be seen above each individual bed on which the person's name is written along with that of his or her "named nurse". There is a hope that if names are filled in, a relationship exists. Of course, the sad reality is that a quick glance at the whiteboards will often reveal that they are completely empty, and in observations undertaken it has often been the case that if names are written in, they occasionally bear no relationship either to the person in the bed or to the person looking after them! A "person-centred approach" is a perfectly rational and humane perspective, but one that breaks down conceptually in that it holds a view of the person which takes the "un" out of "unconscious" and leaves itself working at the level of conscious thought alone. Why is this, and are there ideas within the field of psychoanalysis that can help to explain what it is that leads to the often complete breakdown of person-centred care at the point when it is most needed in terms, for example, of unplanned admissions to residential or nursing homes, or precipitate discharges from acute beds back home following a hospital admission?

Freud and his revolutionary method of treatment for understanding the conflicts of the heart and mind has often been criticized for being individualistic and reductionist. But in revising his theory of mind in 1923 with his introduction of the structural model of the mind, he catapulted us into a world of what has come to be referred to in analytic jargon as the world of "object relationships". What a peculiar word to use when referring to a human relationship! Yet it has stuck to this very day, and means simply human relationships—one person relating to another person. So far so good, and, on the surface, nothing out of kilter with a person-centred approach. But if we go beyond the surface there are profound differences. A person-centred approach, as it is understood in contemporary theorizing in the care of older people, links to understanding the individual and responding to him or her, in his or her entirety, with respect and dignity (NICE Clinical Guideline 42: NICE, 2006). And who could argue with that? But numerous inquiries into the abuse of older people indicate that the practice of such a principled approach often breaks down.

I hope this book will contribute to a deeper understanding of why this may be, in exploring the role that unconscious factors play in the training, continuing professional development, and working lives of health and social care professionals working with people who are older. While each transition point in the lifespan offers opportunities for development, in old age there really are limits of time and mortality, which adds an edge to the therapeutic work. With that in mind I hope interested readers will be encouraged to continue working in the area of old age and find the following chapters helpful as a resource for the development of innovative and sustainable interventions within their own workplace.

PART II

MAINLY DEPRESSION

CHAPTER 2

The metapsychology of depression

Cyril Couve

In this review of some key psychoanalytic ideas about depression, I shall be using Henri Rey's (1994b) notion of a depressive psychic organization that constitutes a kind of fabric of the experience that we call depression. This depressive psychic organization has two interrelated elements. First, it emerges in relation to the loss of an object. The term "object" here refers to a person, a loved one, a loved attachment, a relationship, or a country or also to what can be called a self-object, such as an ideal, a standard, or an expectation about oneself (Freud, 1917e [1915]). The second element refers to a sense of personal responsibility, conscious or unconscious, about the loss itself. Without the presence of this psychic organization it is difficult to make the diagnosis of depression. This should not be taken to mean that causes that do not fall within the psychic domain—such as biological causes of depression—are excluded. It is perfectly possible to hold a psychoanalytic view of depression and include other causes. Rather, it should be taken to mean that without such a mental structure it would be difficult to make the diagnosis of depression.

Another point needs emphasis. The connection between loss, separation, and depression is quite accepted today, both within and outside psychoanalytic writings on the subject. However, the connection between loss and depression is not an automatic one. What determines whether depression follows a loss or a series of losses depends on what the child or the adult has made of the loss and how he or she has reacted to it. Depression is one way of reacting to loss. From within the psychoanalytic tradition, *depression is not seen as a result of loss but, more specifically, as a result of an inability to deal with loss or as a result of an inability to do the work of mourning*. Here, an important distinction emerges between mourning and depression. The capacity to mourn and to grieve is a kind of psychic insurance against depression. Depression is not an automatic consequence of loss. Depressive feelings are usually present in mourning, but they are transient and not fixed.

Freud's 1917 paper "Mourning and Melancholia" is the foundation for the psychoanalytic understanding and formulation of loss and depression. It is a complex paper, which moves on different levels. Freud compared the state of mourning to that of melancholia in order to understand melancholia, by which he meant psychotic depression or manic-depressive psychosis. The state of mind that we call mourning has various features in common with the melancholic state of mind, according to Freud. In both mourning and melancholia there is an extremely painful dejection, a loss of interest in the outside world, a loss of the capacity to turn to new relationships, and a turning away from activity not connected with the lost one. However, Freud was keen to single out major differences between these two states.

In a state of mourning, the mourner is preoccupied, almost exclusively, with the psychic work of thinking about and remembering the lost object. According to Freud the world feels impoverished because the object is no more. By contrast, the loss that has led to the pathological reaction of melancholia is much more difficult to detect. This is due to the disproportion between the nature of the melancholic reaction, which can be quite catastrophic, and the loss itself. Whereas the mourner feels that the world is impoverished without his or her love object, the melancholic is far more preoccupied with the impoverishment of his or her own ego. This impoverishment takes the form of an intense, relentless, and merciless self-castigation and self-hatred, which can achieve delusional proportions. Freud singled out the delusion of self-belittlement as being the crucial distinguishing feature between the state of mourning and that of melancholia. He also pointed out that the melancholic does not hide his self-hatred but, instead, proclaims that he is a sinner, a criminal, that he is rotten, and so forth in a rather exhibitionistic way. So there is a definite narcissistic and exhibitionistic element to the melancholic's relentless self-depreciation and masochism. In addition, although the dejection of the mourning process is extremely painful, the mourner eventually comes to know that this is a normal reaction that will pass away with time, once the work of mourning has been done. Freud called it the "work of mourning" in order to stress the psychic work and mental effort and energy that goes into the process of mourning.

Freud's conceptual strategy in his paper is very interesting. He puts forward a hypothesis that in the case of melancholia there has been a loss, but the loss is an unconscious one. The way he comes to this hypothesis is very ingenious. He says that if one listens to all the self-accusations and the intense criticisms of the melancholic, they do not seem to apply to the person of the melancholic but could very well be directed to a significant figure in the life of the melancholic. This intense self-hatred, Freud thought, linked once to a hatred of an object outside the self. The crises and anxieties generated by this very intense ambivalence are such that the hated object is taken into the self through a process called "introjection". Through the process of introjection, instead of hating the object the melancholic hates him/herself, now identified with the object. Freud, drawing inspiration from the writings of his colleague Karl Abraham (1924), describes this mode of relating to an object as a very primitive one, whose prototype involved an oral incorporation of an object in fantasy.

Freud's paper is a foundation paper, a pioneering paper, but also one that is full of gaps and uncertainties. Nevertheless, it contains many implicit and explicit truths that are very important. First, it establishes a clear link between the state of depression and the internalization of an object or figure that is relentless, punishing, and merciless. In other words, it establishes a very important relation between depression and the sense of responsibility or guilt, which can take extreme forms such as persecutory guilt in cases like melancholia and severe depressive states. Second, it is also implicit in Freud's paper that the introjection of the hated and hateful object inside the self means that the object has not been let go and remains within the self, with terrible consequences. In contemporary psychoanalytic theory these primitive introjective identifications, with their omnipotent character, would be understood as functioning as a defence against separateness and loss. Third, what is also interesting about "Mourning and Melancholia" is that although Freud uses the parallel with melancholia to understand melancholic despair, he ends up with a dynamic view of severe depression and still very little insight into what constitutes what he calls the work of mourning. Freud quite candidly pointed out that the reason why the work of mourning should be so difficult actually eluded him.

He understood the work of mourning as a conflict between a part of the self that, through memory and through a revisiting of memories about the object, kept the object alive and a part of the self that had the capacity to submit every one of these memories to the judgement of reality. Reality says the object is no more; it is dead or is lost. Freud conceived of the work of mourning as a process of maintaining attachments to the object through memory while at the same time detaching oneself from the object by a process of reality testing. After a while, the reality ego prevails over the pleasure ego. While this is interesting, it leaves us, in the main, with an economic view of mourning regarding quantities of attachment and abilities to detach, but not with a fully fleshed-out psychodynamic view of the process of mourning.

The depressive position

This is where the work of the psychoanalyst Melanie Klein on the depressive position is of great interest and value. Klein's theory of the depressive position allowed her to provide a structural explanation for states of mind present in severe psychotic/melancholic depression, but also for the state of mind associated with normal mourning. According to Klein, the situation of loss and mourning revived the conflict of the depressive position and is an occasion to continue the working-through of such conflicts. The state of mourning, according to Klein, is a transient "depression", with a crucial difference: *in successful mourning, it is possible to bear guilt, it is possible to engage in reparation proper, and it is possible to re-establish a good relation with the loved object and good internal object.* Although Klein established a rapprochement between the work of mourning and the state of depression, she also maintained a very important distinction between the capacity to mourn and the incapacity to mourn, which led to depression. While Freud hinted in the direction of this distinction, I suggest that he was unable to give us a dynamic explanation for it.

Melanie Klein referred to the depressive position as a major structure in infantile life inaugurating a new mode of relating to objects, a new psychic reality, a new experience of the world, and the emergence of what she called depressive anxiety—a new form of very primitive anxiety, with its own group of defences. A mixture of internal and external factors allows the very young infant to negotiate some of the conflicts of the earlier paranoid–schizoid position, which Klein thought occurred during the first few months of life. According to Klein, the paranoid–schizoid way of relating to the object means a relation to part-objects. The splitting mechanisms are such that the object that gratifies—the "good" object or the idealized object—is kept wholly separate from the object that frustrates. The frustrating object is hated and, by projection, becomes hateful and persecutory: the "bad" object. The crux of the paranoid–schizoid mode of relating is that idealized and persecutory objects are kept wholly separate, so that both the object and the ego are split. This results in a part-object mode of relating, and in such a world there is no place for loss. The anxiety that dominates is that of being persecuted by the bad object and contains fears of psychic dissolution, of disintegration into bits in relation to bad objects. The omnipotent possession of the idealized object is a desperate defence against this awful state of persecution.

If the infant has been properly contained and mothered and has internalized a sustaining object, then there is movement to whole-object relating. This means that the loved object is also the object who is hated and attacked. When development goes well, there is an increased capacity on the part of the infant to bear frustration (e.g., when the mother is absent), depending on whether a sustaining object has been introjected. This enables an increased capacity within the infant to feel separated from his or her objects such that there is more of a distinction between him/herself and others. In this entry into the depressive position, emotional ambivalence is experienced towards the object, together with an enhanced capacity to integrate feelings of love and of hatred stemming from the same self, initiating emotional whole-object relating. This inaugurates a new psychic reality: the anxiety of loss of the object that is loved.

It is important to point out that, for Klein, entry into the depressive position is not dyadic in nature: it is triadic. With an increased awareness about the mother as a separate person, the new object world that is entered into involves the mother's relationship with a third object. The object who is hated and attacked is not simply the mother but, rather, the mother's link with others. In her work with young children, Klein showed with great clarity the concrete nature of the child's fantasy. Here, the fantasies about triangularity and the triangular psychic space have as their new object the mother's body and what is inside the mother's body. In terms of the contents of mother's body, this can include milk, other babies, and also some link with father, a very primitive type of father, which Klein calls the father's penis.

Since it is the link to objects that is attacked, it also means that the anxiety is very great, because it is all the objects that are attacked. The depressive position is particularly poignant emotionally because it is triangular, which also means that it is not only one object that is attacked or split, but it is all the objects that are damaged in phantasy. Hence, she refers to the notion that in the depressive position the object world is in chaos. She pointed out that while the anxiety is of a more persecutory or paranoid nature (i.e. there is a fear that the objects that have been attacked will retaliate, hence leading to a considerable amount of persecutory anxiety), it is also depressive in nature in that it inaugurates a fear of loss, a concern for the object who has been lost or damaged or whose loss is feared, and guilt because it is the same loved object or objects that are also hated and attacked in fantasy. So, in the depressive position, the child or the adult in later life has to confront both paranoid anxiety and depressive anxiety. The coexistence of paranoid anxiety and depressive anxiety leads to a structure in which guilt can easily become tinged by a very persecutory quality. If paranoid anxiety is still dominant, then guilt will tend to achieve a more persecutory character. The major defence against this new form of anxiety is what Klein calls the group of manic defences. While there are other defences in the depressive position, such as the important obsessional defences, I shall focus on some essential aspect of the manic defences.

Characteristics of the manic defence

1. There is omnipotent denial of need and dependency. Since need and dependency occasion an exposure to the pain of being separate and also to the pain of exclusion in the new triangular relations, this can lead to a very conflictual relationship to the world of objects. Need and dependency are omnipotently denied and omnipotently triumphed over.

2. The triumph over need and dependency is also achieved by a triumph over the object. The importance of the object is devalued, belittled, and demoted, as a way of avoiding what Klein calls "the perils of dependency".

3. It is not sufficiently understood that the triumph over need and over one's object is absolutely central to what Klein calls omnipotent or concrete reparation. One way of attempting to restore the damaged object is to omnipotently rid oneself of one's needs for objects and one's dependency on objects that occasioned conflict

and destructive attacks in the first place. Fantasies of manic repair are often expressed in terms of omnipotent and narcissistic fantasies of self-sufficiency, whereby the need for the object and the importance of the object is demoted or radically denied because one has all the resources oneself. By being perfect, big, and omnipotently grown up and resourceful, the self avoids the risk of ambivalence and destructive conflict, which lead to depressive anxiety and depressive despair.

4.   Under the pressure of the manic defence, a splitting of the object and of the self between alive and dead takes place. The damaged object is dreaded and, instead, the alive part of the self and of the object are idealized. Manic states are usually characterized by grandiosity and overactivity and a forceful but brittle liveliness; they can also be highly sexualized states to ensure the triumph of aliveness over the dread of deadness.

5.   The problem with manic defences, which are essentially triumphant and defeating, is that they themselves constitute attacks on the object and on the self, which leads to more guilt and to more persecution. In working with a person in a manic state, the change from a feeling of being completely devalued to one in which one is intensely concerned for the brittleness of a patient can be quite startling. Mania protects the patient against the feared experience of depressive despair, of psychic pain, and of persecutory internal figures.

The psychic task of the depressive position is gradually to be able to bear guilt and to engage in what Klein referred to as "reparation proper". Reparation proper means that one cannot put absolutely right the damage one has caused to the object in phantasy. But excessive guilt and despair give way to the emergence of concern, of love, or of pining for the objects lost. In other words, reparation proper allows the self to reinstate a good and loving internal relationship with the lost object. This can only come about when depressive guilt can be faced and not fled from with omnipotent defences, denials, and mechanisms. For Klein, reactions to loss will depend greatly on the way the conflicts of the depressive position have been worked through and negotiated. If loss mobilizes persecution and despair, then melancholic states or severely depressive states will most probably result.

The work of mourning is difficult because the loss re-evokes the conflicts of the depressive position—that is, the loss of a loved one re-evokes the guilt occasioned by one's own death wishes and attacks on one's early objects vital for psychic survival and development. If these conflicts are still virulent, then mourning cannot take place and a pathological reaction to loss is likely. If the conflicts are less intense and more attenuated, then the loss of a good internal object is only temporary, transient, and the trust in the individual's capacity for concern and capacity to face guilt, along with a capacity for reparation proper, leads to the reinstatement of good and loving feelings towards one's own internal objects. This, according to Klein, is the crux of the work of mourning: to be able to restore a loving relationship with one's internal good objects.

Clinical illustration:
Twenty-session psychotherapy with Mr D

The difficulties experienced in the work of mourning can be seen in the following psychotherapy treatment with Mr D, a patient whom I saw for twenty sessions, who was unable to fully mourn a tragic loss. D was in his early sixties and had been prescribed a variety of antidepressants over the previous five years. He had become dependent on them, even though they didn't help his depression. As a builder, he moved around and managed to obtain medication from a variety of GPs until he met a psychologically minded GP who fortunately felt he needed psychotherapy and not just medication.

The narrative I am going to give is a result of the twenty sessions and was not obtained in one go. D's attendance and punctuality were very erratic, especially at the beginning. Whenever he started to tell me about the loss, he would sob very painfully, which often meant he could not carry on telling me what he had started. As a result sessions were very disjointed, especially at the beginning. D told me that he had lost his wife seven years ago in the most tragic of circumstances. They had been married for over twenty years, a very close couple, both Catholics, and had three children, now in their twenties and late teens. As Catholics they used natural contraception: abstention, or coitus interruptus during ovulation. His wife had become anxious because of a lump in her breast. She consulted two different GPs and was reassured that the lump was benign and did not need to be removed. His wife went along with the diagnosis but was not entirely reassured by it. One night they made love, unprotected, and then he ejaculated inside her. It was a mistake. His wife told him jokingly at that moment: "now this is it, you have killed me." Things then happened very fast. She fell pregnant, the tumour was malignant, and, with the pregnancy, the cancer spread and she developed a secondary. Tragically the pregnancy bought life and death at the same time. I think that the juxtaposition of these two extremely contradictory and antithetical events of life on the one hand and death at the same time most probably complicated the process of mourning considerably.

Mrs D was placed in an intensive care unit for much of the pregnancy. In a desperate attempt to save the mother, they had discussed abortion, if this might help. But it was too late. And anyway, even if this could have helped, their Catholic principles would have made them decide against it. My patient saw his wife die gradually. However, some of the memories of them together in the hospital bedroom were recounted with an extraordinary vividness and presence and with an unbearable sadness that made me feel close to tears. Their son was eventually born a healthy baby, and before her death two weeks later his wife had asked him: "Promise me you will look after our baby as I would." He had promised.

D received no bereavement counselling but was told by a consultant who had worked on the case that he should not think of making any new or major move in his life for at least nine months, for his own and also for the baby's sake. Interestingly, he followed this advice to the absolute letter. I felt, as therapy developed, that he had heard it and had reacted to it as if it were a kind of edict or an injunction. He gave himself exactly nine months, not a day more, not a day less, and then moved his entire family to a region just north of London. Building work was abundant there, so he could make good money and give everything he had promised he would to his children and the baby.

He worked hard during the day, and also at night, when he would look after his infant son. During the day, childminders were used to help. Despite the hardship in his life, he felt that he was doing pretty well and that he was overcoming the loss of his wife. However, when he could make better use of his sessions, he also presented the other side of him that did not cope so well. He described states of utter exhaustion, culminating in moments of total impatience with his crying young baby at night, sometimes shaking him angrily to try to get some sleep, expressing considerable guilt in depending so extensively on his elder daughter to help care for his little son.

After one year of being in London, he met a woman, herself a relatively young widow with two children. They became friends, and lovers, and soon decided it would be better to live under the same roof with their combined families. It was from this point on that he started to feel badly depressed, constantly tormented by thoughts telling him that he should commit suicide. The very fact that such thoughts came to him increased his sense of guilt because of his Catholic morality. He did not get these thoughts when at work. Usually they came at night when he could not sleep or on his way to or from work. As he downed his tools, he would be invaded with guilt and fear about what he may do while driving back home. These depressive moods and thoughts descended on him, and he felt that he would be condemned to live this kind of misery for ever. He would think about his wife and her death and would sob uncontrollably but without much relief. When he was prescribed antidepressants, he soon became addicted to them. When I saw him, he was taking the pills at will to try to stop his depressive and suicidal thoughts. As soon as he would have them he would take an antidepressant. Antidepressants helped him a bit initially, but after five years he was still depressed and afraid now that he had become addicted to medication. By the time I saw him he also mentioned that his sexual relation with his new partner had become virtually non-existent, and this worried him a great deal in case she thought he was just with her to replace his dead wife. (This narrative makes it sound simple and self-evident, but it was not. Information came in very disjointed bits.)

When we started treatment my patient was very sceptical about how talking to me could help him. He felt that he had remembered all the details of his wife's death so often, and had gone through them so often, that it was not as if there was anything he was hiding to himself. So how could talking to me help him? Whereupon in the session he would tell me something about his wife and then start to weep and to sob uncontrollably. The pain and sadness were so intense that he could not carry on telling me what he had started to talk about. When the session would end, he often was in a heap and would leave in a state of despair. I was left feeling terrible, caught up with the devastating pathos of his tragic loss, but also with a sense of impotence and anxiety about how he would cope with such sadness over the next week. I was never seriously worried that he would commit suicide. But he evoked in me great concern about his state over the following week until his next session. After a while, by using and listening to my countertransference, I started to understand how this man could get antidepressant medication from his GPs, because he very subtly evoked in one a combination of intense sympathy and caring and also a kind of helplessness and anxiety at the same time. This helped me start to think about the distinction between what was pathos in this man—and there was plenty of pathos because of the tragedy—but also to consider what was pathological.

For example, after a while I started to perceive increasingly that when he remembered with such intense vividness the memories of his wife's illness and death, he was perhaps keeping it alive in memory, in the manner that Freud (1917e [1915]) suggested, and that this vividness could be a way of defending against the guilt he felt about his wife's death. The question that came to me was: what kind of tears was he having when he cried so uncontrollably in the session?

I also remembered one of the first things that D told me. He said, "I did not know anything then. . . . All I ever had is my hands", which he showed me, builder's hands, well worn by work. "If only I knew then what I know now." And then he showed me his hands again and said, "These are all I've got." Increasingly in the course of our sessions I came back to this communication and started to see it as a very condensed communication with different layers of meaning, a bit like a dream. On the one hand, it sounded like an apology, the protestation of innocence: "If only I knew this, it would not have happened, but I did not because I am an honest worker who doesn't know much, and the proof is there in my hands. I am an honest worker with honest working hands. My hands are clean." Now clearly this was both an admission of guilt and a protestation of hard-working innocence and ignorance.

Gradually he started to miss sessions or to came late, and I started to perceive a more negative aspect to the transference with me and a kind of subtle arrogance about the lateness when he failed to ring to tell me he couldn't come, hardly excusing himself when I saw him again. He seemed to behave as if all this was par for the course, that there was no sense of loss, that it didn't mean much to come or not to come to a session, while on the other hand he remained plagued by despair, by suicidal, intrusive thoughts, and also by this dependence on antidepressants, which he was very unhappy with. I started to take up the way he mistreated his sessions, the way he made no allowance for any sense of loss in missing his session, or the way he seemed to be subtly contemptuous about his need for my help and about the help that I could give him. I interpreted how he took refuge in his work instead, which provided him with very good excuses for not attending his sessions and not attending to his depression. I started to see a different meaning to his "all I've got are just my hands". His hands, his zealous activity at work, his doing very well financially—all of this was part and parcel of manic defence. It was also a way of denying that he had a mind and that things happened in his mind, a way, too, of denying the possibility of knowing what took place in his mind and the fact that he needed me to help him understand what had gone on in his mind leading to his depression.

D did much of the reconstructing by himself of what had happened. At times I would also help him to put things together about what had happened to his wife and what he felt in relation to her. Gradually he started to treat his sessions much more seriously, and after the tenth session he did not miss any of the subsequent sessions.

I shall now list what felt like some important landmarks in the progress D was making in his brief therapy once he had become more reconciled with his real needs as a patient. In his ninth session he told me that he had decided to stop the antidepressant medication and was surprised at how easy it had been. I think he was able to cast off his unhealthy dependency on medication because he understood that a more healthy emotional process had begun in his therapy which allowed him to make better contact with his very unresolved grief. In other words he had begun to trust the value of his sessions.

Soon after, he made a very interesting self-observation: he said that he had thought about his wife at the weekend and had cried. But it was different this time, because after he had cried he felt relieved, whereas usually when he cried he felt depressed and little relief. This insightful self-observation, which confirmed my sense that D had up to then suppressed his capacity to think and understand out of his unconscious tormenting guilt, indicated that he was beginning to understand by himself the important distinction between the pathos in his situation and the pathological in his depressed state. Depressed tears serve to evacuate mental pain and guilt but do not relieve the patient, whereas tears born out of sorrow follow the reinstatement of love for the lost object and bring relief to the mourner who can now let go of the lost loved one.

One month later he told me he had been able to take his new partner over to Ireland on the anniversary of his wife's death. This was the first time he had been able to bring her directly on one of his trips to his wife's grave and in this way bring his two partners together instead of hiding the one from the other out of guilt. Shortly afterwards he voiced for the first time his concerns for his youngest son's emotional state. I learnt that the latter had been experiencing difficulties at school and recently had been statemented. D wanted me to help refer him and his son and the whole family to a child guidance clinic. I saw this as an acknowledgement of the damage and mess he realized his manic denial had left behind and had caused to his son, who was not properly looked after in his early years. With the acknowledgement of his need for help there was a decrease of omnipotence along with an increase of more truly reparative urges and tendencies: he was feeling more able to face his guilt and put it right instead of fleeing away from it like a haunted man. Finally, in the penultimate session he announced to me that he was planning to marry his partner, which he had avoided all this time because of his guilt.

Some psychodynamic features of this case

In conclusion, I shall outline some of the more salient psychodynamic features of D's inability to mourn the loss of his wife and how this brief spell of analytic therapy allowed him to begin to face internally and externally his tragic loss. The effectiveness of this brief psychotherapy is in itself a testimony to the fact that D had no severe underlying personality problems which usually complicate both the experience of loss and can cause a more protracted and complex depressed state that is less accessible to psychotherapy.

D felt that unconsciously he had killed his wife. The loss of a loved one inevitably evokes the unconscious ambivalent feelings that the mourner has had towards his primal objects of infancy and childhood.

One's guilt at the damage caused to these objects is revived by the more current loss. This brief psychotherapy precluded an understanding of these more unconscious factors. However, what seemed clear was that D felt that his impulsive sexual desire and the unprotected sex had killed his wife. His sense of guilt was most probably exacerbated by his own Catholic morality and attitudes about sex. But the words of his wife had become absorbed by his internal tribunal, which proclaimed that indeed "he had killed her".

It is possible to see how this internal tribunal was active in the way he heard both his wife's wish and the recommendation made by the consultant who treated his wife. He heard both as edicts or strict injunctions that he felt he had to follow to the letter, in the manner of a sentence without parole passed by a tribunal.

Pitted against such a sense of guilt and inner torment, he tried to escape and protect himself by relying on a manic state of mind. He attempted too quickly to replace his wife and to deny his own needs for her as a husband and a father of a baby boy.

He worked zealously, seeking a new beginning and acting as if he could be both father and mother at the same time. He cleansed his builder's hands by making more money than he had before and in this way by looking after his family as if there had been no loss and limitations. But internally his sexual hands felt guilty and persecuting. I think D felt devastated but also angry with his wife for leaving him through her death. His anger and resentment exacerbated his already strong sense of guilt and his reliance on manic overactivity and omnipotent fantasies of self-sufficiency. Later he could acknowledge his guilt towards his daughter for his overreliance on her and indeed recognize that he had not done a very good job on parenting his young son. If mania protects against loss and depression, the omnipotent denial at the heart of mania creates more damage and guilt.

D's sense of guilt emerged in the form of suicidal thoughts when he actually began to replace his wife with a new woman friend and partner. It was only then that his inability to mourn emerged with greater clarity. The suicidal thoughts were the internal sentence passed for his attempts to replace her too quickly, which itself was fuelled by unbearable guilt. His unhealthy dependence on antidepressants was also part of his manic flight into self-sufficiency and an avoidance of his true psychic pain.

After two months of therapy, D began to give up his contemptuous and devaluing attitude towards his treatment and towards his own needs for treatment. The weakening of his manic contempt and the safety and trust provided by his therapeutic relationship allowed him to restart the work of mourning, which had badly miscarried years before. His depression lifted dramatically and his life could start anew, with a considerably lessened sense of guilt and cleaner builder's hands, which did not prevent him from also having a mind.

CHAPTER 3

Assessment

Rachael Davenhill

In old age services, the task of assessment may focus on the differential diagnosis of dementia and depression, or it may involve undertaking an initial assessment as part of the single assessment process recommended by the National Service Framework for Older People (NSFOP). In this chapter, I describe the psychoanalytic framework for assessment used at the Tavistock Clinic which enables the clinician to gain a picture of the patient's internal world and enables therapist and patient to think together as to whether psychoanalytic psychotherapy is the treatment of choice or not. The assessment consultation is a time to try to develop a way of looking and thinking about the person the therapist is seeing in the first instance, rather than precipitately trying to decide how to treat the patient, which would come more towards the end of the process.

The consultation process aims to allow both patient and clinician enough mental space to gather together a dynamic picture of the person's world and how this conveys itself unconsciously as well as in more manifest ways. A typical frame for assessment consultations in the Adult Department is usually to arrange to see the person for two meetings of about an hour and a half, spread over a couple of weeks, although sometimes it may be necessary to offer a more extended assessment of up to six sessions (Garelick, 1994). This enables patient and therapist to see what the person has made of the first meeting—has it

BIOLOGICAL
(physical, biological changes in the body)

CHRONOLOGICAL
(actual age—external facts of the matter)

PSYCHOLOGICAL
(the timescale of unconscious processes, which paradoxically are experienced as timeless)

Figure 1

been digested or not, does the patient present very differently in the second meeting and, if so, what implications does this have for treatment?

I want to start off with three "aide-memoirs" that I have found helpful in thinking about the psychoanalytic assessment and treatment of people who are older. These are not meant to be prescriptive in any way, but they do link to the development of an internal frame of reference, which can be learned through experience over time and carried into the assessment and treatment contact, in which the freedom to move through different structuring levels in thinking and feeling helps clinicians to make sense of their patients' material. The first is taken from the analyst Pearl King (1980) who, in writing on the lifecycle, refers to three different time scales: biological, chronological, and psychological (Figure 1).

Let us continue the image of a small block of flats that King's tiering brings in and move it into the building blocks of why some people may be more rather than less disposed towards, for example, periods of depression. While a psychoanalytic assessment will involve exploring present and past relationships, in terms of past history it would be a mistake to equate very early deprivation in and of itself with psychopathology:

> A vital mistake is made in studies attempting to relate early deprivation to later incidence of depressive illness. All infants do not react in the same way to situations. The rhetorical question is what kind of an infant met deprivation, real or phantasied, and was the deprivation in external reality or was it an experience in internal or psychic reality and constructed by the infant?
>
> It is now necessary to relate the state of affairs to the model of hierarchical supports. If this particular storey in the building—not quite

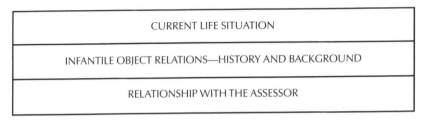

CURRENT LIFE SITUATION

INFANTILE OBJECT RELATIONS—HISTORY AND BACKGROUND

RELATIONSHIP WITH THE ASSESSOR

Figure 2

the basement, which is reserved for schizophrenia, but shall we say the ground floor—is sufficiently pathologically organised, all other floors relating to object relationships will suffer structural distortions. Later in life any loss of any kind as described previously will be structurally and symbolically linked to the earlier experiences through a series of pathologically structured storeys. [Rey, 1994a, p. 194]

How do we discover something about the lived inner unconscious experience of the patient during the time available for assessment? Hinshelwood (1991) highlights three core situations that need dynamic attention in assessment. These include the person's current life situation, history, and the way in which the relationship between patient and therapist evolves within the assessment framework (Figure 2).

Another way of visualizing this is through Malan's Two Triangles (1979) (Figure 3). In assessing the patient, Malan focused on the transference and the development of a psychodynamic formulation that

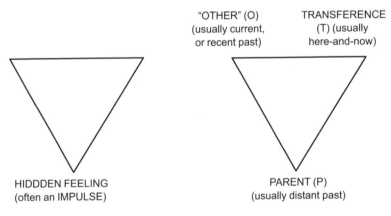

Figure 3

could inform intervention. Hinshelwood explores the potential in an assessment consultation for a strengthened clinical capacity to put together the components of a psychodynamic formulation by looking at the way in which the patient describes both his or her current life situation and history. The way in which the patient describes his or her history and background is always informative when seen through the lens of the unconscious and unconscious phantasy. Here, external reality is not neutral but is in constant interaction with and affected by the internal meaning given to it. So often, a particular view of, for example, a piece of history containing a description of mother or father will be conveyed in a particular way in the assessment—for instance, a father who is very critical. But once the patient is in treatment, the picture may change over time, and it will become apparent that it was, for example, an aspect of the patient's severe superego that was projected into the father which was being communicated in the assessment. During the assessment, the therapist is aiming to let his or her mind freely move across the interplay of internal/external, conscious/unconscious in order to put together a preliminary configuration in terms of both the patient's history and the way in which this applies to the transference as it emerges over the assessment consultation. The transference can be understood through the countertransference response, which in psychoanalytic work is the guiding compass in terms of orientating the therapist to the patient's unconscious communications. Freud thought that the patient transferred feelings from important past relationships into present ones and that there was a compulsion to repeat: "If we throw a crystal to the floor, it breaks; but not into haphazard pieces. It comes a apart along its line of cleavage into fragments whose boundaries, though they were invisible, were predetermined by the crystal's structure" (1933a, p. 59). Old age is an area where the lines of cleavage can fracture apart very suddenly, as highlighted in chapter 1 in terms of the impact that a fall, for example, can have.

What determines the transference configuration is a complex mix that Klein (2nd unpublished lecture, 1936) described in the following way:

> Being guided in our exploration by the transference situation . . . we can observe how the processes going on in the deep unconscious, and the phantasy productions they result in, are modified by the activities of the mind starting from the other end, namely, the influences from without and from reality. This constant interaction between conscious and unconscious processes, between phantasy

products and the perception of reality, finds full expression in the transference-situation. Here we see how the ground shifts from real experience to phantasy situations and to internal situations—by which I mean the object-world felt to be established inside—and again back to external situations, which latter may appear in either a realistic or phantastic aspect. This movement to and fro, which derives its power and intensity from the depth from which it departs and to which it returns, is connected with an interchange between figures, real and phantastic, external and internal which the analyst represents. [Klein, 1936]

If the assessment is approached openly in the way a new piece of music is listened to, then what will become apparent to a sensitive ear is the home key. The music will go through all sorts of variations, but one way or the other will always return to the original chord (Richard Rusbridger, personal communication 2001). Part of really listening to a new tune is not necessarily striving too hard, but letting go of preconceptions enough to allow in the full tone. Sometimes there may be an interrupted cadence in which the unexpected takes the listener by surprise—in music it may be a sudden unexpected rhythm, in assessment it may be a particular personality trait that suddenly appears—but always an overall pattern will emerge, even if it is one of atonality or discord. So it is with the leading components of the patient's internal world that we can listen to and become familiar with in the assessment process or later on in treatment.

Assessment in a dynamic sense is very different from assessment in a psychiatric sense, and a dynamic understanding of the symptom a patient presents with in the assessment would also be different. The symptom can provide an important clue to the underlying problem the patient is struggling with. For instance, an older woman with brittle bones came for a consultation and repeatedly used the words "shattered" and "shattering". She felt "shattered" on arriving in the room; she was "shattered" when she realized that this was an assessment meeting not ongoing treatment, which there would be a wait for. I found it almost impossible to follow what she was saying in the consultation as it was so broken up. I felt she was giving me some indication of a very primitive catastrophe that had taken place in which there was a shattering of her experience into shards. She refused to acknowledge the brittleness of her physical or mental condition and became increasingly paranoid as the consultation went on. Between the first and second meetings she fell, and it was at the point her body shattered that the fragile carapace surrounding her

Referral process

Does the patient want to come?
    Needs of the referrer (e.g. becoming overwhelmed by the patient)
    Fantasies of the referrer (e.g. idealization of therapy)
    Patient carrying projected parts of another (e.g. aspects of parent or partner)

What does the patient want?
    Clarify in relation to psychoanalytic psychotherapy (e.g. understanding
        and alleviation of mental illness,
    promotion of growth and development, symptom removal).

Educational aspect

The patient having an opportunity to experience
    a psychoanalytic approach
    the exploration, understanding, and reformulation of the presenting
    problems

**Addressing the core aspects of the psychoanalytic assessment
and its unconscious determinants**

The psychodynamic formulation:
    The internal relationship to the child within
    How to repair damaged internal objects
    Identification of defences and disavowal

The trial aspect of the assessment

    Monitoring reactions within and between assessment meetings
        (including regressive potential risk of breakdown)
    Further elucidation of defences
    Capacity and will for growth

Treatment recommendations

    Negotiating treatment recommendations with the patient
    Matching patient's needs to what the service can offer
    Is the service the appropriate setting? Or if there is some other ongoing
        therapeutic work, should this be encouraged or supported?
    Should one refer the patient on to a specialized agency? Or as a possible
        patient to a training programme?

Letter to referrer

Psychodynamic explanation and informed advice.

Figure 4.   Core factors in assessment for psychotherapy.

mental structure shattered too, and she had to be admitted for inpatient treatment.

Garelick (1994) has outlined a "pathway" through assessment which can be helpful in mapping the full assessment consultation (see Figure 4).

An important factor to bear in mind when assessing is that a psychoanalytic approach is not neutral, and, like any procedure, it contains risks. Milton (1997) points out that psychoanalytic approaches are invasive—operating at depth not surface level:

> In medical terms, "invasive" is a term describing investigations that mean breaking into the body in some physical way. . . . We have to have a good reason to do a psychological investigation that tends to break into the inner world, piercing defences and potentially causing mental pain and upset . . . just as we would not wish an inexperienced clinician to perform a dangerous and invasive medical investigation on us, so too we would want to regard psychoanalytic assessment as a relatively advanced procedure not to be practised by the novice without careful supervision.

The function of second-opinion assessment in relation to the patient and the referrer

So far I have been addressing the work in assessment with patients who may go into psychoanalytic treatment or, through the process of assessment, be referred on for another form of psychological therapy that may be more appropriate. I now want to highlight the function of what I have termed "second-opinion assessment" as a further key element of a particular form of consultation offered by a specialist psychotherapy service. It is not unusual to receive a request for a second opinion from colleagues in another service at a point when they feel their patient is at screaming pitch, and they too may feel at screaming pitch, in their contact with the patient. The patient may have experienced severe mental distress throughout his or her life in the form of severe and refractory depression or borderline difficulties. Reaching retirement age does not give any relief, in that the individual knows he or she is unable to retire from lifelong difficulties. While the referred patient may or may not be suitable for psychotherapy, the process of a second-opinion assessment gives a breathing space in which the patient's dilemma can be thought about afresh. Developing a psychoanalytically informed opinion through the assessment consultation enables the assessor to think with the patient, the referrer, and the local service about what structures may best contain the situation if formal individual psychotherapy is contraindicated.

The final part of this chapter describes the working-through of an assessment consultation with Mr E, a 78-year-old man with borderline difficulties living over two-hundred miles from the clinic. The GP's letter was curt, saying that Mr E had recently registered with the practice and was insistent on being referred to the Tavistock. In the past the patient had been seen by the local psychological therapy service and been offered supportive contact with nurses from the community mental health team (CMHT), as the assessor felt that formal dynamic psychotherapy was contraindicated.

I sent Mr E an appointment and meanwhile contacted the GP and spoke with the original assessor in the local service. The assessor expressed irritation that the GP had gone ahead with the referral. The GP was irritated with the assessor for not keeping Mr E, as he put it, "off his back", and with the patient for refusing to leave the GP's surgery until he had agreed to refer the patient to the Tavistock. From my conversations with the assessor and the GP, it emerged that Mr E had been struck off virtually every GP's list in the locality at one time or another. He had also become increasingly disabled with a chronic but not life-threatening condition over the previous five years and had repeatedly demanded investigations and second opinions at specialist clinics locally and in different parts of the country. Mr E had eventually been seen by the local psychological therapy service after becoming increasingly agitated and depressed. After a protracted assessment, the assessor—a qualified psychotherapist—thought that the patient was unsuitable for formal psychotherapy but had the possibility of stabilizing with ongoing help from members of the CMHT for older people. This was arranged, but Mr E told one person after another, in no uncertain terms, to stop visiting him after seeing a programme about the Tavistock Clinic and deciding that this was where salvation lay. Prior to coming for the first appointment, Mr E wrote the following in capital letters on the back of the self-report questionnaire that new patients are asked to fill in: "I CAME INTO THIS WORLD SCREAMING AND I'LL LEAVE IT BLOODY WELL SCREAMING."

Mr E, a grey-haired and smartly dressed man, came to the first meeting in a wheelchair. Once in the room he sat with a very determined look, a walking stick looming large in his hand, with his chair blocking the front of the door. He held my eyes in a steely gaze and said that now he was here, he wanted to make it clear to me that this was the best place for him to be and that he hoped he wouldn't have to waste my time or his time in having to complain before getting what he wanted. He thought if he came here every week, that should do the trick.

I was aware of feeling trapped and momentarily frightened. He went on to say that he felt there was nothing to redeem his situation other than his dog—the dog was more reliable than any of those so-called do-gooders. The dog was "a Yorkshire terrorist". He corrected himself and said he meant a Yorkshire terrier—did I know the sort of dog he meant? Well, did I? The reason he wouldn't kill himself was because of this dog. The dog was completely unfriendly to other people—even to Mr E sometimes—and wouldn't let anyone come through the front door, which set those do-gooders straight anyway. Having said that, Mr E sometimes got frightened by the dog as it was so unfriendly and could bite. He'd wondered whether he should have the dog put down, but then felt the dog deserved to live.

I commented that perhaps he felt the only way people would see him was through his terrorizing them into seeing him and then his real deprivation of feeling so trapped and frightened got masked over. Mr E took his glasses off and started to weep. The atmosphere softened, and he went on to say that he had been unwanted and been told that as a baby he screamed constantly and refused to be fed. Both parents died in the patient's teens when a bomb dropped on the family home. Mr E went to live with an aunt and uncle who both sexually abused him until he left home. In his twenties he self-harmed, made repeated suicide attempts, and was a psychiatric inpatient on and off for many years. Eventually he spent time in a therapeutic community, which seemed to have stabilized him sufficiently that he was eventually able to get a job in a residential home for adults with learning difficulties. This seemed to contain aspects of Mr E's fragmented character, with the presence of a kindly matron-like manager who appeared to look after Mr E as well as the adults in the home. When the manager died, Mr E felt his world—which, in its way, had offered an unofficial inpatient setting—shattered.

I enquired about his earliest memory and whether he had a recent dream. A patient's free associations to the query about an early memory and dream can enable a clinician to deepen his or her understanding of the unconscious experience of the patient. Mr E remembered a dream from the previous night. In the dream *he found himself in his wheelchair, which was spinning faster and faster out of control*. His earliest memory was of his mother drying her dress in front of the fire and one of the buttons getting so hot that it burnt her. This reminded him that he had got in such a rage the previous day that he had smashed up all the smoke alarms in the house with his walking stick.

I saw Mr E for a second consultation and throughout the assessment was trying to piece together as truthful a picture as was possible of the internal-object relationships experienced by Mr E. I could draw on what he told me about his current life situation and his past history and by attending to the affective experience of the transference–countertransference movement in the session. In doing this, I was attempting to inform and flesh out a psychodynamic picture that could help guide me in thinking about how to proceed.

I thought that the central configuration he was conveying to me was linked to the inadequate parenting of a shattered child. His desperation then escalated when this experience was repeated in the response of those around him—the GP, for example, who ended up feeling bullied and inadequate and wanted to refer the patient on. I thought Mr E's first communication to me in the questionnaire was right in terms of the ongoing scream that had been successfully projected into all those surrounding him. It seemed to me that what Mr E made clear was that even if there were all the resources in all the world, ultimately he felt they would not be sufficient. The problem we were facing was that although there weren't all the resources in the world, there certainly were some considerable resources in his own locality in terms of a social worker, a community psychiatric nurse (CPN), the GP, and an experienced psychotherapist.

Mr E had told me that the only reason he hadn't killed himself was because of his "Yorkshire terrorist". I thought this represented a major defence—his rage and hostility were necessary to keep him alive. I thought that if this defensive structure collapsed, there would be a very strong risk of suicide; I was in agreement with the local psychotherapist, who had recommended ongoing supportive contact by the CPN and social worker, with supervision provided by the psychotherapist. From my contact with Mr E, I thought there was some confirmation for my hypothesis that whatever was provided would be experienced as damaged or would get quite a battering. In thinking about Mr E's history, along with the here-and-now situation in the immediacy of the contact with me, Mr E had told me of his mother, a possible source of warmth, burning her button. I thought in part that his unconscious phantasy was of a feeding breast that was damaged. Mr E desperately wanted some warmth, but if he got closer to the other person, then damage set in. Evidence of this came into his account of the situation before coming for the first assessment meeting, where Mr E told me that he had smashed all the smoke alarms in his house with his walking stick the night before. I thought that this connected to the omnipotent phantasy the patient held that a referral to the clinic would resolve all his difficulties; I also thought that the smashed-up smoke alarms represented the local CPN, social worker, and psychotherapist, whom Mr E wanted to knock out of the picture but, in fact, were crucial as his safety net which needed resecuring to enable him to survive the fine line he traversed internally between terrorizing and terror-stricken aspects of his personality.

In this example of Mr E, my assessment of his internal world was worked through in my own mind and in discussion with colleagues, and then in my contact with the referrer and local team back in the patient's home town, rather than in any direct interpretative work in a sustained way with the patient himself. I said to Mr E that I thought if I saw him, it would only add to what I thought was an illusion of there being some ideal solution somewhere for the tortured psychic world he found himself inhabiting. So long as he held on to this belief, it meant that he was unable to make any use at all of the not-inconsiderable support that realistically was available to him locally. Similarly, once we were able to arrange a review meeting of all the clinicians in contact locally with Mr E, it was possible to think about, rather than enact, the patient's phantasy that somewhere there would be an ideal answer. This led to a strengthening of clinical identity. Once the notion of cure was replaced by one of thoughtful care, it meant that a realistic long-term care plan could be made to support those clinicians in regular, sometimes daily contact with Mr E. A key aspect of this included timetabling-in intermittent review meetings for clinicians working with Mr E with the consultant psychotherapist locally. The use of psychodynamic understanding in assessing both the containment needed by the patient and the containment needed by staff in meeting the needs of the patient has been noted by various writers (Arden 2002; Martindale, 1989; Stern & Lovestone, 2000) and may include weekly work-discussion groups or consistent but less frequent review meetings. With this in place, it meant that the team were able to not discharge Mr E from their books, in the full understanding that the years ahead would inevitably be difficult ones. This capacity to not discharge is one that is given very little acknowledgement or recognition within many existing service structures, where there is structural pressure to discharge, and it does need to be acknowledged as a form of active containment and hard-won achievement by often hard-pressed staff teams.

CHAPTER 4

Individual psychotherapy

Rachael Davenhill

"Experience has taught me that the complexity of the fully grown personality can only be understood if we gain insight into the mind of the baby and follow up its development into later life. That is to say, analysis makes its way from adulthood to infancy, and through intermediate stages back to adulthood, in a recurrent to-and-fro movement according to the prevalent transference situation."

Melanie Klein, "Envy and Gratitude" (1957, p. 178)

or to put it another way:

FATHOMS
Young I visited
this pool; asked my question,
passed on. In the middle years
visited it again. The question
had sunk down, hardly
a ripple. To be no longer
young, yet not to be old
is a calm without
equal. The water ticks on,
but time stands, fingerless.

Today, thirty years
later, on the margin
of eternity, dissolution,
nothing but the self
looking up at the self
looking down, with each
refusing to become
an object, so with the Dane's
help, from bottomless fathoms
I dredge up the truth.

R. S. Thomas, "No Truce with the Furies" (1995, p. 10)

One of the leading themes in working with people who are older is the weighting of external realities in old age such as illness, accumulation of loss, traumatic history, sheer life experience, and so on. It is impossible to get away from the facticity of age—there really is a concrete representation of loss in the older person who has experienced the actual deaths of many others. Freud, in his early paper "On Psychotherapy" (1905a) thought that the sheer accumulation of lifespan material contraindicated analysis as a therapeutic method in old age. He, of course, disproved his own point of view by continuing to develop his own thinking and writing about his ideas right up to the end of his life. Freud's own theory of mind, along with contemporary psychoanalytic thinking, emphasize the need to free oneself from the, at times, overwhelming amount of external reality that can enter into a patient's session in order to be able to function in role as a therapist, where the work task is to understand, interpret, and think about the patient's psychic reality. The psychoanalyst Wilfred Bion thought that when working with so much reality, it was important for the analyst or psychoanalytic psychotherapist to extricate him/herself or there can be pressure to become something other than the analyst. This is one of the most difficult areas in the countertransference response. Readers may identify from their own experience in working with a particular patient the pull to respond as a social worker or daughter or son or mother and start to operate outside the transference. Of course, it is important for the therapist to be open to the patient's transference and temporarily step into whatever pair of shoes the patient requires the therapist to fit into at a particular point in the session—that is the basis for empathy on which normal projective identification rests. The problem arises if the therapist cannot step back out of the patient's shoes and into his or her own, at which point the patient has lost her or his therapist.

Areas personal to the therapist may affect the countertransference response.

Many clinicians, as they start to work in a therapeutic capacity with people much older than themselves, may still be facing issues in connection with separation from their own family of origin. The "sandwich effect" of simultaneously having and taking care of young children while taking care of a career outside the home may well coincide with parents becoming more frail and dependent . While this is very common, it is worth taking account of in terms of the peculiarly vulnerable set of internal and external circumstances that clinicians themselves may need to notice and be aware of.

> For example, a therapist described in supervision her feelings of panic after hearing from the wife of a 70-year-old man she was seeing for once-weekly psychotherapy that her patient had been taken into hospital following a minor illness. The patient had stabilized well and would be discharged over the following few days. The therapist found herself offering advice to the patient's wife on the phone and then immediately went to visit the patient in hospital. She was perplexed by her own behaviour and degree of upset, but in supervision she realized that while there was inevitably some anxiety in relationship to the patient, her leading anxiety that had driven her into action was actually in connection to her own father who had become ill very suddenly and died in hospital some months previously.

Caper (1999) draws attention to the internal constellation of the clinician regarding the relationship the therapist has with her or his own internal objects. Understanding more about what belongs to the therapist and developing a capacity to differentiate this from what belongs to the patient is a core part within the NHS of specialist training in psychoanalytic psychotherapy, which includes at its heart the experience of a personal analysis or psychotherapy.

The search for psychic truth is part of what makes us human, and one aim of psychoanalytic psychotherapy is to allow the individual to reclaim disowned aspects of their personality through understanding. One way in which this understanding comes about is through enactments in the relationship between therapist and patient in the treatment process itself, which allows for an unconscious repetition of past and present forms of relating to external figures such as parents in the past, as well as to partners and colleagues in the present, and so forth, but also to internal figures. Freud thought that the past had to be approached a little like an archaeological dig—if you kept going through the layers, an accurate reconstruction of memory and history would eventually come about. However, current psychoanalytic thinking would suggest that the past is not a series of facts from much earlier times, but something that is alive and well in the present and can be experienced directly through the therapeutic relationship, so that "in psychoanalytic treatment we can observe the psychic structures that keep the past in the present—we don't just construct the past, we construct internal object relationships in the present" (Feldman, in press).

Unlike classical psychoanalysis, where an individual attends sessions four or five times a week over a number of years, the basic framework for psychoanalytic psychotherapy in the public sector is much briefer. It may include an extended consultation of two to four sessions; brief psychodynamic psychotherapy, which is usually twelve to sixteen sessions; individual once-weekly psychotherapy of usually about one to two years' duration; intermittent open-ended treatment on a fortnightly or monthly basis; and psychoanalytic group psychotherapy, which may be time-limited (usually one to three years), or more open-ended if the therapist is running a slow/open group. It is important before treatment begins for the therapist to be clear in his or her own mind what the treatment frame is and to communicate this clearly to the patient.

In terms of formal psychoanalytic psychotherapy, it is important to establish a secure frame that will contain both the therapist and the patient. Quinodoz (1992) points out that this basic frame

> helps to bring out the three-dimensionality of the analyst–patient relationship: I am thinking of everything a violation of the setting, or any need to make an exception to the rule, can reveal about a patient's psychical mechanisms. Now in order for a setting to be violated, there must first be a setting; and to make an exception to the rule, there must first be a rule.

Within the secure containment of an agreed setting, the relationship between patient and therapist can begin to unfold. At the very least, the setting—as a representation of the clinician's state of mind—needs to be a neutral space, protected as far as possible from outside distraction, in which patients feels free to bring their thoughts and the therapist is open to whatever the patients brings into the session. In terms of the therapist's state of mind, Klein (unpublished lecture) described the analytic attitude as one in which:

> Our whole interest is focussed on one aim, namely, on the exploration of the mind of this one person who for the time being has become the centre of our attention. . . . If we are not bent on labelling our patients as such and such a type, or wondering prematurely about the structure of the case, if we are not guided in our approach to him by a preconceived plan—trying to evoke such and such a response from him—then, and only then, are we ready to learn step by step everything about the patient from himself. . . . This rather curious state of mind, eager and at the same time patient, detached from the subject and at the same time fully absorbed in it, is clearly the result of a balance between different and partly conflicting tendencies and psychological drives, and of a good co-operation between several different parts of our minds. . . . Our critical faculties undoubtedly remain active all along, but they have, as it were, retreated into the background to leave the way for our unconscious to get into touch with the unconscious of the patient . . . fruitful analytic work . . . will only be effective if it is coupled with a really good attitude towards the patient as a person. By this I do not mean merely friendly human feelings and a benevolent attitude towards people, but in addition to this, something of the nature of a deep and true respect for the workings of the human mind, and the human personality in general. [Klein, 1936]

Problems of abnormal or failed mourning are very common in many of the people who are older referred for assessment and treatment to old age and psychological therapy services. While Freud thought that it was impossible to contemplate one's own death, Klein asserted that the fear of death was present in the unconscious from the beginning in terms of primitive fears of annihilation. The psychoanalyst Hanna Segal wrote the first detailed published account of a psychoanalysis with an older person in her classic 1958 paper "Fear of Death: Notes on the Analysis of an Old Man", and she suggested that many people in later life come for help because they are unable to face the death of others or the prospect of their own death. This mirrors very early difficulties in facing ambivalence with regard to loss and separation in early childhood, and therapists often raise anxieties with regard to ending treatment with a patient who is older.

Time is a crucial concept in thinking about old age, where a key representation of time is death. Bell (2006) noted that it is far more common to locate persecuting rather than peaceful fantasies in our representation of time, while Birksted-Breen (2003) sees that "time as non-repetition is particularly hated because it is immutable, inevitable and leading to loss and death". She pointed out that the therapeutic setting is a representation of time, with a beginning, middle, and end to each session, and finite reality being confirmed with the eventual ending of the treatment itself. The therapist is the "guardian of time", and the fact of time in the therapeutic encounter is what Birksted-Breen calls "the third element", which stops the "folie à deux" in terms of the illusion of treatment going on in some infinite way. She links this to the oedipal situation, in which "With the toleration of the oedipal situation and of the depressive situation, time can 'elongate'. Memories replace 'reminiscences'; thought replaces action; The past can be faced, accepted as past and distinguished from the present. Equally the present can be lived in the present as distinguished from an idealised or persecutory future" (p. 1507). In order for this to take place, the dead person has to be relinquished through mourning in order for the individual to find and strengthen her or his own internal capacities. This is a very different process from identifying with the dead person (lost object) as a way of hanging onto that person, which forms the basis for many of the cases of failed mourning seen within old age services or in older adults seeking out analysis in later life.

Clinical illustration: Mr E

Mr E was a man in his late sixties who was referred for help with his depression following the death of his wife, who had been killed in a traffic accident while they were on holiday four years previously. He was immaculately presented, to the degree, he said, that his doctor had once joked with him about it and enquired whether his house was as tidy as he seemed to be. In talking with him, he described in detail the circumstances surrounding his wife's death as though it were yesterday. This, of course, is a very clear feature in trauma and conveyed immediately to me a sense of timelessness that rendered him unable to move on at any level. He survived but felt he was no longer living his life. This was true, as he was identified with an object that he felt he had to keep hold of in a particular way in his mind, which ultimately evaded the painful work of mourning. During the course of brief treatment, Mr E brought the following dream:

He was standing inside a large impersonal room, a bit like a terminal. At one end of the room was a large, glass window, which made up the wall.

Outside he could see nothing other than a red ether. He thought that it looked a bit like a Rothko painting. A figure emerged from the ether, slightly shapeless at first, like a genie emerging from a lamp, and somehow seeped through the glass into the lounge area. He knew the figure was going to land somewhere and that its name was "Guilt". The patient stood frozen to the spot and the figure went into his wife standing next to him, who curled up like an old shrivelled foetus. He knew she was dead.

In his associations to the dream, Mr E thought that it was guilt that would kill him and that if only the figure had gone into him, then it would be he who would have died, not his wife.

Mr E had been married for forty years, and his dream vividly brought in the guilt of the survivor—after such a long marriage, following his wife's death he felt unable to live with the guilt of carrying on living, and he continued to deny himself the possibility of new relationships or experiences. Guilt can take different forms, both depressive and persecutory, and it is possible to see in this example the way in which Mr E was consumed with persecutory guilt, which left him in a state of terrible isolation.

Limits and possibilities in an individual psychotherapy: trauma, remembrance, and reparation

In his book *The Emigrants* (1996), W. B. Sebald described his discussion with his factional character, the artist Max Ferber, who moved to Manchester from Germany in 1942. In their conversation, Ferber described the way in which:

> It grew steadily harder for me to write my letters home or to read the letters that arrived from home every fortnight. The correspondence became more of a chore, and when the letters stopped coming, in November, 1941, I was relieved at first, in a way that now strikes me as quite terrible. Only gradually did it dawn on me that I would never again be able to write home; in fact, to tell the truth, I do not know if I have really grasped it to this day. But it now seems to me that the course of my life, down to the tiniest detail, was ordained not only by the deportation of my parents but also by the delay with which the news of their death reached me, news I could not believe at first and the meaning of which only sank in by degrees. Naturally, I took steps, consciously or unconsciously, to keep at bay thoughts of my parents' suffering and of my own misfortune, and no doubt I succeeded sometimes in maintaining a certain equability by my

self-imposed seclusion; but the fact is that that tragedy in my youth struck such deep roots within me that it later shot up again, put forth evil flowers, and spread the poisonous canopy over me which has kept me so much in the shade and dark in recent years.

Ferber then gives Sebald a brown-paper package containing his mother's memoirs. These were written between 1939 and 1941 and showed, said Ferber,

> that obtaining a visa had become increasingly difficult and that the plans his father had made for their emigration had necessarily become more complex with every week that passed—and, as his mother had clearly understood, impossible to carry out. Mother wrote not a word about the events of the moment, said Ferber, apart from the odd oblique glance at the hopeless situation she and Father were in; instead, with a passion that was beyond his understanding, she wrote of her childhood. . . . In the time that had passed since they were written, said Ferber, he had read the memories his mother had committed to paper only twice. The first time, after he had received the package, he had skimmed over them. The second time he had read them meticulously, many years later. On that second occasion, the memoirs, which at points were truly wonderful, had seemed to him like one of those evil German fairy tales in which, once you are under the spell, you have to carry on to the finish, till your heart breaks, with whatever work you have begun—in this case, the re-membering, writing and reading. That is why I would rather you took this package, Ferber said, and saw me out to the yard, where he walked with me as far as the almond tree. [pp. 190–193]

I want to describe something of my experience with a patient who came from a not dissimilar background to Max Ferber and part of "the package" that I think he needed to hand to me in a very particular way in the early part of the treatment. The issue of survival and its impact on the individual and those around the person, including, in this case, me as the therapist, are explored in the following account of once-weekly psychotherapy over a one-year period with Mr F:

Background

Mr F was an 80-year-old man referred to the clinic by his GP. The practice counsellor had seen him briefly for difficulties arising when his much younger wife had left Mr F with their three children, the youngest of whom was in his late teens and still living at home. The counsellor had been concerned at the degree of anger and distress voiced repeatedly in the family sessions with Mr F's repeated query, "Who will look after me as I get older?" At the point he sought help, he was clinically depressed, finding it difficult to sleep at night, with early morning wakening, uncontrollable bouts of weeping, and various reported difficulties with memory loss. Mr F moved himself day after day into the waiting-room of his GP practice or onto the bench outside the GP's surgery. He felt he now had no buffer to deal with so much of the past that still invaded his present and impacted on those around him—particularly his children. When I first saw him, his nights were spent in an agitated, sleepless state in which he felt tormented by his wife's departure, was emotionally labile, and wept constantly. The GP conveyed a sense of helplessness and irritation with Mr F, who insisted on talking to him every time he left the surgery. The GP had suggested repeatedly that his 80-year-old patient be seen within the old age services, and Mr F had repeatedly refused, only accepting a referral to the Tavistock because it was to an outpatient adult psychotherapy service.

Mr F was born in Eastern Europe to a prosperous Jewish family. His brothers and sisters had been born at different points before, during, and after the First World War, with father away in the army throughout most of the war. Mr F described to me his escape from his country of origin, telling me that his father had arranged for him to work his passage on a ship that eventually arrived in England. Mr F ended up in Manchester and was then, because of his country of origin, immediately interned as an "enemy alien" for the duration of the war. At the end of the war he learned that both his parents had perished in a concentration camp. Mr F quickly built up a successful business and went on to marry three times. On each occasion, he married women literally half his own age, and it seemed, as he spoke, that his wives and the children they bore him contained his projected youth, through which he felt secure that his world could continue indefinitely.

The shattering of this perspective came in three ways. First, upon his retirement; second, when his wife left him to live with a man her own age; and third, his fear of the loss of his youngest son, who would soon be leaving home. Mr F said that while he knew his youngest son's leaving home eventually was natural and inevitable, he was afraid that he would respond in some catastrophic way in terms of some unbearable constellation of pressures in himself being triggered off, connected to his own unnatural and precipitate leaving of his own parents at the age his son was now. Mr F was quite specific in the first meeting that he could not afford to wait until then, as he felt it would not leave him enough time to deal with what he termed "the soreness" inside himself. He said he felt he suffered from the loneliness of old age. By this I thought he was referring to both the external reality in terms of his marriage breaking down, but also to what Klein calls "This state of internal loneliness" which, she goes on to describe,

> is the result of an ubiquitous yearning for an unattainable perfect internal state. Such loneliness, which is experienced to some extent by everyone, springs from paranoid and depressive anxieties which are derivatives of the infant's psychotic anxieties. These anxieties exist in some measure in every individual but are excessively strong in illness; therefore loneliness is also part of illness, both of a schizophrenic and depressive nature". [Klein, 1963, p. 300]

Klein (1963), Cohen (1982), and Hess (2004) in writing about loneliness have noted that a major fear in being alone is that the individual is afraid of being left with feelings of overwhelming persecution, with no one to project into.

Assessment and treatment

Mr F conveyed both despair and courage in his approach to assessment and treatment with his implicit understanding that issues he had managed to evade in a particular way through the structuring of his work and family life were no longer holding fast, and that while he felt his life had broken down with his wife's leaving, he felt that if he did not gain some understanding of himself at a deeper level, it would completely shatter at the point that his youngest child left home. In our first meeting, Mr F said that he had taken his son to see the film *Four Weddings and A Funeral* and described the phenomenon of reaching a certain point in the lifecycle where the opposite was true—invitations he received were no longer to weddings but to the funerals of old friends and colleagues. Each time he received one of these invitations, he would weep for the friend and simultaneously feel relief and triumph at what he called his illicitly held thought that "at least it wasn't me this time". This, of course, is something many people who are older describe as they look through the obituary pages of the newspaper, but for Mr F it took on a particular meaning in the light of his history.

Mr F went on to say that he wanted to have nothing to do with old people, as he felt they were all locked into their own worlds, with little interest beyond their own narrow confines. Over time I was able to think with him about a narrow, rigid part of himself that he felt stuck and imprisoned with, conveniently lodged elsewhere in those he termed the "oldies" whom he then, contemptuously, wanted nothing to do with. He had been relatively happy so long as his world was populated with younger people—his wife, his children, and, in the early months of his therapy, his at first hidden thought that I might be his young companion throughout his old age. At the time of seeing my patient, there was a great deal of coverage in the papers and on television and radio about the anniversary of the liberation of the concentration camps, and he was approached at various points by museums and film-makers who were keen to record his story. In the early months of treatment, I rapidly became in the transference the son or wife whose role was to act as his secretary and notate his life story (one of the reasons, Mr F had told me in the preliminary meeting, his wife had eventually left him).

I enacted this dynamic by, for example, keeping copious notes at the end of each session, or finding myself upset at the end of each session sometimes, carrying this over into a preoccupation beyond the session itself. Over time I began to see how the quality of Mr F's telling me of his story captivated and ultimately controlled me in a particular way. I became aware that my response was similar to the way I had felt as a young woman when I first learned about Auschwitz and Belsen and had stood in the Imperial War Museum seeing a silent reel of film, repeating again and again the liberation of Belsen, finding myself unable to move away from the screen of the piles of dead bodies, and the living dead. I realized that I had become as consumed with Mr F's past as Mr F felt consumed by his past. With supervision it became possible to think more flexibly about what the experience of his wife and family may have been living with Mr F, and for Mr F what his experience of living with himself may involve.

My ability initially to function with Mr F as his therapist who could understand and interpret the pressures arising in the transference and countertransference was hampered so long as I felt identified with Mr F's external story. And yet the hampering was inevitable in terms of an enactment that ultimately enabled me to understand more about the internal pressure my patient felt driven by, and which he exerted on those around him. In the countertransference I was able to experience and become more aware of how controlled Mr F felt by his inner objects and, in return, how he then controlled others by projecting guilt and responsibility into them. The pressure seemed for me to be the solution, rather than think with Mr F about what solutions there may be to his extreme fear of getting older in isolation, with his youngest child about to leave home and no real friends. Beyond this external situation, I thought Mr F felt haunted, persecuted, and alone with the internal "older ones"—namely, his dead parents.

Earlier in the book I referred to Freud's great paper "Mourning and Melancholia", which gives a detailed description of the internal world of the depressed person in identification with an object that is dead or decaying. With Mr F, I think it possible to understand something about the nature of his identification with the decayed objects—his parents in the concentration camp—and the way in which, at an internal level, he feared the envy of the dead, feeling accused by his objects that he survived into old age while they were unable to. In his initial questionnaire prior to being seen for an assessment for treatment, Mr F had responded to a query about his parents by writing starkly: "They were both murdered in a concentration camp. I am uncertain whether I am coming to terms with this or not." Garland (2002), writing about the nature of trauma and the impact of traumatic events, takes up the way in which, at an external level, perhaps there are some things that we are unable to come to terms with in terms of "getting over" them. The issue for Mr F was not so much the getting over things—some things it is not possible to get over—but more the *getting on* with things. With Mr F, psychotherapeutic treatment was able to provide a secure framework within which he and I could learn more about and understand the defences that earlier on in his life had been a necessary means of survival and, over time, had become rigid and unmoveable. The challenge for the treatment was whether these defences would stay calcified, in identification with the bones of the dead that lived within him and he felt controlled by, or whether there was still the possibility of something more flexible developing in his feeling freer to grow older and plan for his old age in the way his parents had been unable to. "Psychotherapeutic treatment which analyses such anxieties and defence mechanisms may enable the patient to experience ambivalence, to mobilise the infantile depressive position and work it through to sufficiently re-establish good internal objects and face old age and death in a more mature way" (Segal, 1958). For Mr F, this meant the painful task of repairing within and without. Rey (1994b) noted that the object has not got to be restored to the exact condition in which it was before the damage (p. 227). So with Mr F, the damage had already been done, things could not be restored to the state they were pre-retirement, pre his parents deportation, but, to some degree, there always remained the possibility of reparation. An indication of this at a follow-up meeting two years post-treatment was to hear that he had negotiated the emotional challenge—which at the start of his therapy he thought would lead to a catastrophic breakdown—of allowing his last child to leave home freely. It seemed that Mr F's capacity to leave go of controlling his objects ("I will die if you move away") paradoxically allowed in a warmer relationship between Mr F and his children as well as with his ex-wife. Rather than continue to identify with the internal objects he felt haunted by, Mr F managed, to some degree, to separate from them and in this way regain the life available to him with his children in the present.

CHAPTER 5

Couples psychotherapy: separateness or separation? An account of work with a couple entering later life

Anne Amos and Andrew Balfour

A t the Tavistock Centre for Couple Relationships (TCCR), there are many referrals of couples who are entering later life. They are often partnerships that have been together for many years, but facing retirement and old age together seems like a hurdle too far. Intimate relationships, in which children have been reared and family life with its vicissitudes has been borne, are still, nevertheless, a receptacle for much emotional distress and mental suffering for the individuals concerned. Illness, incapacity, retirement of both or either partner are challenges to all partnerships. With increasing longevity and with a more psychologically minded population, organizations that work with couples are also increasingly concerned with those in later life.

In this chapter we are concerned to explore, using a case example, not so much the end of life, but more the losses involved in entering later life and how these can challenge a long-standing relationship. The changes and adjustments that are required may be more, or less, possible for one or other partner. It is a truism that living life necessitates facing loss and limitation. Declining physical abilities, loss of a work role in society, no longer being required as a parent, waning intellectual abilities and energy levels, as well as disappointments about the life that it wasn't possible to lead, are all losses to be borne. These concretely experienced losses trigger our earliest infantile experiences of loss and separation, and perhaps never more so as when approaching later life. The dependency that belonged to our infancy becomes, once again, a reality that cannot be escaped from by "growing up".

Tavistock Centre for Couple Relationships: models of marriage

At TCCR, a model for thinking about difficulties in couple relationships has been developed that is an application of psychoanalytic thinking. It involves seeing the couple together, at a regular time each week, sometimes extending for as long as several years. Often, as in the case we shall describe, the couple will see two therapists working together as a therapeutic couple. From this method of work, an understanding that couples share an unconscious phantasy has developed. Often this centres on a shared infantile terror, and in their relationship the individuals concerned develop a shared system of defences to deal with these fears and anxieties. The defences can harden to such an extent that they exert a stranglehold on emotional openness and spontaneity in each individual, and sometimes this leads to a situation where all sense of individual identity can be lost. The purpose of the therapeutic work is for the couple to face in the consulting-room, and in their relationship with the therapist/s, these early anxieties, in order that they can begin to understand how they use each other to avoid their own individual difficulties.

An early example of such thinking is elaborated in the work of Lily Pincus (1976) entitled *Death and the Family: The Importance of Mourning*, where two types of defensive pattern were described as operating in a marriage. The first is a marriage based on identification, where all good things are kept in the marriage and all difficulties projected outside their relationship. The couple are very identified with one another, like identical twins. The second type of defensive pattern in a marriage is based on projection, where one partner has all one set of characteristics and the other the opposite. Together they seem to make a whole, as if one partner is only complete with the other. Pincus showed how in both these defensive patterns loss of individuality strangled a marital relationship, so that in the event of the death of one of the partners the grieving process of the remaining partner was seriously impaired. Most partnerships are a complex combination of these patterns.

A further notion in marital therapy is that of "marital fit". This is a way of describing how partners in a relationship fit into each others' needs, often in the most subtle ways. Even in what might appear, to the outside, as the worst of relationships, the individuals concerned might be maintaining their own individual mental equilibrium. An intimate adult relationship satisfies many emotional needs, not just for love and dependency but also to ward off and deal with difficult, troublesome, and ill sides of the individual. Projective identification is a universal phenomenon. It is a psychic mechanism through which one person might, so to speak, "put part of him/herself" into another person, attributing to that person some feared or disavowed aspect of his or her own personality. This is usually an unconscious process and is part of the glue that holds the couple together. In an intimate relationship, part of the self can reside in the other so that it is not entirely lost. This can be seen in the situation when a partner marries in the hope of improving this or that unacceptable characteristic in the other and thus can be a way of trying to improve something in another person that is actually troubling to oneself. Relationships typically have a dominant atmosphere created by the interaction of the two individuals, and by what they transfer to one another of their own individual internal worlds, their inner objects. In trying to understand this, we speak then of the "dynamic structure" of a relationship, which has its own underlying shared or complementary unconscious phantasies.

In the following example, it is possible to gather a flavour of the emotional currency or dynamic of a marriage even as it reaches its end. In his novel *The Heather Blazing*. Colm Toibin (1992) conveys the tension between a wish to make amends, to sort something out, but the intractability of the personalities involved and the pull to a familiar "marital fit". He describes the relationship between the central character, an elderly judge, Eamon, and his wife, Carmel, who has already had one stroke, leaving her speech impaired. She has become incontinent and excruciatingly ashamed having to be cleaned up and taken to bed by her husband. Once in bed she fears having another stroke, and after a withdrawn and agonizingly cold and distant silence between them, she says she wants to talk to him. This is what she says:

> "Eamon, please pay attention to me now. We talked about this years ago, I don't know if you remember. I still feel we are not close to each other. I am sorry that I am boring you. . . . Maybe I am the one who's cold. Maybe I made you like that. Can you understand me? Maybe we looked for each other and found a match, each of us. . . . I used

to love how reserved you were, but I know now that it was wrong of me to want you like that. And I have long ago given up arguing with you. Everything I think I keep to myself now. I want this to change. I want you to listen to me."

He replies "I'll think about what you said."

He then returns to the living-room where he looks out of the window at the lighthouse. [p. 154]

Colm Toibin then describes, through the lighthouse, Eamon's state of mind:

the fierce beam of light [which] came at intervals. He [Eamon] watched for it, it was much slower than a heartbeat or the ticking of a clock. It came in its own time, unfolding its light clear and full against the darkness which was everywhere outside. [p. 155]

The judge seems to feel deeply the heartbeat that is the consistency of their relationship and a connection to the baby in the womb experiencing the beating of its mother's heart, as well as the darkness that is Carmel's death and his own, too. This is all conveyed and experienced through the familiarity of the lasting nature of the landscape, not in his conversation with his wife. She, on the other hand, is trying to reach out with her voice before it is no longer possible for her, before she sinks into her own darkness, trying to talk about her own coldness, not just experiencing it as coming from her husband.

Dependency in marriage

Klein describes the primitive, infantile reaction to loss as a fear of annihilation, that we defend ourselves against with the primitive defence mechanisms of projection, splitting, and denial. Unbearable feelings, like hunger or no mother to give comfort, are disposed of by projection, so that the baby no longer feels that there is something good outside that will comfort, nurture, and protect him or her but actually feels that the world outside is bad and persecuting, and he or she feels tormented. This can be seen in a young baby's crying that takes over the whole body and, we infer, the baby's mind too. The baby is tormented from inside and out. The world is bad, and the baby is bad. The dependency that is inherent in the intimacy of a partnership, together with increasing dependency that facing later life entails, augers fear and anxiety reminiscent of that earliest primitive dependency: of a baby on its mother. The anxieties of this earliest dependency can lead to claustrophobia, feeling trapped in a horrible tormenting, bad world and therefore misunderstood and badly treated. This claustrophobic world can be concretely experienced as the marital relationship, as was exemplified in the following example of Mr and Mrs E.

Clinical example: Mr and Mrs E

Mr and Mrs E seemed in many ways to have so much, yet, despite their considerable financial and career success, not to mention children and grandchildren, they could see nothing hopeful ahead of them. Encroaching older age seemed to them to be felt to be a point beyond which development stopped; there was nothing to look forward to. They could not enjoy what they had, and when they presented for help they were in a desperate state. Past success and happiness seemed to be denigrated and forgotten, their current life seemed deadly, and the future could not be thought about. In Mr E's words, "the past is grim, the present is grim, and the future is grim". We now describe something of the clinical work we undertook together with this couple, who came to us weekly—apart from the usual breaks at Christmas, Easter, and in August—for nearly three years.

Assessment and initial stages of treatment

Mr and Mrs E were French. Mr E was an international lawyer of some fame and standing in his field, and Mrs E had retired from her position as a teacher. They had been living in England for a short while because of Mr E's work—he had been offered a work challenge that he was eager to take on. They looked like an archetypal middle-class, elegant, older couple, but they presented in a desperate state after more than forty years of marriage, children and grandchildren, and two successful careers. Things had been difficult since Mrs E's retirement two years previously. They had recently bought a retirement house in France and came to London during the week, staying in their flat while he worked and she tried to occupy herself with cultural activities such as trips to galleries and theatres. In some ways they appeared to have it all, and yet they were desperately unhappy, both of them depressed, and he at times seemed at risk of suicide. Their retirement plans had stalled: he had kept working despite promises to the contrary, and they had never properly moved into the beautiful retirement home outside Paris that they visited at weekends. They conveyed vividly their inability to move into and inhabit together the territory of their old age.

In the normal course of the work at TCCR, self-report forms are sent to each partner before their first appointment. When Mr and Mrs E came, they told us how neither of them had read the other's form, both of which were sitting, out of sight, side by side on our desk, "in parallel", so to speak. These forms, each one unknown to the other, sitting like this on the desk, seemed to reflect the parallel lives this couple lived, and this was echoed in the way in which they each took it in turns to address us in the session, having no direct contact, no exchange with one another. It was as if they had ceased to see the other as a separate individual and they no longer had anything left to discover about one other.

On the forms themselves, each had complained that the other one was depressed—Mrs E, in particular, had emphasized her worry about his depression and complained that all he did at home was fall asleep in front of the television. We expected, therefore, to meet up with a withdrawn man. In fact, he presented initially as a rather suave, commanding figure, and we were struck, instead, by Mrs E's considerable grief and sadness. She was tearful and aggrieved, and it was our impression that she was the depressed one who was left waiting for him and frustrated at his unavailability. She complained that, taken up as he was with matters of European law and developing the European Union, he was always very late when they arranged to meet up, and she felt neglected and ignored. At weekends, she complained, he only wanted to surround himself with people and entertain in their French home and did not appreciate how much work it was for her trying to run two homes. He told us of an old family friend, a woman in her nineties, who had recently left to live in Australia, and with admiration he said, "Now, that's life for you". The feelings of grievance and depression seemed to be lodged entirely in Mrs E—partly, at least, provoked in her by her husband's behaviour, his withdrawal into the world of work, and the way in which he distanced himself from her. We suspected that a very depressed part of him was lodged in her, so that she might then be thought of, at that moment, as the one carrying a "double dose" of despair—her own feelings and his. This is an example of the projective mechanisms mentioned earlier.

At this early point in our work with them, we asked ourselves why they sought help now, and we wondered about the role of retirement as a trigger. It seemed to us that it might threaten a defensive cleavage that they had maintained until this point in time, their parallel forms representing their parallel lives, where work could function to provide for their mutual need to keep a distance from one another. With retirement facing them and simultaneously being avoided, it was as if they feared being thrown together. Being in contact with these feelings of depression, lodged in the other, with no escape into anything else seemed to be an underlying fear for both of them. They took care, as it were, that there was no chance of their becoming depressed at the same time, when they might become completely overwhelmed—"both go under at the same time", as they later said they feared.

A first glance at their situation might look as if Mr E's attitude was very positive, as he was continuing to be involved at the "cutting edge" of development in his area of expertise. However, what emerged was a much more disturbing picture. He was under enormous pressure, inside himself, to work harder and harder, so that he slept only a few hours each night, driving himself in a ruthless way, without any regard for ordinary human need for rest and recovery. She was, we thought with some reason, concerned for his health and his survival. His doctor, too, we learned, was concerned about his high blood pressure. He expected only high performance from himself. He was at the top, he had to be responsible, and he felt that a lot of people's livelihoods depended on him. There were increasing and insoluble problems in his work, and this meant he had to work longer and longer hours, reflecting, we thought, the internal pressure in his mind. At this time we feared that Mr E was in such a withdrawn state that he could make a suicide attempt, so identified was he with the failures and serious problems at work. Any human vulnerability or struggles, in his mind, were the equivalent of failure and evoked powerful self-condemnation.

By understanding the cruel tyranny Mr E put himself under, we were able to reach something more human in him. Over time, he began to refer to this internal condemnation that drove him so remorselessly as a "cancer" that grew in his mind. This led to him painfully revealing just how empty he was of feelings for his wife. He cared for her, he said, but his feelings of love had vanished. He could not force them to come back, and now he felt tortured, just like at work. "His lack of feelings had beaten him", he said, "the way nothing else had ever done." He felt he could do nothing about this, he couldn't bring back the feelings however much he tried. Mrs E seemed to be in an equally tortured position—endlessly waiting for him to make up his mind, to commit to her, or not. Her feelings of anger and frustration at this were thinly disguised in sniping comments about his incompetence. Each seemed to have entirely lost any notion that there had ever been any good in their marriage and felt stuck in what was referred to as a "twilight zone of perpetual misery", where nothing changed and no change felt possible. This is how the sessions felt to us, too: there might be a bit of liveliness, a hint of some movement, in one session, but this would be lost by the next one, and we would be faced with the complaint that things were just the same and they were stuck in the same old groove. Unsurprisingly they felt that we were not helping them either, and we had to face that we were stuck, just as they were stuck.

Middle phase of treatment

Any lively, spontaneous, or overt feelings seemed to have disappeared, and yet behind their elegant, polite façade we sensed simmering and explosive aggression. Slowly it was possible to show them their angry feelings towards us for the way in which they felt we were failing them. For example, on one occasion they turned up for what they thought was their usual session, but actually it was our holiday, and we had given them ample warning we would be away. They denied being put out by this, even though they told us in many other ways of the enormous inconvenience it had been for them, so that eventually even they could not sustain a polite façade. As we were able to accept their anger and criticisms of us and talk to them about those feelings, slowly we began to hear more about their complaints and fears that we were untrustworthy and didn't care and had maybe even overlooked telling them of our holiday. On reflection, it occurred to us that the fact that they could not hear of a change in our routine with them, that we left to have our own holidays, demonstrated something of their shared inability to face change because of the disturbing feelings that this provoked.

Following this, there was a period when one or other of them was unable to come to a session and the other would come alone. At such times, each of them would comment on how much freer he or she felt, able to say things now that he or she couldn't when the other was present: each was convinced the other would be "devastated" if he or she were to hear what was being said. While these revelations never felt particularly remarkable, what was more striking was their mutual attribution of vulnerability and "devastation" to the other partner. On one such occasion, Mr E commented on what he felt was his difficulty in "speaking from the heart" to his wife, because she could so easily be devastated. It felt there was an echo here in the way he talked of having to be careful with her, of his treatment of us, his therapists. We noticed that when he was angry with us, he would comment, quite out of the blue, that it was not that he felt furious, not that he felt he was going to explode—even though no one had said that he was, this negation often being our first sign that this was precisely what he felt. On this occasion, when this was taken up with him, he said that he could easily devastate us, as if sure of his own intellectual and verbal superiority. We suggested to him that he tended to think of himself always as potentially devastating, never devastated. It then emerged that he had been very upset recently when in fact his wife had been the one to angrily comment that they should split up, and in telling us of this he became tearful. He said that it made him think of his son's comment, which he had been surprised by, that his mother would manage if they split up, but not his father. We caught a glimpse of Mr E's vulnerability, and he commented on his real uncertainty about himself. He told us that he felt all his success in life was because he worked hard. It was not that he was brilliant like many of his colleagues, and the trouble was he could no longer maintain this level of hard work and others were overtaking him. It was a painful and distressing moment for this apparently highly able and defended man to show us such raw emotion. It was at this point, when he seemed to glimpse some of his own vulnerability, that his feelings about being with his wife emerged. In his mind, she expected such high standards from him and, like him, she could not bear a worried and anxious man who might fail. No wonder old age and retirement were terrifying.

This material seems to lead us towards an understanding of their shared underlying unconscious anxiety: that emotional contact could lead to what was most feared: "a devastating explosion". There was a phantasy operating that if nothing changed, there would be no contact, no explosion, and then nothing would be lost, particularly not the sense of oneself as a self-sufficient individual. Each of them denied awareness of their need and dependency by projecting it into the other so they did not have to face their own frailty. If time stood still in the way they complained so bitterly about but actually maintained by their actions, there would be no development. Emotionally speaking, this was a small price to pay to maintain the denial of feelings of dependency and loss of competence. Keeping themselves apart seemed to be an attempt to obviate or circumvent any knowledge of the other's difference. Neither could see the other as someone who would have the capacity to care for him or her if he or she were needy and dependent, and each failed to recognize his or her own individual need for love and concern. There was no intimacy as, paradoxically, they were not separate individuals and the main method of communication between them was that of projective identification, disposing of, and despising, vulnerability and emotional neediness in the other.

Strikingly, given this was marital therapy, there was no discussion of their sexual relationship. Similarly, there was neither discussion of their past nor anticipation of impending retirement. This loss, like so much of their emotional lives, was unthinkable and not discussable. Mr E's response was to take on new projects and work ever more frantically, to ablate any knowledge of the reality of his impending retirement. Eventually we heard of Mr E's prostate cancer some five years previously. Initially they claimed it made no difference to them as a couple, it was unrelated to their difficulties. But actually his response, as we would now expect, was to cut off and work ever harder, in a painful and vain attempt to regain youth and potency. It became, in this phase of the treatment, more apparent just how much he had withdrawn into an idealization of self-sufficiency and away from his vulnerability and dependency. He nurtured "dreams" of being off on his own in which he was a kind of existential anti-hero, on his own in some romantic foreign city. How unreal Mr E's dreams of separation were became clear. He was entirely bound up with his wife and could not go away on his own except to work, where, of course, he felt equally shackled. With this knowledge he withdrew further and no longer wanted to do anything with his wife in public, did not want to be seen connected to her. This could now be taken up as an angry attack on her for her exactingness, which, of course, was also his exactingness projected into her. It was just these sorts of projections that made their inseparability increasingly evident.

We heard of the lists of tasks that she would regularly, at the start of the weekend, put out on the kitchen table for him to achieve. Mrs E told us of her distress at being cuddled by an old disabled man for an act of kindness by her, and she said how much she wished this had been her husband. While this seemed to be painfully true, it also seemed like a surreptitious attack. She seemed to want nothing more than for him to be a good boy and do what she wanted, yet she complained that even an old disabled man could do what he couldn't—give her a cuddle. Neither one of them seemed to really need the other. We heard of their earlier married life, when she went along with his wish to take risks and do exciting things but actually resented all that she was left to deal with, particularly an ill son. Mr E also resented the way in which she ran the family, and he felt there was no room for him. It took months of work with this couple for them to begin to be more open in their resentment of each other, resentments that had built up over years.

This defensive arrangement of keeping themselves apart, silently resenting the other, and maintaining their own very separate world of work or family seemed to allow each of them the sense that they presided over their own "fiefdom". This arrangement was threatened by the thought that they would both retire and share one space. This mobilized anxiety because their defensive structure was threatened; their projections onto each other were coming too close for comfort. This further added to our picture of this couple's unconscious phantasy: a belief that intimacy could only mean the domination of one by the other.

In the sessions, he often dominated, making much of his feeling of being "to blame" for the situation. She largely seemed to go along with this. This stuck state and immobility had the quality of obsessional hesitation, between two alternatives: the world of marriage or work. His preoccupations dominated her: she patiently waited for him to make up his mind, but did not make a claim, did not assert her own mind much. Her passivity seemed to add to his persecuting sense of guilt. Her position was subtly very critical of him, so filled up was she with silent grievance. She rarely became full-bloodedly angry with him, and so the quality of her attacks on him made it difficult for them to be recognized. They were then treated by each of them as invisible and could not be thought about, known, and forgiven. He could not help her with her grievances as he could not answer them in a robust way, which might have helped to stop them building up. She was left alone with her sense of hurt and grievance, which he felt persecuted by, confirmed in his belief that nothing could be done, nothing repaired, and it was all his fault as he could not love her.

They once described our function as psychotherapists as being to provide a "fire blanket" for them, as if our task was to put out the dangerous rage they both felt with each other. This perception of us also described how they behaved with one another. Any sparks of passion or conflict, which might lead to something more explosive, seemed to be dampened down in them. They did not follow through on their thinking, did not allow any conversation about what it meant that he no longer loved her. In that way, although there was much agony, there was little sense of a struggle, involving both of them. This would mean contact and intimacy, which seemed to be disallowed because of a shared fear of too much heat. As he once put it, referring to his announcement that he did not love her, he had "made the wound, but couldn't withdraw the knife". It was as if a feeling or thought was a thing, in this case a knife physically put into the other. This is an example not of communication as discussion and thinking, but of projective identification, putting something unwanted into the other and fearing the consequences of its return. So the agony continued, of no contact and no resolving of anything, no healing. The stuck situation was damaging but, in not being resolved, reflected their fear that nothing could be made better, as to do that would mean facing all that had been lost and damaged. He seemed to retreat in the face of the experience of a persecuting sense of guilt when he was with her, which she reinforced with her complaints. Together, they seemed to be organized to avoid a situation of feeling regret at what was no longer possible, so as not to have to face the harm they had done to one another in their marriage by seeing each other as an unwanted part of themselves. Instead, they lived in a "perpetual present", where they avoided knowing about the reality of ageing and the actual limitations of the life that was available to them.

Facing and experiencing loss and separation

As time went on, and with our help in facing their resentments with us for "not helping" and their resentments with each other, there was in fact movement. She, tired of waiting, challenged him. She would no longer hang on, keeping a vigil at their flat in London. She was moving to France, into retirement, and, if he wanted, he could come too. She showed her independence in other ways, by starting to do more on her own—for example, going on holiday without him—part of which she enjoyed. There seemed, in her challenge, to be a possibility of separateness, a glimpse of a situation in which they could exist together, not entirely bound to one another. Mrs E seemed to be moving on from this stuck state where they were both unable to feel anything other than that the other had to change, to a situation where there was some idea that there were really two people in the marriage who might have separate needs. However, as she moved, his position seemed to harden; his solution to his difficulty in achieving a sense of separateness from her turned into a consolidation of his position that this could only happen if they actually separated.

They did separate physically. She moved back to France, to a town that they had lived in when the family were younger, gaining a sense of belonging from this, of being in her own "mother country". We had two final meetings with each of them on their own. They seemed to engage with their painful feelings of loss on their own with us, in a way they could not manage when they were together. Mrs E, while explaining her practical struggles to move into a new home, was touched to discover that she met people walking down the street who had hardly noticed she'd gone, but she added, "I know I am older". She seemed to have nostalgia for her old family life with her husband, when he and she had both been members of the community, and this included grieving for its passing. Time had not stood still, and she felt older and sadder.

Mr E seemed unable to give up his retreat into self-reliance, which had seemed to intensify for him as things had started to fail him, both in terms of his physical capacities and his career, which had ceased to be the "shining jewel" for him that it had been in his younger years. Although in our final meeting with him he claimed to feel lighter, happier, and freer, we were aware that there were sad feelings very close to the surface, not just the *mea culpa* that we had heard so much about. Mr E felt he had support from his children and seemed much more able to make contact with them of his own volition. He felt we had helped him do something that he could not have managed to do on his own, that he had gone along with an unhappy state of affairs for so long, and, although he was lonely, he felt better. He did still think of his wife as the vulnerable one. She was having an operation and still needed his support in sorting out her new home. It was as if some of the projections had been withdrawn but not all of them.

This was a painful ending to bear, and we were left with a sense of the enormity of the loss involved, of a marriage that had lasted almost a lifetime that we could not, in some fairytale way, make a happy one. We had to face our limitations just as Mr and Mrs E had to face theirs: despite all the external riches this couple had accumulated together, they were emotionally impoverished and stuck. Their solution to this was actually to separate, and it seemed this was the only way in which they could begin to mourn and move into their own old age. The power of their shared unconscious phantasy that intimacy and dependency were to be avoided meant they were unable to move into the shared territory of their old age together as individuals linked together in marriage.

Separation or separateness?

In this example of marital work with, Mr and Mrs E, a couple facing later life, we show how they had to actually end their marriage before they could face, as individuals, many of the losses involved in growing older. They seemed to need to separate concretely because of the power and intensity of their mutual projections into one another, which left them unable to mourn and work through loss in any other way. Without being able to do this, they were so palpably unable to lead a full life and enjoy all that they had in their lives. For Mrs E, her husband seemed to personify all her denial of her own vulnerability. He seemed to trap her in a world of endless waiting for his attention, in the vain hope that all would come right. When she could face more of her own involvement in this, she was able to make an internal move to be a more separate individual and face her own pain and sadness that her husband, far from being able to save her from old age and death, had in fact needs of his own. For Mr E, his wife's physical presence seemed to remind him of his ageing body and failing abilities—in fact, the vulnerabilities that he had been running away from for much of his life. He felt trapped by her presence, by this painful reality. He seemed to need to escape in order to begin to face, possibly in a more diluted form, his own pain at experiencing loss.

Perhaps this example has shown the power and grip of a marital relationship and its link with the mental health of each of the partners. Without this working through, Mr and Mrs E would, we think, have faced further and more serious depression, with greater restrictions in their emotional life and with the obvious consequences for their children, grandchildren, and their future carers as their dependency needs increased. For them, the companionship of an intimate marital relationship was not possible at this point in their emotional development.

Simone de Beauvoir (1972) wrote:

> our private inward experience does not tell us the number of our years; no fresh perception comes into being to show us the decline of age. . . . When we look at the image of our own future provided by the old, we do not believe it: an absurd inner voice whispers, that that will never happen to us—when that happens, it will no longer be ourselves that it happens to.

The partners in a couple might be said to reflect to one another the reality of their ageing, literally representing, in the older body now in front of them, the reality of time passing. The prospect of loss and illness, the difficulties of caring for another human being, of retaining one's own separate identity while allowing closeness and dependence on others, all of these things, and the anxieties they bring, are not unique to old age, but they are very much a part of it. The knowledge of time passing may be a stimulus to couples to want to work on long-standing difficulties, to address long-avoided areas—an opportunity for development. But the trigger for seeking help can also be the breaking-through, in later life, of long unresolved issues, when old ways of managing them are tested as losses impinge more, and long-standing patterns and defences may no longer hold up.

CHAPTER 6

"Tragical–comical–historical–pastoral": groups and group therapy in the third age

Caroline Garland

"Love triangle at old people's home led to shotgun ambush of rival, 67"

Report in a London evening newspaper, March 2007

What does it mean to be old?

The residents in the Emma Lazarus retirement home in uptown Manhattan are preparing a production of *Hamlet*:[1]

Hamburger and I arrived precisely on time and found the troupe already assembled. As we entered the library, the twittering stopped. It was a sobering moment. Hamburger must have sensed my nervousness since he gave me an encouraging pat on the shoulder. But to my consternation, the director's chair was already occupied, and by a man altogether unknown to me, a white-bearded fellow with glasses and wearing a sweater, corduroy trousers and loafers (no socks!). He was slouched cater-corner into the throne, one leg draped casually over an armrest. When he saw me looking at him, he smiled cheerily and gave a little wave.

My first directorial crisis! The troupe was agog, waiting to see how I would handle it. A false step now, I knew, could mean a permanent loss of authority. I merely shrugged and walked deliberately toward a vacant chair, one located, ironically, just beneath an early Selinger, an eviscerated purple cat on a green-splotched chrome-yellow background. "Wherever the director sits," announced Hamburger, acting in a kind of choral capacity, *"that's* the director's chair." The tension, at any rate, was eased.

Our newest resident, it turned out, was a certain Gerhardt Kunstler. He had arrived only this afternoon and was still finding his way around. (The ladies in the troupe were glancing at him speculatively.) He had dropped in, he explained, merely to get a sense of our activities, to meet a few new people, to see what sort of nonsense ("no offence intended") we were up to. We should just carry on and pay no attention to him. What he hoped to do was arrange a poker game, but that could wait.

I called the meeting to order, said a few flattering words about "our little family of thespians," explained that in my view a director should not be confused with a dictator, and then announced the cast changes: Hamburger would play Horatio, Pincus Pfaffenheim the Ghost, Salo Wittkower Polonius; the Red Dwarf would be promoted to First Gravedigger, and Freddy Blum had agreed to accept the role of Claudius. This last caused some grumbling (Blum, as we know, has his enemies), particularly from Salo Wittkower, who had survived two directors as the villainous king. Still, Wittkower was somewhat mollified when I told him that the use of musical motifs was still under consideration, and, in the event we determined to use them. "Pomp and Circumstance" would be equally appropriate for Polonius and would remain his. Then I turned to my conception of the play, which, I said, differed from Adolphe Sinsheimer's in only a few respects. La Dawidowicz, I could see, was becoming edgy, but she remained silent.

"I want to tilt the emphasis to bring out the important theme of adultery," I began, and as simply as I could, I presented my arguments.

There was, I am happy to say, general assent, even admiration. For example, Lottie Grabscheidt said, "Wow!"

"That has real possibilities," said Wittkower generously.

"There *are* no possibilities," said Kunstler suddenly.

Obviously this fellow is a troublemaker. Watch out, Korner.

"Tell me, Mr Kunstler", I said. "Is there some contribution that you might be able to make to our little production? We're always happy to welcome new talent."

"Funny you should ask." He had not noticed my sarcasm. "Years and years ago I worked the colour wheel in summer rep. Boulder, to be exact; that's in Colorado. Three shows I've got to this day word-for-word." He counted them off on his fingers: *"Hamlet, Lizzie Borden,* and *Rose Marie.* 'Give me some men who are stout-hearted men.' That's how it went. 'Shoulder to shoulder and bolder and bolder':

they loved that bit in Colorado. Well, I was young. I needed money for paints, for a hot dog, for beer. I hadn't had yet my big break, the mural in the mezzanine of the Exchange, down-town Topeka, *Fluctuationa*, 1951. Could be you've seen it. The rest, as they say, is history. But acting, no, that's not my line. If you want, I could paint some scenery for you. Just give me the word."

"We already have beautiful scenery," said Minnie Helfinstein, at the moment a Lady-in-Waiting but in the event that Tosca Dawidowicz walks out, a shoo-in for Ophelia. "You should see the set for scene one, Mr. Kunstler. A person could count every brick on the battlements."

"Representational? That went out with the dinosaurs!" Kunstler laughed so hard he began to cough. "Cigars," he explained. "Don't worry, I can paint over it. What I see is a black background interrupted by a few asymmetrical shapes in muted colours."

This passage, taken from Alan Isler's brilliant novel *The Prince of West End Avenue* (1996, pp. 162–164), is salutary as well as entertaining, since the men and women he describes are in their late seventies and eighties. The anxieties, rivalries, competitiveness, attention to style, concern for self-image, wit, intelligence, and sexuality are undiminished, even if their execution is rather shakier than it used to be. Earlier, and much in the same vein, Oscar Wilde pointed out that the tragedy of growing old is that one doesn't. It is worth making the point repeatedly. All that the old have in common with each other is that death is much closer than it used to be. In all other respects, the particularity of the individual is as present as ever, and the uniqueness of the wishes, phantasies, and impulses is as present and undimmed. Indeed, in some respects they are enhanced, or at least more visible, since the original defences against allowing such impulses and phantasies to emerge into consciousness tend to wear thin with great old age, much as the pile on a carpet wears away with age and usage to show the basic weave—the fabric of self. Both sexuality and aggression may become more overt. However, the tastes, style, personality, intelligence (or lack of it), and defensive propensities survive the years and will largely determine how each individual faces the prospect of diminished capacities and eventual death—with bitterness or humour, with resentment and envy, or with generosity and courage.

There are, of course, age-related issues arising in group treatment, but it is a mistake to think that the preoccupations of an older person taking part in a therapy group are likely to be completely different from those they worried about twenty years earlier. The problems that are brought for examination, or dug up to be struggled with, are as much to do with the individual as to do with the age group. Moreover, the fact that all older people face a death that will come sooner rather than later does not necessarily make for a warm fellow-feeling. It may aggravate rivalry and competition. It is hard to mistake the triumph in an old person's voice, as well as the sadness, as one hears of the number of contemporaries' funerals that have been attended.

Younger therapists may be tempted to compose a group of older patients only, but this is an impulse that needs to be examined carefully and the reasons for it laid bare. It might be the only population available, as in a residential or nursing home for older people; in that case, what is the function and task of the group? What purpose does it serve? Is it to be an activity group, a social group, or is it to be a formal psychotherapy group? Is it to be as lively and passionate as the geriatric production of *Hamlet* described by Alan Isler? If a decision has been made to run a group purely for people who are older when there is a mixed population to draw from, the younger therapist will need to question the possibility of there being a wish to split off some of his or her own feelings about death by projecting it into the patients, bundling them together into a "old age group" and obliging them to deal with it there on the therapist's behalf. None of us finds the prospect of death easy. As far as therapy groups are concerned, and if circumstances allow, it may well be better to place one or two older patients in groups containing a spread of ages, reflecting the spread of the generations.

An older woman
in a multigenerational psychotherapy group

In this group, Dora, a woman in her mid-seventies, is some fifteen years older than the oldest of the rest of the members. She came into the group because of chronic and severe depression. She had lived most of her life in a state of moral superiority, which she employed as a defence against allowing herself to be vulnerable to loneliness and regret—in fact, to strong feeling of any kind. At first she described what she viewed as the chaos and muddle of her contemporaries' lives when younger—"always falling in and out of love and then being let down by stupid man. I don't know why they do it. I've got my nice little flat just as I like it, and I don't want great muddy footsteps messing it all up, thank you very much!" She had never had a boyfriend, never allowed herself to be kissed. "It wouldn't have been right unless we were going to be married, and I never met one I wanted to marry!" At first Dora was shocked at the sexual and profane language used by the younger ones in the group (in their early twenties) and would complain about what the therapist was exposing her to. After a while, it was pointed out to her that there was a group specifically for older patients running in the clinic and perhaps she would feel happier there. "What are you talking about?" she snapped. "I'm not going into a group for *old* people." The group then pointed out how much of the time she spent complaining about their youthful manners (or lack of them) and habits. At the same time, they began to modify somewhat the more extreme turns of phrase that had been, for them, run-of-the-mill—able to hear their speech for the first time through someone else's ears.

In the following brief extract from a session, two women in their thirties have been facing difficulties over conception. One, Jo, is afraid she has conceived as the result of a one-night stand and is terrified that she has become pregnant, which will mean an abortion; the other, Amy, a lesbian, has been trying without success to conceive via IVF and an unknown sperm donor.

Jo is feeling and looking better, and her period has started, which means she can now face Amy and admit to what she had been doing, and how terrible she would have felt if she had been pregnant. Amy does not like this. She feels she can manage her own difficulties in conceiving, and if she doesn't conceive she is going to adopt, she's decided. She doesn't want Jo feeling sorry for her. But she's glad Jo isn't pregnant for Jo's sake, not for hers. Dora is listening to them intently. Her face mirrors some of the expressions on the two younger women's faces. She is amazed at the emotional pain they are prepared to risk. She wants to dismiss them as foolish, but it is clear she is very engaged with their dilemmas. The girls say to her, "Sorry, Dora, to go on about these sorts of things, we know you don't like it—I bet you think we are stupid." Dora becomes quite emotional. Suddenly she speaks about how much she regrets never having taken risks in her life—never, either practical or emotional. She thinks Jo and Amy are brave rather than just stupid. It is awful to feel she's left it too late. Now she feels she is going to die, to end her life feeling she has wasted it. Amy and Jo are shaken by this sudden and unexpected display of feeling. They speak to Dora about the risks they run and the pain of getting things wrong, but Dora is adamant. She is suddenly able to feel she would rather have got into a mess and into a state than to have nothing to show for her life. This statement of real feeling allows her to move, emotionally speaking, into the same kind of territory inhabited by the other younger group members. They "adopt" her as one of them. Jo says that Dora is the granny she'd like to have had. Dora says, in a way that makes them all laugh, "Well if you'd got me as your granny, you'd never been born, would you!" Dora is now engaged in a more emotionally real life than she has ever been able to have before.

The excerpt illustrates some of the difficulties, as well as some of the rewards, for an older patient in a mixed-age group. What may have to be faced are regrets, not merely for the life that has been lived but as well for the life one did not live. For any of us, regrets for what was not done are in some ways more poignant than regrets about what one actually did. However, what may be gained is a new status in relation to the young, in which their regard and even affection is valued rather than dismissed. Dora's *modus operandi* was grumbling, and though it never quite went away, it lost its edge. Instead it became her role in the group: the one whose job was to chide the younger members about their immoderate language, the coffee cups left around the room, the unwatered plants. She took it on herself to look after the plants, beginning to do something for others as well as for herself, and it was appreciated. The sense of transmission between the generations, of being able to pass on experience or wisdom or a sense of having failed to take advantage of important opportunities, offers a taste of immortality. Something of oneself has taken root in the young and is being valued. In many respects, Dora came to have closer relationships with the younger members of the group than she had achieved with her own parents

Basic elements of group structure

In this section I describe some important features of the basic structure of any group intended to provide something helpful or constructive for its members. Such groups would include staff support groups, occupational therapy groups, groups for the purposes of remembering, recalling, and even recording personal histories, activity groups (e.g., cooking, or listening to music), as well as the formal psychoanalytic psychotherapy groups, on which the second half of the chapter focuses. These features fall under three headings: the *territory*, the *time*, and the *task*.

Territory and time

The properties of territory and time establish the boundaries of the group, which need to be protected. The group takes place in the same room each week, at the same time, with the same furniture, and free of interruption from outside agencies. The external boundary needs to be secure because in one sense it is what enables a collection of individuals with a task in hand to become a group. The boundary (both of territory and time) marks the edge between the inside and the outside, demarcating the membership of the group from the membership of the whole of the rest of the world. The group leader's job is, among other things, to protect that boundary. Strangers, non-group members, will be excluded. When the group's time and space is protected, what goes on inside the group feels more solid, safe, and contained, allowing for the taking of emotional risks and the expansion of individual limits and boundaries. In the same way that there is a physical territory, there is in a therapy group an emotional boundary. What takes place in a therapy group remains private to the members of that group. It is not taken outside the group as gossip.

In a hospital setting, sometimes medical staff will want to extract a group member on a particular day for what seems to them like a good reason. The therapist needs to be clear, and to make it clear to colleagues, that group time is protected time: there is no going out and no coming in until the group session is over. In the same way, the overall period of time for which the group will run needs to be known beforehand. The group might last for a specified number of sessions, with a closed membership, or it might run on an open-ended basis with a slow turnover of membership: when one member leaves—which may mean dies—a vacancy is created for a new member. (This is a topic that *The Prince of West End Avenue* deals with both wittily and profoundly.) With an older population, it can in many respects be helpful to run groups for a limited and specified period of time. Ending a group—indeed, ending anything in a clear-minded way—is both very difficult and very productive. Because an older population has to face a final ending, in which there are no chances to *get it right this time*, it can be very helpful to talk about and work through the ending of the group itself, as a kind of preparation for having to work through the ending of life itself. In a nursing home for people who are older, everyone has to deal with death, not only with the loss itself, but also with the sense that it will sooner rather than later be one's own turn. Facing the ending of a group can, if sufficiently recognized as important by the group's leader, be dealt with thoughtfully and sensitively as a kind of dry run for death. Too often, illness or a sudden emergency can catapult the older person into a continuing-care setting in an unplanned and upsetting way, such that neither they nor their families can digest what has happened and find ways of living with it.

Task

The notion of task is crucial. If the group leader is clear about the task of the group, then behaviour that is off-task (cups of tea in a psychotherapy group, for example) can be noticed to be detrimental to the work that the group has met to carry out. The task of a group for recalling and recording memories, or making up a photograph album, is clear. The task of a therapy group is harder to spell out, but a good start is that *group members should get to know each other and should permit others to get to know them.* Such a task encourages reflection, talk, and the sharing of thoughts and feelings.

In the following section, some features of psychoanalytically based group therapy are described, as a basis for determining whether or not group therapy may be the treatment of choice for one or more older patients.

A psychoanalytic view of development

The primary group

The smallest of all possible groups is composed of three individuals. Although a baby is born to a mother, we could say that the arrival of a baby makes a threesome out of a couple. Even if the conception is achieved by artificial insemination, there is always a donor of that sperm somewhere in the world with whom that mother has a relationship, at the very least in her own mind. This means that the baby is always relating to a mother who has in her mind "the father of the baby", whether or not she actually knows who he is, lives with him or not. This primary group of three forms an important part of the structure of our mental lives. A triangle is formed in which each member will have a relationship with both other members, and at times each member will be excluded from what goes on between the other two. Sometimes, the father will have to wait while mother is feeding the baby, or the baby will have to wait when mother and father choose to be alone together. How the baby responds to the shifting and rotating nature of this triangle—now in, now out, now with the other two focusing on the baby as the centre of their attention, now with their turning their backs on the baby and focusing on each other—will influence the development of the individual's mental structure and subsequent characterological strengths and vulnerabilities. It is also the basis of the baby's lifelong ambivalence to his or her loved figures.

Thus there are both intensely positive and intensely negative impulses experienced in relation to the same primary figures in every infant's life. It is through the discovery in action that ambivalence exists, that hostility exists even towards those who are most loved, that complex desires can exist even in relation to those that are hated, that the possibility of integration becomes real. Klein (1946) writes vividly and movingly of these processes as they emerge in early infancy and, in particular, of the power of unconscious phantasy in the infant's life. The black-and-white nature of early relations, in which figures are felt to be either wholly good or wholly bad, can, if things go well, give way to a more depressive recognition of the goodness and badness recognized to be inherent in each of those same figures. At that point a more real concern for others can develop and, with it, a wish to repair some of the damage done, either in phantasy or in reality. This process involves a shift from what Klein called a *paranoid–schizoid* mode of operating to a position that she felt showed a *depressive concern* for the infant's objects.

Thus in every group situation there are three protagonists: the individual member, the group therapist, and the group itself, reflecting the triangularity of that primary group. Understanding the triangular and shifting nature of relations between the three parties is an important part of the work of group therapy. Often it can be seen that the therapist acts as the link between the member and the group itself. At other times the individual member may feel painfully excluded from what he perceives as the therapist's intimate relations with the group. In the group session described above, Dora felt that the therapist preferred the younger members and that she was a burden and a drag on the group's activities. These feelings were able to be examined in the sessions themselves, and their reality tested. It was important for Dora to recognize that she could indeed behave in a burdensome way with her endless complaints, but that the complaints could be alleviated through the understanding of their origins in infantile anxieties.

This kind of transformative process is never completed once and for all: it is a repetitive cycle of internal work. Thus its derivatives may often be seen in unmitigated form in adulthood, and they may emerge with renewed psychological vigour in extreme old age. The kind of dependency that great age can bring with it evokes many infantile feelings and many unresolved infantile conflicts, which may well be lived out in relation to family and to care staff. When no one—neither the older person, the professional carer, nor the family—understands the origin of such feelings and impulses, such aggressive or possibly sexual behaviour may evoke bafflement and hostility in return. "Why does she always take a swipe at me when I am trying to help her?" In this kind of situation, work discussion groups for care staff may be particularly helpful. Young workers need a chance to express their puzzlement and resentment at those who can react violently to their ministrations, or who become very regressed and infantile when the transference is more positive. Understanding something of the origins of the behaviour they are exposed to may help them cope with it better. This is part of the purpose of groups for both staff and patients.

Group therapy

Talking groups can be immensely helpful for people who are older. They provide an opportunity for the clarification and expression of unresolved conflicts and passionate feelings, clearly visible and vigorously at work in the setting provided by the therapeutic group. Group therapy is a form of treatment in which these issues and dilemmas can be seen in live action between the individuals in the room and can be addressed directly in the here-and-now by both group members and the group therapist.

It is not appropriate to the subject of this chapter to give a detailed review of the development of group therapy over the last half century in the Tavistock Clinic, but it is well worth mentioning the work of Wilfred Bion (1961). Bion developed most of his interest in treatment groups in the Adult Department of the clinic, and his approach has underpinned all the department's subsequent developments in group therapy. His fundamental thesis is that any group (of any description) will always contain two ways of functioning—that which is addressed to the work in hand (the Work Group) and that which represents primitive forms of defence against work (the Basic Assumptions). The presence of a predominance of Basic Assumptions (Dependence, Fight or Flight, and Pairing) lets the therapist know that the anxieties present in the group are, at that point, too great for it to continue with its proper task. This provides the therapist with food for thought, rather than with wordy formulations or abstract interpretations. This theoretical basis for group work is perhaps particularly useful in helping the therapist think about the work with groups of the elderly, in whom habitual social defensive strategies may have worn so thin that the underlying anxieties become quite apparent. Sometimes the way in which the elderly might position themselves in a wholly dependent stance towards their family, or the staff in a care home, may be entirely necessary and appropriate (physical disability, incontinence, immobility). If, however, they are able to attend a therapy group at all, then some of the work will consist of facing and examining that very dependence, as well as the many complex and painful feelings about it. An enforced and genuine helplessness in one who has always taken a pride in being independent may be hard to bear. Irritability or apparent ingratitude may be ways of fighting or fleeing from the hatred of dependence, as may the idealization of one particular carer or family member (pairing). The paranoid ideation that can develop in the elderly is often aggravated, even produced, by the fear and resentment of that enforced dependence.

However, in those who are still capable of reflection and thought about their situation, group treatment can be a very positive experience. Psychoanalytic psychotherapy groups in the Adult Department are run on the basis of seven or eight individuals coming together on a regular basis for one and a half hours a week, over a period of time (ranging from one to three years) in order to understand better the ways in which they relate to each other both consciously and unconsciously. There is of course no reason why such groups should not meet twice or even three times a week, perhaps for a rather shorter period of time—perhaps an hour and a quarter. The understanding of the less conscious aspects of thinking, feeling, and behaving is achieved, with the help of a trained therapist, through an examination of the minutiae of the interactions of the here-and-now within the group, including the mood and atmosphere in which they take place, at both the surface and at deeper levels. This examination may be linked with the historical contexts in which these behaviours developed, as with the infantile feelings described above. As well as relations between individuals, each member's way of relating to a shared object, the group, is examined, as is the individual's and the group's varied stance towards the therapist over time.

When placed in a group setting, internal objects become strikingly apparent externally, as is apparent from the above extract from a session. The advantage of a specifically therapeutic setting, whether group or individual, is that usual social constraints and inhibitions are set aside so that it is permissible and helpful not only to notice these idiosyncratic modes of relating, and the associated phantasies, but to do so with a view to modifying their more unhelpful aspects. However, the mechanisms of change, or modification, require both understanding and the wish to change matters for the better. Change in characteristic modes of relating is the hardest of tasks for human beings. There is a built-in aversion to the kind of pain involved in real change. Some group patients will wish, and will fight, to use the setting for the purposes of re-enactment rather than for change. Relinquishing behaviours can be painful and frightening, and the existing modes of relating may offer gratifications (e.g., the extreme helplessness of infancy, on the principle that *if you can't beat it, join it*) that new ones do not possess. Understanding these factors in therapeutic treatment without adopting a moralizing or nagging stance towards the patient is part of the therapist's task. (Here, personal experience of treatment is an invaluable basis for becoming an effective therapist in any modality.)

Maintaining high standards of commitment and reliability

The therapist needs to be consistently and reliably present and on time for each session, and to end the session on time. This behaviour forms part of the therapist's attention to the importance of boundaries—those of time as well as territory. To start a session two minutes late will affect the mood and the material for the entire session, and if the anxieties are not heard and responded to, they will reverberate for many sessions to come. To end a session five minutes over time may seem considerate on that particular occasion—a patient is distressed, for instance, or in the middle of recounting something important—but group members will respond to the event by attempting to engineer it on many further occasions. Their unconscious view of the therapist as someone who can be pushed around will diminish the therapist's authority and the stability and safety of the structure that the therapist provides. All patients are aware of the approaching end of the session, which is why they may sometimes try to override it: all endings carry with them some pain.

The therapist's language

The way in which the therapist speaks to the group, the *you* and *I*, is important. "Interpretations" may be a special category of intervention, but they do not require a special class of language, a special tone of voice, or a special vocabulary. Technical language or solemn pronouncements do not belong in the treatment setting. If the interpretation cannot be formulated in ordinary everyday language, then it has not been fully grasped by the therapist and is not ready to be said out loud. The therapist might say to the group, "You are feeling a bit left out of the good things you feel I'm probably up to at the weekend ", but not "You are struggling unsuccessfully with your oedipal anxieties". The second says more about the therapist's own anxieties than about the patients'.

Helping members to say what is on their minds

Rarely, if ever, is a member helped to say what is on his or her mind with a direct question. Instead, the therapist can make an observation about a particular state of affairs and then go on to comment on the fact that the group itself, who must also have noticed this state of affairs, is avoiding its investigation. This way the therapist is constantly reminding members that ordinary social reticence or discretion is not applicable in group therapy (although courtesy is), and that it is permissible and helpful—indeed necessary—to express curiosity and concern about each other, to discover more about each others' states of mind.

Clarifying the feelings and anxieties that underlie preoccupations and behaviours

The assumption is that puzzling behaviours are provoked by underlying anxieties, which may be more, or less, conscious. In the example of the multigenerational group given earlier, it was possible to see the way in which Dora's dismissing of the value and importance of relationships in her life was a defence against her anxiety that no one would find it possible to be close to her. In a psychoanalytic psycho-therapy group, the therapist's job is to think about and to come to an understanding of these anxieties, based on his or her understanding of unconscious mental functioning, and then—most importantly—to help the group to arrive at this understanding for themselves. Clearly this is a complex task, for which training is always useful.

Interpreting anxieties and defences to the group

In the early stages of group treatment, the therapist may have to be more active in interpreting anxieties and defences to the group than in the later stages, when members know more and are more adept at understanding each other and putting that understanding into words. It can be a revelation for group members to come to notice and use their own countertransference—to discover that their own subjective responses to the nuances in each others' speech, posture, gestures, and facial expressions may provide useful information as to the state of mind of the other. In time, the use some members come to make of their countertransference can be highly sophisticated, in that the feel-ings are registered, held on to, thought about, and finally made use of in the form of a comment.

The therapist also needs to be aware of the importance of timing. Premature knowing by the therapist usually delays understanding in the patient. Listening, waiting, and thinking are often more important than uttering. The longer the therapist can bear to wait, particularly as time goes on, the more work may be done by the group members themselves. Group therapists often come to find that, if they can bear to hold on to the interpretation for a while, it gets made by one of the members.

Group therapy offers certain specific advantages

It is important for the therapist to be clear about the value of group therapy as a treatment modality with advantages of its own over and above its obvious cost-effectiveness. Patients offered group treatment may at first feel they are being fobbed off with something second-best. A therapist offering a group can be seen as pushing bucket-shop modes of treatment, and in the state of intense need experienced by patients at the outset, the anxiety is often that having to "share" a therapist with six or seven others may aggravate an existing sense of deprivation. If the therapist is aware and confident of the value of group treatment, patients' fears can be contained by the therapist's own knowledge of the eventual considerable benefits to be had. These can be several.:

1. The existence of other patients in the room diminishes the sense of isolation, failure, and shame that can attach to the need for treatment. Although this same sense of failure can make individuals initially reluctant to accept a group as the treatment of choice, since they fear revealing these feelings in public, once in the group it becomes a different matter. An expressed and shared vulnerability can become a source of comfort and hence strength.

2. Having more than one patient in the room means that the inevitable attempt to externalize and make manifest each individual's internal object relations will ensure that incongruities and discrepancies between one individual's view and another's becomes material for discussion and understanding. Jo's wish for Dora to be her granny was at odds with another member's dislike of Dora's carping complaints about the way he swore. Spelling out these differences offers vital food for thought.

3. Dependence upon the therapist alone is diminished because of the existence not only of fellow patients, but of "the group" itself. Dependence on "the group" can often be tolerated, whereas dependence on the therapist is resented and denied and may lead to an envious rejection of the therapist's understanding and point of view. Group patients are strikingly able to bear plain speaking from fellow members better than they can from a therapist. Moreover, fellow patients often put things more directly and bluntly than a therapist could risk. As Dora's group said to her, "Well, stop moaning about us then." This may not rate as a psychologically sophisticated interpretation but was both fair and effective in the particular circumstances.

4. Patients without a particular interest in or capacity for psychological insight may nevertheless gain a great deal from the internalization of others' curiosity about motive, impulse, and feeling. Over the course of time, a distaste for psychological insight can diminish to reveal a real sensitivity, often defended against for years. Patients may discover in themselves considerable talent for understanding others' difficulties. The process of objectification—discovering what is in oneself through first seeing and understanding it as it

takes place between others—is immensely helpful when it comes to helping patients see what part they play in their own difficulties. Often that work is done by patients in relation to each other and does not require specialist therapist intervention. Dora became a woman who could grasp other's difficulties as well as her own. She came to have a helpful perspective on others' troubles and they turned to her for some aspects of the comfort that was missing in their own families. When valued, Dora became genuinely valuable. In order to love, one needs to be loved.

5.   The group offers a particular structure in which each member is not only a patient, but is also part of others' treatments, and is in this sense also capable of coming to function as the therapist does. In psychoanalytic terms, this acts to reduce the envy of the breast as the provider of all goodness, since each patient is both baby and *also* part of the breast that nourishes and supports the other babies. Psychic nourishment is easier to take in when one may also be capable of providing it for others.

6.   The capacity to see what is going on between others leads to an increased sensitivity to others' difficulties and an increased ability to respond flexibly to others' needs. This increase in flexibility is both the outcome of a reduced tendency to project unwanted aspects of the mind and personality, and also in turn a cause of further re-introjection of split-off aspects of the self. As in all forms of analytic treatment, the re-introjection of lost parts of the mind leads both to a greater mental capacity to tolerate pain and distress and to a fuller and more integrated personality. Unappreciated emotional intelligence is discovered and used. This can lead to some quite unexpected side-benefits, apart from the amelioration of object relations in general—the patient may discover new interests in the external world, such as an increased appetite for the job or for literature, music, or physical or social activities.

It was possible to see this happening in the group described earlier, in which group therapy enabled the older woman, Dora, to develop an increased interest and capacity in her relationships with other people, rather than simply in those she had had with her cats. It diminished her narcissistic withdrawal from the world of others and enabled her to go and find some part-time work in a charity shop, which brought her into contact with people from many different cultures and socioeconomic backgrounds.

Specifically age-related issues in therapy groups

One of the most painful features of growing old is that one can be shamed by one's own body, including the brain. The inability to perform some task that used to be taken for granted—for example, walking, or to remember what one went to the shops to buy—can be deeply upsetting. Sometimes this will be pointed out by others even before it has been recognized by the ageing individual. A young woman told her mother that she felt her mother was no longer a safe-enough driver, in terms of eyesight and speed of response, to be driving the grandchildren around. The younger woman felt she was pointing out something both obvious and natural, but it came as a deeply painful shock for the grandmother to realize that in her daughter's eyes she was no longer competent. The shame is not only the loss of function, it is that it is simply a product of age. The mother felt discriminated against on grounds of age alone; it took her some months to come to terms with the realities of what ageing means in practice. Often, old people do not recognize or feel they are old until they are told as much by the young. Children, too, feel the shame of ageing parents. These are the kinds of issues that it is difficult but profoundly helpful to have raised in groups specifically designed to be therapeutic.

This point underlines the value of multigenerational groups. However, clearly sometimes it is not possible to form a mixed-age group. Care homes tend to have populations within a limited age range; the population of the Emma Lazarus home in Alan Isler's novel were all over 70. Yet even with a restricted choice in terms of population, it is possible to create working groups: perhaps a reading of a Terence Rattigan or a Noel Coward play, popular a couple of generations ago, with some rehearsing of individual parts beforehand; perhaps a "music hall evening", in which anyone who is capable performs a little song, reads a poem, or talks about what in the day's news has irritated or pleased them most, while others form an audience. This audience may or may not be appreciative. The point is not to do such things well, but to *do them at all*. Passivity is the curse of old age, and it is easy for family and staff to collude with it: it makes "managing" the old person an easier job. Yet the silent resentment of old age itself can communicate itself both consciously and unconsciously to everyone within range, leading to an equally silent resentment at having to shoulder the burdens of caring. Better to struggle with an ambitious project and fail than give up and wait for death—one's own or someone else's. This, for all concerned, is soul-destroying. Of course, groups may be created for many different purposes—such as occupational therapy, staff support, family groups—and each is capable of being productive in a different way.

Closing comments

Ideally, as in the case of Dora, many old people who are still mobile are best treated in therapy groups that span two or three generations. In this country, the large extended family is now a relative rarity and, distressingly often, old people are hived off from the life of the larger group and warehoused in enclaves specifically designed for the old. For those from other, perhaps less urbanized countries, this is a puzzling phenomenon. A young woman from China described the situation in her own home.

> "We are not a nuclear family. We are a big family—there are three or four generations living together at one time. The old always sit in the middle when we are taking a picture, and there is a form just like a tree, like the old are the roots and it spreads out on all sides. And although there are more and more nuclear families these days we all manage to meet together every week, the generations together, my family and my children with my parents and with theirs. We sometimes think about why. It goes deeper than culture—*it is what we do. It is what we are.*"

In this kind of setting, the family—actors in the drama that is every family's life—have "their exits and their entrances, / And one man in his time plays many parts".[2] In terms of large-group phenomena in society and small-group phenomena in the extended family, we need to reconsider why it is, since all of us will be old one day, we deprive ourselves of that chance to live out the last of our allotted ages as a part of the great tree of the family: its roots.

Notes

1. The quotation in the chapter title is from Shakespeare, *Hamlet* (II, ii), in which the players are describing the kinds of scenes they can perform.

2. Shakespeare, *As You Like It* (II, vii). Jaques is describing the seven ages of man.

CHAPTER 7

The experience of an illness: the resurrection of an analysis in the work of recovery

Ronald Markillie

In March 2003 and for the next three months, I went through the worst experience of my life following an operation to replace an aortic valve. Although a successful operation, it was followed by a profound and bewildering regression such as I had never experienced before. I offer this account of my experience because I believe that what went on in my mind deserves as much attention as that which my body received. Both were involved in recovery. Two things make this account individual: my personality structure, which was tested by this onslaught, and my experience of a good analysis from fifty years before, which became a living memory to help cope with what was going on and to give meaning to it. I think it would be wrong to regard this episode as reflecting unfinished or unresolved matters from that analysis, since the intervening fifty were, in the main, happy and stable ones. My analysis had examined and helped me modify but never fundamentally to change personality organization and this can be regarded as the expectable outcome of a good-enough analysis.

The operation itself had been no problem at all. I was amazed by the absence of pain and discomfort following it and how well and easily it had passed in spite of my being 85 years old at the time. As I see it, that is concordant with how my personality operates. My son, who saw me two days afterwards, says he could hardly believe that after such an operation I was very much like my normal self, despite some oedema of the legs and some disturbance in my visual fields, persistent coloured patches, and hallucinations of machines with rotating shafts. However, to all intents and purposes I appeared to be doing very well in the circumstances. I think that some vascular changes in the cerebral blood supply during the operation were implicated in these disturbances, but they made it almost impossible to read for a time, a major defensive strategy for me.

A week later my son reported that I was a wreck. I became overwhelmed in that time by extreme physical disability, followed later by an intense black depression and hopelessness of which I had had no personal experience before, other than having seen it in depressed patients. I am less sure why the physical reaction came when it did, though I can convince myself that developing severe Clostridium diarrhoea triggered it. My son also dated my decline to this incident. I was already compromised and vulnerable, but this was a double-edged sword. It made me feel ill; but worse, by producing appalling incontinence that was humiliating in the extreme, it accelerated a very unwelcome regression. In no way did either the nurses who had the mess to deal with or the doctors who were all comforting and reassuring foster that. My blood electrolyte balance went haywire and was extremely difficult to stabilize. One's brain cannot function well at a very low sodium level. Daily blood tests became increasingly unpleasant as my veins collapsed. I developed severe oedema of my legs and feet, which led to fluid-intake restriction and a powerful diuretic regime in an attempt to reduce it. Suffering from urgency of micturition normally, being made to pass more compounded my dread of being incontinent, with its ensuing embarrassment. The final straw came when the cardiologist said my electrolytes were too unstable and I required too much specialist nursing care to be transferred to the nursing home that I had booked for my rehabilitation. I hated him for saying it but I knew he was right, and I sank further into hopelessness. I had to stay nearly four more weeks in hospital, which, in spite of its excellent care, felt anything but secure. It seemed larger, the distances to the toilet greater, the ward less hospitable, with almost nowhere to rest if you were in trouble away from your bed. As I fell a few times, that feeling intensified.

Alongside the physical collapse, I became aware how much my thinking or, rather, fantasying had changed. It was foreign, and some of it became frightening, for it seemed to be psychotic in character. I remember few details, for time has healed. It was not overtly paranoid. It was persecutory, in the sense that it was intrusive and insistent; my thoughts seemed outside my control and vaguely threatening. It is reported that I was much more irrational than I remember, and I was, I am sure, difficult at times. I felt increasingly unhappy, even lost in the hospital. I was being kept on with a receding discharge date, while all around was a faster turnover of patients who came and went. My son reported that I often spoke as if I was floating outside my body. I do remember that I phoned the matron of the nursing home to try to persuade her that I was fit to be transferred and that she would be able to give the special care I needed. I remember a fantasy while speaking to her of being carried into the home on a stretcher, floating or possibly borne at shoulder height as a coffin is carried. Towards the end of my stay in hospital, one male patient in particular disturbed me. I must have heard him fifty times talking about his future operation to all and sundry in a way that betrayed his anxiety by constantly denying his uncertainty about what might be going to be done, its outcome, and his real fear of future death. My disturbance was at his failure to learn, because he was clinging to denial in the endless repetition. There was a whiff of righteous indignation at the adverse effect he may have been having those who did not understand his denial, and, in that, I assume there was a great deal of projection about my own behaviour. Although I knew the valve change had been successful, I did not know whether my hope would ever be restored.

Over these weeks I lost a great deal of weight and most of my musculature. This meant that I was extremely weak and had great difficulty in moving or helping myself and needed other people's help to carry out any personal task. Some of this resulted from my not eating, and I complained a lot about the food. I was still in a hopeless and despairing mood after I moved to the nursing home. After my first day there, I began to think, with false logic, that my home and my friends there might pull me back to health by giving me hope. I tried to arrange a transfer much nearer home, to a rehabilitation centre that I had positively disliked previously. Fortunately my son refused to act on this. I challenged my treatment, especially when unknown, unexplained, and unpleasant drugs were presented to me without comment. I was very suspicious of one of the sisters, who seemed to me to wish to adhere to a diuretic regime that I thought had already become excessive. As my condition deteriorated, the nursing home, which had been a good place in my mind, was increasingly felt to be a hostile one. Memories began to surface as I attempted to stay outside the turmoil and bewilderment that I feared might engulf me. Memories of a much earlier hostile hospital environment emerged and can now be seen to have had an important role in the feeling of depression and isolation that I began to feel. It was entirely appropriate and saving for such affect to surface again and be recognized in the service of recovery, for the reality was that the present nursing home was my salvation.

Analytic reflections

The apparently easy early passage of the first few post-operative days had matched what might be termed my premorbid personality organization, which has always been confident, assured, coping with difficulties and outwardly handling crises calmly. It had proved itself, down the years, to have been sufficiently flexible yet stable and adaptive to get along successfully. I am normally introverted, stable, curious, agreeable, and reasonably directed. However, I have always responded psychosomatically, rather than neurotically, throughout my life, and there is a strong family history of psychosomatic disorders. My main reaction was asthma, which has been very rare in later years although I suffered an attack not long before this experience started, not unrelated to my wife's death. Another reaction in later years, polymyalgia rheumatica, contributed to my physical downfall. I have thought for a long time that the roots of psychosomatic ills are at a primitive if not psychotic level. At the end of the Second World War, I had a wonderful opportunity to attempt to treat many cases. The transference problems that arose during treatment and the general difficulties of interpretation were the chief cause that led me to seek analytic training. When that started, being analysed by a woman—Eva Rosenfeld—was not without its problems, for as a woman she enshrined the first phase of my problems. She was Viennese but had lived in Berlin before she came to London. Although a friend of the Freud family (a good-enough reason for some envy—I do remember making remarks like "You and your Freud"), she had later courted disapproval by venturing to understand more of the Kleinian direction. My analysis was terminated before the end of its fifth year because of her ill health; I accepted this because of the financial burden and made plans to move back to the north of England. I have speculated often about what I might have gained had I sought more analysis. It feels now as if I have regained something more though fifty years later.

My mind tried to puzzle out what was going on as I collapsed (and that does not capture the urgency and intensity at times). I am convinced now that the nursing home had become a place in which all hope was fading, a hostile place, which in reality it was not. In that context, things from my analysis began to come back. Once I was conscious of this, it resurrected an old thought that analysis never stops. Things were exposed that indicated a deeper personal disturbance than I had thought before, yet at the same time it was constructive and comforting. I now regard what happened in this highly compromised time as, if not a resurfacing of unfinished business, then a revisiting of matters that needed attention. It gave me an opportunity for fresh working through, which was presumably part of my attempt to reassert control, to stay outside and not be sucked in, a parallel healing process to the somatic one. I began to think, as I had never done before, that my early personality organization must have been triumphant, omnipotent, and much more primitively—even psychotically—based.

I am going to describe some of the memories and fantasies that I recalled as I struggled to grasp what was happening to me. Working through them became a fundamental means by which I recovered.

The first incident was one that arose early in my analysis and was not based on a true memory of mine but on what I must have been told. On my second birthday, I ran away from home. I was found forging ahead about three-quarters of a mile from my home. I was picked up by someone and, I presume, returned to my distressed mother. It may be significant that this was the road, almost a mile long, that my father walked to the station to go to his office. (To give an idea of how different the world was then, although lined by houses there would have been not one parked car in all that distance, nor any real danger, far less than now). The stimulus for that adventure was that two of my mother's cousins had arrived who had attended the birth at home of my only sibling, a sister, seven months before. Had they come to admire my sister, Jean? I think not; they probably had come to see my mother and me, as it was my birthday. I have only the vaguest feelings that I might have felt excluded when she was born and thus reacted against them, but that was taken up in my analysis and much else in active oedipal terms and in those of sibling rivalry.

My insight in hospital was that my behaviour then must have had an omnipotent component to it, a triumphal one, which was much more primitive than ever emerged in my analysis. I hesitate to mention what I am sure would be a legitimate association on the couch, but I keep picturing a professionally taken photograph of me from this time. I am in my Sunday best, standing alone, and I seem to be a very self-possessed young man. That seems to fit the personality that I have just mentioned, which certainly would not have been true of the one I displayed a few years later in my latency. I wish now that this episode could have been analysed at more than an oedipal level, though training analyses must reflect their time and must have changed in fifty years.

One of my most powerful enduring character traits is linked with that memory and gives a clue to my inner defences. I need to know where I am if I possibly can. I have always been curious about where roads and railways went. Recently in the nursing home in an area new to me, I was quite unsettled as I had no map and was thus unable to know where any of the roads went that I could see. I was much relieved when I was taken out and traversed them and knew where the villages were that the staff talked about. An important early fantasy game, with no more than an old pram wheel and an orange box to simulate it, was that of driving a bus, especially with my grandparents as passengers. When quite young I knew where every bus route in London went, and there were at least two hundred of them. I have always said that if I were as good at other important things as I am at finding my way, or working out where I am, I would be brilliant. Confidence, assurance, and ascertaining the facts whenever possible have been my overt strengths. Another detail is that very often, on long car journeys, I have an unseen passenger to whom I explain the landmarks and any significant historical or topographical information. The strength and intensity of this behaviour, I am convinced, shows it was and is part of an active control system to contain (or perhaps to project) the primitive anxiety of being at a loss.

My self-analysis during this compromised time led me to believe that, while omnipotence and omniscience were important factors in my character which protected me against overwhelming loss, the genesis of this structure belonged to the earliest period of my life and not essentially to oedipal conflicts. A pertinent memory that surfaced at this time was that when I was 5 years old I spent an afternoon at a mother-and-baby clinic with my grandmother and her youngest sister, who was running it, the district nurse of her village. Because I was alone and not needed or involved in any of the proceedings, envy stirred up violent fantasies. I ripped open pregnant bellies, tore out their contents, swung babies by the heels, and dashed their brains out against the walls—as happens in all too many brutal wars. Although I had no knowledge of the existence of that behaviour either in history or at the time, I somehow shared in it. (So much for the legal presumption of infantile innocence.) I cannot remember losing my temper in life, but I have always known what violence felt like and presumably have defended strongly against it. External aggression I may not have shown, but fantasies of extreme and lethal destructiveness are an old and lifelong familiar. Not surprisingly, I was a timid little boy after this, and shame was never far away. Other links with pregnancy occurred down the years and during my analysis. Examples are a pattern of skin disease appearing on my flanks more than once during analysis, and the only time I have experienced colic was when my wife had gone down to London to have our first child and I was alone awaiting the news.

I am convinced that my running away was a reaction to the significance of women and, most importantly, their capacity to bring life into the world. It was also the first sign of a difficulty and defensiveness that formed my character. That was what seemed to make sense in hospital. The presence of these fecund and baby-handling, caring women was more than I could cope with, particularly as I was now needing care as never before. At the age of 2, it created an envy and I suppose frustration and rage, which I could only handle by running away, or perhaps by joining the men. That envy persisted, though later it was handled in a much more egosyntonic way than in the examples that follow. I remembered a primitive fantasy that my mother had a penis-like appendage from the middle of her chest through which she suckled. Clearly I possessed one too, yet I cannot have been in ignorance of her anatomy. She had been feeding my sister. A masterly manufacture maybe, but a pathological way of denying the obvious and my lack of it.

Only very recently have I begun to wonder about my reaction to being brought back home, for I had always thought of it as a successful venture. Now I realize how precarious I was then. How long would it have been before I felt lost or in some need? Had that already started to happen? A very recent event has, I think, thrown some light on that. Prior to my more recent move to a nursing home, I had lived in a serviced apartment for eleven years. A reorganization of the services to the apartments led to the provision of breakfast and supper being withdrawn. Intellectually this was no problem, but I was surprised at the unreasonable feeling of anxiety and depression that I experienced before my first self-prepared meal. It was dramatically relieved when a kind neighbour arranged for my lunch, which I had missed, to be kept for me to eat in the evening. The depression rolled away while that meal was produced and eaten. It caused me to remember the depressive anxiety I would feel when on a journey if I had no fixed place to stay the night, and that feeling would go completely once I had eaten. I am in danger of trying to make out a case, but my strong conviction is that the intensity of this reaction said something about the precarious state I was in at age 2. I have no memory of how I was found or of what state I was in, distressed or not. I have liked to fantasize that I was reluctant to return as I was triumphantly striding away, but the truth more likely is that I was already in trouble. I suspect that I had stressed the running away in its positive aspect as a manic defence against depression and helplessness. The feeling of depression is a form of memory.

I have so far described the changing insight I gained about the basis of the wish for omnipotence and omniscience in my character. Alongside this thinking there was a further working through of an earlier experience. At the age of 6, I developed scarlet fever and was sent to an isolation hospital, which at that time meant just what it said. I can still see clearly the ambulance arrive at our front gate and knew it was for me. I also remember the strained secrecy towards me of my mother and our doctor, who had never been an ogre to me. I caught rubella as well while there, which led to two more weeks of total isolation, altogether six weeks. I recaptured that disappointment and relived it as my recent discharge date was moved back. That then had been a painful time, but its only traces until now were that down the years I could experience a feeling, particularly on a fine, still summer afternoon, of everything seeming to have stopped, suspended in time, silence, being alone. Triggered by stillness, it was no longer frightening, but acutely reminiscent.

One further memory from that time was painfully available, and its significance to my recent plight came to mind as I suffered. There was a ghastly daily ritual of being given a laxative, whether you needed it or not. I quickly learned to take the one least foul in taste. I remembered soiling my bed on one occasion because the nurses were so slow in coming when I called. It was only weeks after my recent crisis that it occurred to me that the last straw in precipitating my hopelessness had been being made to take potassium chloride. I think the feeling of isolation and of the almost hostile space that I experienced in hospital when my departure was postponed, together with my reaction to being made to take foul medicine, was intensified by that earlier hospital isolation. I think of this whole recall as an actualization of an experience, not just a painful memory. I mean by this that being able to link, in a meaningful way, the past and the present was my way of handling something in a constructive way, part of my personal maintenance.

Apart from this episode, my attachment to my parents was never broken or even severely damaged, but there is plenty of evidence that I have protected myself against being vulnerable to the potential separateness of others. When I first read Winnicott, I recognized his description of a capacity to be alone, but it is only more recently that I have distinguished this as being achieved by the internalization of an object rather than via more omnipotent means. I have tended to value being alone, a strong solo, not in the presence of my mother. I could say that is where I introduced God, but I will turn to this in a moment.

My capacity to be alone was tested, but never beyond endurance. On the first evening of a family holiday in new surroundings when I was 7, I remember us going out onto a hillside to enjoy the view, when quite out of character I collapsed into a strange state and had to be carried by my father. That incident rapidly recovered and, I would have said, left no obvious trace. I know that often when I have gone away eagerly enough from home in adult life, I have experienced an internal pang, rather like a red warning. In analysis this incident was related to my oedipal reactions to the fantasized sexual closeness of my parents on holiday. I can't deny that, but I have only just established from family photographs that this holiday was the one following my stay in the fever hospital. I am sure that the previous year's traumatic separation was involved in this, though why the link had not occurred to me before I cannot say. I should stress that my relationship with my mother was a good one. I used to call her out at night to ease an asthma attack with a primitive nitrite smoke. I needed it, I needed her. She came uncomplainingly, leaving my father, and yet I hated the smoke, and her closeness in some way repelled me.

My most recent memories suggest that my very strong need to know where I was in space and, as far as possible, to be able to determine that and thus control it, together with what I referred to earlier as an omnipotent or triumphant organization, was the polar opposite of depression and a form of manic defence. There is more resonance to come about this. Some of these thoughts came only after I started to write down my experience since leaving hospital, and I have strung these associations together in a way that seems to make sense. During my analytic reflections I began to review the way in which my personality had influenced a change in my final career choice. At first I had wanted to become a locomotive engineer, but medicine called. I had to be persistent to persuade my father to let me do it, as it was hard for him to afford. There is no question that getting closer to women, possibly gaining entry into, or seeing into, or sharing more of their world, was a primary factor in my choosing and working to become a doctor.

It is probable that my desire to know where things went is also related to my mother's hidden inside. When I became a medical student, post-mortems were held at lunchtime, and I went to a very large number long before I needed to. When scientific curiosity is bonded with voyeurism, it makes a powerful and stable combination, but it can exist on its own nonetheless. Such motives have sorted themselves out with time. In my first hospital job I did a number of post-mortems myself, which was not usual practice, though it was a fine learning experience of a sort, and valuable for the hospital. The motivation had been legitimated. It exemplifies control and is also omnipotent in the sense of necessary violence and desecration. This time I really was ripping open bellies, but in a very controlled way. I can still feel the satisfaction of opening a skull elegantly without damage to the contents. I assume that a good marriage permitted an imperceptible working through of much of this. I know it permitted me to work through that ambivalence to close contact with my mother. I could have been a good surgeon but despised their attitude then towards their patients. I was more interested from the start in persons and not just bodies. Fortunately we had a much richer and lengthier contact with patients than most students have these days, and when I decided to train as a psychiatrist, my first job was looking after the male wards, followed by the army, which I enjoyed.

As I lay in hospital and tried to understand the frightening state I found myself in, these links came to my mind more powerfully than ever before. Some of my unfinished business had to do with breast or womb envy. Fecundity rather than femininity is a better term, though woman as the receiver is also important. If your understanding of metapsychology is early Freudian and some of it modelled on penis envy, then it may not be so easy to switch into opposite concepts based on maternal or female attributes, when they surface, as I am convinced they do here. If your concern is not spotted and taken up hermeneutically in analysis, you may not be able to grasp and configure it quickly enough as a patient. If it receives no analytic recognition, you may begin to discount it by default or in collusion. That is the direction in which I found it was necessary to go. In what may look like a criticism of my analyst, I have two analytic memories expressing hostility and one reparative one. I understood the anger in the first two, but not the envy at the time they happened. I remember cocking a snook at her by triumphantly lauding that I had impulsively and extravagantly bought something. In the second, I described a sexual experience, which had been an acting out of sexually humiliating and degrading her. The third memory is of the only non-analytic response of hers that I recall, and it has always stuck in my mind. Only very recently have I come to think that it may throw some light on what I have just said was missed and why it may have been missed. I remember quoting a line of a hymn, though I can't remember with what it was associated. "I thank thee Lord that all our joys are touched with pain." There was a quiet but firm "No" from behind the couch. Maybe those gentle words I uttered were like a stiletto that penetrated to her pain. I didn't understand it then, and it was only after her death that I learned that she had lost, I think, three young children, including especially a daughter. In such circumstances, fate had not given her much encouragement to think that fecundity was enviable.

I have described how the enforced regression produced by hospitalization and what ensued totally undermined my fundamental assurance and led to deep depression and despair. For a time I was nursed in maximum dependency but all the time cut off from my entire familiar activities and surroundings. There was much sensory deprivation. Requiring assistance for almost every activity, the humiliation of incontinence of urine and faeces in public, even gladly wearing nappies (diapers), being dependent for all treatment and care on others (none of whom ever protested or made me feel bad) wore me down. In spite of a great deal of attention, I felt increasingly lost and isolated, in total contrast to the triumphant mood of my primitive organization. You need a degree of strength, ability, and confidence to get away with a triumphant mode. You cannot do so if your skeleton has collapsed and you are more like a deflated balloon, or like a car robbed of its wheels. I begin to understand why triumph in history needed those complex, grandiose carriages, archways, and other designs. It needs a ritual form or structure to exhibit it, to actualize it, and my potential for creating structure had been hit for six.

I recently re-read Paul's striking metaphor, at the end of Ephesians, of putting on the whole armour of God. I had forgotten that one phrase in that passage always signified more for me than any other part: "Wherefore take unto you the whole armour of God, that ye may be able to withstand in the evil day, and having done all, to stand." That last phrase has always impinged on me. It was that invincibility, that capacity to endure and still to remain standing when the battle had passed, which registered most for me. That brought back another familiar fantasy. Throughout my adult life I have pictured a lighthouse on a rock surrounded by tempestuous seas, just standing and serving, unbowed by the storm. I think that that says more about my omnipotent personality organization than anything else—part denial, of course, but also a goal. During my illness, that figure of the lighthouse was threatened as it never had been before. I was unquestionably helped in overcoming it not by having had an analysis in the past, but by having a living personal encounter alive though dormant in me. I might have denied my need for a source for such inner strength, but clearly I did have it and an old and valued relationship came to life.

In the past, my first line of defence has been psychosomatic, but this did not lead to understanding, nor to memory and actualization. I had an asthma attack about a month after my wife's death. I am in no doubt but that that was part of a mourning process and it cleared the air, but it led to no fresh insight. Memories and fantasies are different and to be effective must have their source in psychic reality. Memory has to be actualized, recreated, for it to be real, worked through in the present, experienced in the area of the patient's omnipotence where he or she can take constructive action. Understanding one's true involvement, one's responsibility, frees one from having to remain a victim. For me this process was the continuation of analysis in which I had to play my part, if there was to be a parallel recovery in mind as well as body.

The record would be incomplete, and I would not be honest if I did not mention something that did not fail: my experience of God. Religion seems almost to have become respectable in psychoanalysis lately. To me it is private and personal, and I have had an active faith since my teens, but in a strong dissenting tradition. This took a beating during my analysis, but the greatest difference afterwards was that prayer was never the same again. Praying was much more like letting go on the couch to an unseen figure—real enough, but at the same time a composite fantasy figure disfigured by my projections. Can I say, prayer was more real because of that? That requires believing that one is heard, and by whom. In the loneliness of my illness, I was not alone and my relationship was much richer. But with whom was it? One has no objective evidence of God's existence, and it may look as if there is nothing to show for it, yet, by faith, He is. The feedback in it feels as real as that in any other relationship. It is an experience of Grace, *charis*, an unmerited gift that gives it a reality strong enough to be tested for what it is. In no religious sense, and certainly in no mystical one, I suggest that a good, effective analysis is an experience of Grace. The patient who, from envy of the analyst, or whatever else, has to do it himself or control it all himself receives no *charis*. He cannot admit to his need. The therapist who has to treat compulsively, or who does so to satisfy his own needs, purveys no *charis* either. To ache to help someone could lead to invasion, worse still if the helper is compelled to succeed. By contrast, the suspension of memory and desire with a patient is not rejection but, effectively, *charis*. That seeming therapeutic reticence may be a painfully acquired skill, but when experienced it is a gift that could never have been initiated by the patient alone.

This exemplifies the way a capacity to be alone works for me. One is not alone, because alongside is a powerful good internal object. Surely that refers to an internal living person that has a reality, however composite. Regarding God, He may be a delusion but feels alive, as real as if actual. My experience of Grace comes across like the feedback does in any other authentic relationship. Throughout my illness, that bond remained intact and was a source of strength, though it was tested and did not provide much hope. Popular images, like passing through the valley of the shadow of death, registered but were of little comfort because the valley seemed to have no end. I was never depressed enough to believe psychotically that God was either dead or I too wicked for Him to save. This internal relationship was one strand of the restorative process going on within me. It is not prescribable, nor is it a form of cognitive psychotherapy. It is what was happening, and that could only be experienced, endured, and ultimately overcome. In fact, and increasingly in my mind, I was not alone but wonderfully supported, by human goodwill, by encouragement and hope from those staff and friends who were not just mouthing "Have a nice day". I cannot be sure, but I think that it is the *charis* in a good analysis which permits it to continue on in the future. It is not analysis that persists, it is an analytic relationship.

A therapeutic regression can only work towards recovery if the therapeutic relationship facilitates it, so that a minimum of hope and trust emerges. Then growth and new development can start. That happened almost by stealth through the loving care I received and could later enjoy. I had a nightly bath ritual in the nursing home. The kind, motherly carers, by bathing me, leaving me to soak, and then drying me, produced an unplanned effect. It was an infantile regression in the best sense, especially as they showed every sign of enjoying it and of not carrying out a chore. It was intimate, sensuous, and erotic in the sense of the erotism that pervades mother and son early in care. To be tucked up in bed and this intimate person care was, I am sure, immensely healing and a valuable early stage in rehabilitation. It was a healthy climb out of the pathological dependence and the traumatic collapse into hopelessness, through a real dependence lovingly met.

Not all my help was emotional. In my depression I sought the help of an antidepressant drug, even though I had been dismissive before of their overuse before taking an account of the person who was depressed. After the first dose of Paroxetine, I felt as if I was being held. It was so immediate that it was probably a placebo effect. The warmth and quality of the nursing home I moved to from hospital was an inspired gift. It exceeded expectations and ultimately won me round to being able to trust it and enjoy it. The reassuring sincerity of the caring staff fell on sceptical ears at first. In my ignorance I was even more dismissive of physiotherapists, but the self-evident rationality of their exercises, plus their encouragement and their reaching the troubled spots, soon had me improving, to the delight of those looking after me, and the waning of my scepticism. Most of all, I experienced—and still do—the reversal of regression, a healthy progression, development.

It is within the relationship with my carers that my analysis survived in me and switched from dormancy into action. This must be linked with my feelings about women. I have realized only as I have written how important a part separation and depression have played in my life. They were denied in the need to assert triumphantly my freedom. There is no question that that forms one interpretation of my relationship to God; it is there also in some of my references to the capacity to be alone, that is when it is based on omnipotence rather than on the internalization of loving, thinking, people. I think now that the ache about women that was so strongly motivating in my life was an attempt to deny a feeling of unbearable separation from women that could not be repaired. As a little boy I fantasized violence, as a man I even used my profession to handle this issue.

I am left somewhat amazed but grateful that all this resurfaced in the course of an illness, and still goes on at times. I had not thought previously that I was vulnerable. My personal learning in relationships had been good enough to outweigh defects. Experiencing and receiving *charis* enabled me to give, and not in any restless, compulsive sense. I was a different, easier, and more tolerant man after my analysis. I feel a different man now after this troubled journey, and much more at rest, largely, I think, because of Grace, which before had been too exclusively a Christian concept for me. It is best described as what you receive when you are freed to express a need in an environment that is loving, concerned, willing to help you to meet it. Thanks to good internal-object relations, and to excellent external ones in the shape of the very objective care I received, I did not collapse. The significance of what went on originally, as well as now, has come into the foreground during my analysis and has been acknowledged and internalized. It seems like a bit of personal rehabilitation. Time will tell if that is true. I am in no doubt, but I still cannot recommend such an illness as a means of learning.

The next stage: living precariously

This now must be my last lap, whether it lasts months or years. My faith may have given me great support, but it has not spared me misfortune, nor was I expecting it to. One thing, though, has changed. Before, to have been confronted with the need to go into care in a nursing home would have been disturbing and resisted. External circumstances have now so changed that I can accept this need and its restrictions with relative equanimity. Paradoxically, that will provide more freedom than being independent on my own but held back by a disability without external support. That is what I said to myself before it actually happened. What follows will show whether or not my predictions were correct and how they differed from reality.

Seven weeks after leaving the nursing home and returning home, a new situation and a challenge began. I began to feel better than I had done for a long time and continued to do so even after disaster struck. My left knee became increasingly painful as I had stopped taking Diclofenac. I had taken a high dose for years as it was effective in reducing arthritic pain. It had produced gastric bleeding, enough to cause severe anaemia just before my cardiac operation. I assume that stopping ceased to mask the encroaching failure of both my knees. The left patella fractured spontaneously from being ground away from behind my arthritic processes, exacerbated by my physiotherapy and my more active lifestyle. I had to be readmitted to hospital as an emergency, and the patella was removed. This time my experience of hospital was totally different—frustrated, of course, yet relaxed; concerned about the future, but enjoying much of the present circumstances. My earlier experience made dependence much easier to accept. It was easy to resist the pressure to succumb to the false dependency-making ward routines, for such a mode does not make for a rehabilitative one. I was able to walk easily with crutches afterwards. Sooner than was desirable, but because of the pain, the right knee was successfully replaced. After another small complication, a few weeks later during rehabilitation the quadriceps tendon above the knee ruptured. It could only be repaired by tying the muscle and the patella together with string and hoping that it would hold. Things have stabilized, but I have not been able to walk since, as neither knee can be locked.

I returned home, where I had excellent daily care and assistance to get across to meals, and this mishap had much less impact than might have been expected. Apart from altering the layout of my study bedroom, I continued with my old lifestyle and my companions unchanged. This was not to last, as that holding environment crumbled. As a result of unwise management, the organization running the house went into solvent liquidation and sold it as a going concern to a new company. They rightly raised the rent considerably, but sadly removed much of the service and provided only one meal a day. That, I realized, I could not easily manage, and I knew that if new residents arrived, one old rule of the house—that a wheel chair was not welcome in the dining-room—would reapply. I decided I must move into care, and then a chain of events started that has much more bearing on the process of ageing than did the experience of my operation. My first thought was to return to the home that I already knew, as it was well run, the food was excellent, the care staff did the caring, the hospitality staff looked after the meals, activities, and outings, and the cleaning staff cleaned and looked after your room. I knew that I would only be able to afford a small room and dreaded having to get rid of most of my library and its musical counterpart.

What seemed like a chance event followed, though I prefer to think of it as unmerited Grace for I benefited from a foreknowledge that I did not have. The new home rang to say that they could not show me the room on the day that we had arranged to view it. Rather than waste my transport, I went to look at another house. It was delightfully situated, the room that I was offered there was far larger than I had dared hope, and I decided almost on the spot to take it. What I did not know was that it was within a lively village into which I could travel. I have since joined a number of activities, made friends, been overwhelmed by the kindness and assistance freely offered, and have a freedom to come and go unknown for the best part of two years. I knew of the limitations of the first house, but I had not appreciated what a prisoner I would have been had I gone there, neither had I thought how much a prisoner I would have been had I stayed in my old home, for both villages had no amenities and the roads were narrow and dangerous on a scooter. This experience has been a very important buffer against the loss of freedom entailed in becoming an inmate and has helped greatly in working through the old crisis that ensued.

I recalled something my cardiologist had said to me in a characteristically laid-back way: if the heart surgery was possible and successful, I could kick cardiac problems into the long grass for fifteen years. I remember replying, "Good Heavens, I shall be a hundred by then, so I shall have to die of something else!" It took on a different significance when I entered the home. The average age of residents was getting on for ten years older than the place I had left. I still felt younger than my years, so suddenly to be faced with great age and decrepitude around me was depressing. Shall I have to go like that before I end? The opportunities of intelligent conversation were more limited than I had expected. Partly this was the result of memory loss and degrees of dementia. Positively, I have learned more about dementia than since the early days of my career. The adaptations in the way people suffering from it try to deal with it are fascinatingly varied. But even if you have not demented, being an inmate for any length of time reduces your experience of the outside world and thus impairs your conversational repertoire. Interesting reminiscences work for a while but start to pall on repetition. My reaction has been exaggerated by attending for a long time an elderly day-care centre for physiotherapy. That has been excellent in starting to get me on my feet again, but seeing irrecoverable stroke patients, amputees after vascular insufficiency in the legs, and severe multiple-sclerosis cases, all of us who were containing their problems well, including more general senile problems, make it seem sometimes as if one's nose was being constantly rubbed in decrepitude.

This led to a definite depressive reaction, characterized by early morning waking. Apart from many thoughts about ending it, this was not otherwise full of morbid fantasies; rather, it was more as if the ability for normal fantasying was frozen by anxieties. It would have been much worse if I had not earlier experienced the waiting for care, not knowing when it would come, and the variable lack of communication—some carers being much more sensitive to this than others are—that seems to be an inevitable experience in care. If I had not, I am sure that my reaction would have been more severe.

I began to miss my wife, which I had not done before, not because I was lonely but because I longed for some warm physical contact and a continuing presence, rather than a continuing absence, of any bodily contact. Perhaps unintentionally I have just defined aloneness rather than loneliness. Being addressed as "Darling" is no substitute. Maybe my humour helped to spare me that fate, which I have not had to resist as I would have done. A capacity to quip and respond had also helped. Dr Johnson defined "precarious" in his dictionary as "being dependent on the care of others". Life has become precarious with a vengeance, and this has to be assimilated. There is not even implied criticism in those last remarks. If it is not easy for me to cope with that decline all round, it can hardly be any easier for the staff which has it all day and every day. They must develop defences against any anxiety or depression that this induces, just as nurses have always had to cope with the emotional demands of their work by defensive strategies that ideally should not make the problems even harder to surmount. I inhabit a room that overlooks, and overhears, where the staff sit and take their breaks. It came as a surprise just how much noise was generated by them sometimes, in particular what I must call the cackles. In any group interpretative setting, I would unhesitatingly call this flight behaviour at times. At 7 a.m. and during early morning waking, it was vexatious and soon dreaded. Later, when worked on and understood, that behaviour became something that one could simply sleep through.

This is now part of an ongoing life. I am beginning to stand unaided and to walk. At some point that upward trajectory will meet the downward one of increasing age. Living in a very attractive environment with some social life outside in the village makes life more than something to be endured. Communal living gives some security, but I have always jested that the motto set over all such establishments for staff and inmates alike is: "You can't win." For me, that is most strongly felt about food. Apart from the economy, and health and safety matters, it can be so dreary, so unlike my freely indulged gourmet tastes of the past, but that is what some others want. "Nothing fancy", they cry. In fact, there are a lot of grumbles at meals but these are not pursued, largely because they are forgotten, but also for another aspect of precariousness. You don't rock the boat, for fear of making yourself unpopular and being asked to leave. That may be an irrational fear, but it is there for some residents.

Those words reminded me that Geoffrey Vickers, who ended in the place in which I am now, wrote a book called *Freedom in a Rocking*

Boat. That title has always produced in me a vivid crop of agreeable fantasy of maintaining a balance, control, and an ability to keep in touch with one's environment enough to sample and enjoy it despite the local turbulence. It is not an inappropriate metaphor related to living dependent upon the care of others. One need not only be a victim: some management is possible. That requires acknowledging the boat, from which it is then possible to foster and encourage communication and feedback. More than you might expect, mutuality can develop. That requires an adequate sensorimotor apparatus for the necessary work to go well. Ageing is still the devil, as decrepitude can deprive us even of that. Until then—or does that freedom help to postpone that "then"?

PART **III**

OBSERVATION AND CONSULTATION

CHAPTER 8

Psychodynamic observation and old age

Rachael Davenhill, Andrew Balfour, Margaret Rustin

> About suffering they were never wrong
> The Old Masters: how well they understood
> Its human position; how it takes place
> While someone else is eating or opening a window or just
> Walking dully along . . .
> In Breughel's Icarus for instance: how everything turns away
> Quite leisurely from the disaster; the ploughman may
> Have heard the splash, the forsaken cry,
> But for him it was not an important failure;
> . . . and the expensive delicate ship that must have seen
> Something amazing, a boy falling out of the sky,
> Had somewhere to get to and sailed calmly on.
>
> W. H. Auden, "Musée des Beaux Arts" (1938)

T his chapter illustrates the relevance of the psychodynamic observational method at pre- and post-qualification level for core professions working with people who are older. Psychodynamic observation has been used successfully as a core component

---

An earlier version was published as R. Davenhill, A. Balfour, M. Rustin, M. Blanchard, & K. Tress. "Looking into Later Life: Psychodynamic Observation and Old Age." *Psychoanalytic Psychotherapy,* Vol. 17, No. 3 (2003): 253–266.

of training for child psychotherapists in the NHS since the 1940s and was originally developed at the Tavistock Clinic by the psychoanalyst Esther Bick. She asked her trainees to undertake an observation of a baby, and his or her caretaker, in the first year of life as a means of learning about the basic foundations of personality development. At the time, she wrote that this approach to observation is valuable in helping the observer to: "discover the values of being and themselves becoming a receptive observer. In this exercise there is no obligation to do anything beyond observing. Indeed, one has to refrain from action . . . " (1987, p. 265).

While this sounds a simple task to undertake, in practice it is extremely challenging, as Hinshelwood and Skogstad (2000) point out in their book on institutional observation. What is immediately striking in thinking about staff working with older people is how young, comparatively, the staff group is. Martindale (1989) looked at the anxieties aroused for younger clinicians coming into contact with patients who are older. At a point in the lifespan where individuals may be trying to separate from their own families of origin, establish their own careers, and start their own families, working with older people may arouse unresolved feelings regarding separation, dependence, and independence. In being drawn to work in the area of old age there may be the wish to repair yet often the reality of having to witness deterioration. The difficulty here is that if, in the work setting, repair cannot really take place, then the more omnipotent expectation of providing a cure rather than offering care becomes a burden impossible to fulfil and a source of disappointment. Inevitably in the field of old age, at the more severe end, cure as such is not an option. Despite the wish for neatness conveyed in the 2001 *National Service Framework for Older People* (DOH, 2001a) and other national documents, there remains an ongoing difficulty in the wish for "joined-up" and "seamless" thinking. While a desirable aim, this nonetheless remains an unrealistic one so long as the unconscious factors that so often lead to fragmentation and breakdown of thinking are not fully acknowledged and given a formal place to be understood. Psychodynamic observation provides an accessible framework within which some of the unconscious tensions of later life can be articulated and understood in detail.

Waddell (see chapter 11) illustrates the linkage between the understanding of the very early states of mind of the infant and what she refers to as the "opaque mental states of old age", highlighting the way in which the caregiver's capacity to unconsciously register, reflect, and think can give meaning to the infant's or older person's world through the caregiver's capacity to care responsively. One of the key psychoanalytic concepts crucial to understanding this area is that of projective identification:

> By the mechanism of projective identification the baby/child/ elderly person who cannot understand, think, or talk about his or her fragmentary or fragmenting experience may nonetheless be able to engender in the care-giver some version of that basic experience. If . . . the caregiver can offer a mentally receptive state of mind, conscious or unconscious, the communication can be received, modified if it is one of pain and rage, appreciated if one of love and pleasure, and re-communicated, whether in more manageable or in reciprocal mode. The caregiver's mind functions as a container for, and a sorter of, the projected emotional fragments, which, as a consequence, become "the contained". Care of the very elderly—those so often lacking the capacity to speak, yet so intensely riven by extreme emotional states—requires a painful reversal of the original pattern of container–contained (the young now struggling to offer states of reverie to the old).

Setting up a psychodynamic observation

Psychodynamic observation in an old age setting is a key component of the two-year Tavistock post-qualification course on Psychodynamic Approaches to Old Age. As part of the first-year course, participants undertake an old age observation for a minimum of twenty weeks, followed by a baby observation in the second year. This allows a further deepening and integration of course participants' thinking and emotional understanding of very early states of mind and their relevance for the understanding of both the anxieties and possibilities for further development in old age.

The five key steps in undertaking a psychodynamic observation for the course are as follows:

1. The person undertaking the observation sits in a discreet position in whatever setting he or she is carrying out the observation. This will have been carefully negotiated and agreed beforehand, with informed consent being given by the staff and users of the setting.

2. The observation takes place once a week, usually at the same time, for a minimum of twenty weeks. Once in the observational setting, participants are exposed to the problem of watching an

"unprotected" space and will be exposed to a confusion of feelings in terms of for whom they felt what. For example, they may feel closely identified with a particular staff member, or with one of the patients, or exposed to people coming in and out wanting to engage in some other form of interaction. This aspect of somehow staying involved but remaining sufficiently neutral is a dilemma that all observers struggle with. In psychodynamic observation, the discipline of being an observer is primarily about not doing things. In our everyday work role, we are always acting and reacting in one way or another in working with patients and running services. There is rarely any experience of doing nothing. In psychodynamic observation, however, there is a formal framework that allows the situation being observed to impinge on the observer's heart and mind and allows him or her room to consider what may be going on unconsciously as well as consciously.

3.   No notes are taken at the time.

4.   The observer will write up detailed process notes as soon as is possible afterwards, outside the observational setting. Although this is demanding and time-consuming, it is often the case that, paradoxically, much of the observation may not be consciously observable to the participant until some time has passed, and a process of further digestion can then take place, as things not originally at the surface of the mind come to the fore in the process of writing up.

5.   The further processing of the observation takes place in a weekly supervision group run by a psychotherapist. Each member of the group is able to present an observation in detail on a rotational basis. A major advantage of meeting as a group is that the observer is exposed to the associative process of the group setting. The group allows a multifaceted perspective to emerge, so that by the end of the presentation and discussion, the observer will hopefully feel that it is possible to have a truthful and more rounded picture of the many aspects of the experience he or she has allowed him/herself to be exposed to.

The aim of the observation is to allow the observer to come close to the older person's experience and develop an attuned capacity to see and retain detail. In becoming aware of the emotional impact that the interplay between the individual and his or her environment may produce, it is hoped that the observer will learn from his or her own experience about factors, conscious and unconscious, that can support or impede development and adjustment to transitions in the later part of life.

Psychodynamic observation provides a powerful learning tool for understanding the unconscious as well as the conscious atmosphere of the world of the older person and his or her carers. This understanding itself can have a strong containing function. Psychodynamic observation is quite different from, though can be complementary too, other methods of qualitative observation such as dementia care mapping (DCM). Here, the observer is "looking in" to observe the quality of care in a particular environment at one remove. Although DCM and psychodynamic observation are both forms of observation linked to looking and being looked at, in which vision is a form of action at a distance, the psychodynamic observational method is more intimate. The observer is looking at her or his own subjective experience of what it is possible to look at, take in, and think about at both a conscious and an unconscious level—she or he is learning, in effect, to develop his or her own capacity as internal consultant to the unconscious atmosphere of the observed setting, rather than relying on external feedback from without.

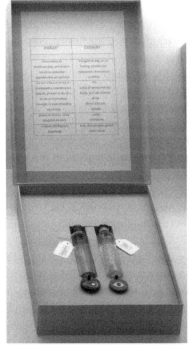

INSIGHT	EYESIGHT
discernment or understanding; penetration; intuition; immediate apprehension or cognition	eyesight; seeing; act of looking; mental view; judgement; observation; scrutiny
the act or fact of seeing or contemplating something not actually present to the eye; mystical or prophetic foresight or understanding; revelation	the action of seeing with the bodily eye; the exercise of the physical faculty of sight
power or activity of the imagination; inwit	ocular perception
wisdom; intelligence; knowledge	look; view; glimpse; glance; observation

Figure 1: "Insight and Eyesight". Detail from Susan Hiller's *From the Freud Museum* 1991–6. The wording from the inside of the lid of the box is reproduced above for clarity.

Looking into later life:
the health centre and the nursing home

Two observations are now described. The first links to more normative aspects of ageing, while the second concerns itself with the difficulties for older people and their carers when there is more physical and mental deterioration. Normally the psychodynamic method of observation is used purely for continuing professional and personal development and, as such, remains, other than for supervisory purposes, within the private domain. For the purposes of confidentiality, therefore, a series of fine-grain observations have been amalgamated from a number of different settings. In the first example, detailed observations in a day centre, a health centre, and a day hospital for older people have been combined. In the second example, observations in a nursing home, a residential care home, and a continuing-care ward have been used. Although each example is an amalgamation it is hoped that the experience of observing conveys itself and remains true at depth.

Observation 1:   The health centre

The observation took place for an hour at the same time once a week for a period of twenty weeks. Each time the observer went, all present in the clinic were asked to read and sign an informed-consent form, which described the purpose of the observer's presence in terms of continuing professional development and made clear that, if there were any objection to her or his presence, the observation would not take place. The centre was a busy multi-purpose building in which various health clinics took place, including an older people's outpatient clinic. The waiting area for this was laid out in a circle of armchairs, interspersed with little tables and the occasional table lamp. To the side of the waiting area was a large communal area where staff, both visiting and permanent, tended to sit and write up notes. Ann, the observer, placed herself there as the least obtrusive place to sit. The daily staff team meeting was still taking place when she arrived, and for the first fifteen minutes Ann felt as though she was observing a stage set. The whole place was still and quiet. An elderly woman with grey hair sat slumped in a chair, seemingly asleep, looking quite deteriorated. Next to her was a woman in her sixties, smartly dressed in a red jacket and skirt, reading a newspaper. There was then a small coffee table, after which sat two more newspapers next to each other—all that could be seen at first—held up by two women. Finally, at the other end of the room sat two more women, side by side, both sitting motionless, like statues, not reading newspapers, looking straight ahead, completely still.

Ann described quickly losing track of time, like someone in transit, only becoming aware of this when staff began to emerge out of a side room following the end of their meeting. The change was remarkable. Suddenly, in one almost synchronized movement, all the newspapers were put down and the room seemed to come to life. Ann noticed that most of the staff members were from minority ethnic backgrounds, whereas most of the patients were white. The two women whom she had originally not been able to see because of the newspapers held up in front of them started to talk to each other about an information leaflet regarding how to prevent further falls. The woman on the right asked the other woman if she had tried doing the exercises on the leaflet—they were very good and did help you not to fall over, she'd really recommend them.

Meanwhile, the grey-haired woman, Miss A, whom Ann had first seen slumped in the chair asleep, had been collected by a young male physiotherapist and taken to a side room. On her return fifteen minutes or so later, she seemed completely transformed. She was awake, alert, slightly imperious, speaking with a heavy Eastern European accent. She started to talk to the woman in red next to her but then seemed to become slightly confused, saying that she was unsure whom she was due to see. She started to call out loudly "Darling! Darling . . . " trying to attract the attention of a nurse. A male nurse who had emerged earlier from the staff meeting was leaning against a wall just behind her and was imitating the woman saying "dahling" in a slightly contemptuous manner. When the woman realized he was there, she called him round. He stood to one side, towering above her. She insisted he come round to the front and move into a position where she could see him, otherwise, as she put it, how on earth could she be expected to speak to him and he be expected to hear her? At this point a more ordinary contact then did seem to become possible. The nurse asked the woman her name. She asked him how long she would be there for. When he shrugged and said he didn't know, probably until the afternoon, the old woman insisted he fetch someone who did know, otherwise, as she pointed out, they were both in the same boat, waiting around not knowing what was going on. Another member of staff then came across and confirmed that once Miss A had been seen by the doctor in the next hour or so, then she could go home. If she wanted, they could call a taxi for her.

While this interaction was taking place, the two women who had been sitting like motionless shadows at the other end of the waiting area had moved. One, Mrs B, was helped to her feet by an occupational therapist and taken for an assessment. The other woman, Mrs C was approached by a nurse who asked if she would like a cup of tea. Mrs C said that she had been sitting there since 8.30 that morning when the community transport had dropped her off, and no one had seen her. The nurse acknowledged how frustrating the waiting must be. She went on to say that the doctor had only just arrived and started to see people. The old people's lunch club was on today—the nurse could get her some nice lunch from there if Mrs C wanted. Mrs C said that she just wanted to go home—she got knotted up in her stomach just sitting there. The nurse asked her if a newspaper would help. No, said Mrs C, she just wanted to get home, that is what would help. The nurse was very kind, but it made it worse, all the waiting. At this point Mrs B slowly walked back to her seat, shuffling slightly as she sought to maintain her balance as she held onto the arm of a Ghanaian nurse. The nurse commented that where she came from it was called the land of six cultures because of the mix of the population there. Mrs B commented that in London, this was the land of forty languages, as it was such a big mixture of everyone. Mrs B and Mrs C then settled back into their seats, but no longer seemed shadowlike. Mrs B commented on how good the staff of the clinic were. Mrs C agreed, adding that although it was true the staff here were good, what was not at all good was the transport. She would get picked up at 8 a.m. then driven around for two hours before getting here, then it would take up to two hours to be taken back home at the end of the day, as well as all the waiting around when they were actually here.

As she left this first observation, Ann described feeling moved and engaged and aware of how much mobility and movement from a more passive to a more active engagement oscillated in and out of the observation for both patients and staff. From writing up the observation and thinking with colleagues about it afterwards in supervision, two areas particularly struck her. The first was her initial response on hearing the two women discussing the information one of them had been given about falls. Ann had immediately thought of Vermont and the deeply coloured leaves of autumn. In the outpatient clinic there were a number of older people who had fallen, and although the falling had an impact, they were far from being shrivelled or dead. The latent capacities of people attending this particular clinic were clearly near the surface and accessible when staff were fully involved with their patients. What was striking in this and other observations was the impact that real engagement from the staff had on the clinic atmosphere or culture, as though the life blood was allowed to flow again. This had been particularly striking in the observation of Miss A.

The clinic were justly pleased with the number of patients they felt were helped back to their "old selves" as opposed to being catapulted into a much older stage of life containing more restrictions. However, despite the overt optimism suggested by in the clinic literature in terms of getting people back on their feet, which conveyed an attitude, in theory, of giving attention to the needs of the whole person, Ann was particularly affected by the experience of sitting in the waiting area and the impact of this "transit-lounge" experience on all involved. What was very clear was the burden of the constant waiting and the way in which, at a deeper level, this must trigger off more primitive anxieties in terms of "what next?"—at what point does the possibility of being able to impact on the object and the environment crumble? This dilemma seemed also to be reflected among the staff group, some of whom were very actively engaged with the frustrations of the patients in their care, whereas others seemed constantly below par, under-functioning, never seeming quite at full capacity—as though in an almost complete identification with the patients in their care. For some patients, the experience of waiting around for most of the day seemed to be containing, whereas for others it was a total persecution, with the space leaving them feeling less and less in control. The difficulties with the transport externally—and this seemed to be a universal phenomenon across all the observations in this kind of setting—could also reflect the dilemma of erratic waiting in the period of recovery following a first fall in the younger older people, who predominated in this particular clinic. The psychic query seemed to be: "Will I get back to where I was originally, and how much adaptation and further development will take place after I have been so knocked off balance?"

The second area that had preoccupied Ann was the land of forty languages. This was connected to the issue of cultural difference in the area of race and also raised the issue of what it meant to enter into the

culture of later life as a younger observer or a younger staff member—
of how there is no one group of older people as such, but an inhabiting
of very diverse worlds that varied enormously from one individual to
the next. This could be seen in the example of Miss A, who persisted in
exerting her insistence on being acknowledged and impacting on the
environment around her, and Mrs C, who seemed to recede away from
her human identity into a shadow state when she felt abandoned by
her environment and unable to assert any potency—two very different
responses to a similar situation.

Observation 2: The nursing home

The home was set in pleasant countryside—slightly idyllic on first
approach, a bit like a country-house hotel. Once inside, the observer,
Dan, felt hit with the overwhelming smell of urine and disinfectant,
and hit also by the thought of such an abrupt contrast between a preserved outer shell and an institutional inside, the urine a reminder
that inside contained more damage than the outer appearance initially conveyed. The layout of the home was open plan, with a central
observation point, a lounge area, with small two-person bedrooms
coming off it. Along each wall of the lounge was a row of seats. Each
time Dan went, the residents were sitting in the same seats, with a
tray on wheels in front of them, positioned too far apart for any interaction to take place. At the end of the lounge area was a large-screen
TV, which was always on and quite loud. There was an atmosphere
of waiting, with people facing towards the empty centre of the room,
which occasionally filled with staff. One of the most striking features
within the home was the patient's physical immobility and the difficulty of any kind of flexible emotional functioning for either patients
or staff. The first example of an observation in the nursing home con-
nects to dependency and the struggle for independence of body and
mind in an elderly man.

Example 1

When Dan arrived in the lounge, Mr A, a large man with thick
white hair, attempted to get up from his usual armchair, located
against the lounge wall. A care assistant came to Mr A, telling him
that he should finish his tea. She pushed him on his shoulder, and
Mr A rocked back and forth and then slid back into his chair. He
picked up his mug of tea and made loud slurping noises as he

drank it. He then slowly pulled himself up to a standing position again, and again was gently pushed back into his chair, with a query, "Where are you going? Not yet, you have to drink more." This happened a couple more times, until the care assistant looked over at a male nurse and made a silent appeal for him to intervene. The nurse went over and put his arms around Mr A's shoulder in a matey way, asking him to sit down. He then pushed down on both of the old man's shoulders firmly, so that he had to sit down. The nurse left, commenting, "You'll have to sit down or you'll fall down."

Mr A immediately stood up again, losing his balance, then re-standing, all in all for eight attempts. Finally he gained his balance. He started to walk forwards, using his tray on wheels for support, like a Zimmer frame. He made it, slowly and painfully, into the middle of the room, Dan noticed that the other patients, who up until this point had been enclosed in their own individual worlds, were all watching Mr A's progress with interest. Dan thought of *One Flew over the Cuckoos Nest* and Mr A's effort to use his remaining strength to defy the immobility that had everyone trapped in their chairs.

The other patients took an interest in his progress, and Dan was gripped by his and the other patients' vicarious involvement in Mr A's struggle for movement and autonomy. By now he is standing unsteadily in the middle of the room, holding on to the tray on wheels in front of him. The care assistant who had previously been telling him to sit down walks past and does not seem to notice. At this point a large group of visiting student nurses come in with the manager of the home. She describes the phone system of the home to them in great detail. They are standing in the middle of the room at the observation desk on which a number of phones are placed. Meanwhile, just behind them, Mr A is taking increasingly unsteady steps into the middle of the room. He is a big man, and Dan described feeling increasingly anxious, imagining how much Mr A would hurt himself if he fell. More nurses came in and milled around. No one seemed to notice Mr A except for every member of the patient group, who continued to track his painful progress attentively.

Slowly the student nurses drifted away, and the male nurse came back. Dan found himself on the edge of his seat, trying to signal to the nurse with his eyes that there was something wrong. The nurse saw Mr A and called out to him, "What are you doing?" He went across and led Mr A back towards his chair. One of the other patients called out, "We're all watching him, not the TV." Another patient replied, "He's the star of the show." This was the most interaction Dan observed between the patients throughout the many weeks of his observation.

From his seated position, Mr A looked up at the nurse with a sideways grin and pushed his tray away from himself as if he were going to try again. This time, however, he did not try to stand up, and very quickly he seemed to be asleep. The male nurse sat down next to Mr A and drained a bag that Dan had not noticed before, which was now visible on his ankle, just below his trousers. The nurse said, speaking to himself as the old man was now asleep, "You just keep on drinking, and I'll keep taking the piss."

A little later, Mr A opened his eyes. The sun was shining through the lounge window, and an occupational therapist (OT) came into the middle of the room, swaying her hips, saying, "Isn't this wonderful, doesn't it make you want to dance? Would you like to dance?" She swayed across the room towards Mr A and said, "Nice shirt." He replied, "Snazzy, isn't it?" The OT said something else and Mr A tried to respond, but the she moved away without waiting for him to answer. She went into a side room, and Dan heard her greeting another patient in a similar way. Mr A put his hand to his brow and frowned and grimaced, looking pained.

The OT's comment "Shall we dance?" could have represented something enlivening, a savouring of what was once enjoyed. But instead, any more real contact is avoided by her quick move away. Mr A did not have a partner for the slow steps that he was in reality able to make, the "dance", in his efforts to move across the room that he did need a partner for, and could have been supported in. In the face of such bodily restriction, it seemed that the tremendous movement of imaginative engagement needed for staff really to be aware of the emotional context underlying Mr A's attempt at physical movement seemed to be too great. This raises the question of the unconscious anxieties aroused for younger staff who are coming into contact with people so much older than themselves. Frequently excitement can be used to shield the self from ever-present suffering. Earlier on in the observation, the mass discussion about the telephone system meant that the painful feelings associated with Mr A's slow and tortuous attempts to imprint his human capacity on his surroundings were left in the eye of the observer, and the central observation desk became a mechanical area devoid of real meaning in terms of what could be taken in. This observation also highlighted how difficult it can be to engage with an awareness of restriction without resorting to the defensive manoeuvre of a more erotized link as a retreat from any sustained emotional contact. In undertaking an observation of this kind, the opportunity is allowed of really trying to understand what kind of relationship to diminished or developmental possibilities can be borne by both the older person and the staff.

A second example highlights the unconscious difficulties this can present to all involved.

Example 2

As Dan arrived at the home, a nurse was attending to a chair-bound woman, Mrs B. The nurse asked Mrs B to lean forward, holding her from the front, trying to pull her forward to insert a pillow behind her. Mrs B was calling out. There was a desperate quality to her cries, and she seemed to be in pain. The nurse tried to supply another pillow in the hope that Mrs B would be more comfortable.

Mrs B shouted, "Ow, it's hurting. Ow, stop."

"Just try and lean forwards, Mrs B", says the nurse.

"I can't. Stop. It's hurting".

This went on for a minute or two, with the nurse struggling and the patient shouting, until the nurse said, "Ok, I'll get some more help." She threw the pillow over the nearby table and then turned back to Mrs B, telling her to eat her breakfast. Mrs B replied that she couldn't, and the nurse continued, "Have some tea then", and left the room.

Mrs B began to wail and called out, "Won't somebody help me . . . I don't know what's going on . . . I haven't got a clue what's happening. It hurts, I can't sit here any more." Dan could hardly make out a lot of what she was crying out. There were no staff around, and the other patients were looking away.

Mrs B called out, "I can't sit here any longer. . . . Won't somebody help me?" Dan thought she may have said "loo" and felt an intense pressure to do something. The nurse returned and said to Mrs B "What's the matter?"

"I want the loo."

The nurse started to wheel her to the toilet, and Mrs B said "Where are we going?"

The nurse replied, "To the toilet."

Mrs B said, "Oh", and suddenly became much calmer.

This observation is obviously disturbing, and was disturbing for the observer to take in. In talking with colleagues in the supervision group later, Dan said that he wanted to turn away from the cries and tune into the television on the far wall, which the other residents had all done when they looked away. What emerged from this observation was how hard it was to be in any ongoing contact with Mrs B's painful state of mind. She made it clear that she could not stand the position she was in. The nurse went to get help, but some time passed before she returned, and Mrs B became increasingly desperate and disorientated. At the beginning, the nurse's idea was that if she gave Mrs B a pillow, she would be more comfortable. However, Mrs B was desperately conveying that she needed something to be taken away, rather than something additional provided.

Melanie Klein made the important point that the breast—by which she meant the mother or primary caretaker, which here the nurse would represent as the primary source of help—is there to function not only as a source of nourishment, but also to take away difficult or bad feelings. Bion, by elaborating Klein's insight, described the psychic mechanism through which this can be done as projective identification, whereby unwanted aspects of the self are projected out and onto or into an individual who is able to function as a ready receptacle for unwanted feelings. A carer who is able to accept such projections and think about their meaning may then be able to respond to the person's unconscious source of distress, as well as its conscious manifestation. In the observation, Mrs B was conveying that she needed to be able to project out an experience that seemed to be connected to some terrible confusional discomfort that was stuck inside her and she needed to get rid of. Under such circumstances, the nurse was unable to give her something to make her feel better.

Mrs B's cries had a piercing quality, and the nurse, the observer, and the other patients all retreated in the face of this, not wanting such distress to be lodged with them. The patient seemed to be internally in the hands of a persecutor: aching bones, too-thin limbs, hopelessly struggling with a deteriorating body. The body had become a source of persecution and burden, and the nurse seemed to be felt as a persecutor. The patient was isolated in her own internal world, and the nurse was on her own. This seemed to be reflected in the empty observation point in the centre of the room. An extra "eye" was needed but was not there. Instead, the observation point seemed to represent an "unthinking eye", a symbol, perhaps, of the difficulty in bearing what is there in front of our eyes. Such difficult states of mind need to be projected out; the nurse involved had no one to turn to, and the patient was temporarily left screaming. All the other patients were immobile and could not get up. Most people may have had at some point in life the experience of coming into contact with a screaming baby where no one knows what the matter is. The mother or father may have tried everything—feeding, changing, rocking, and so on. Doing something does not seem to have any effect, and the important factor then is who contains the container—what support is there for the main caretaker to support him or her in the contact with this screaming infant? The same question is of equal importance for carers and clinicians working at the other end of the lifespan. It says much for the internal resources that the nurse in this example was able to draw on in herself that, after temporarily withdrawing from Mrs B, she was able to re-enter the distressing situation and to continue trying to help the older woman. Although Mrs B ostensibly seemed to become calmer when the nurse took her towards the toilet, in fact—as Dan reported to his supervision group—when she and the nurse got there, she did not actually physically need to use the toilet. This would seem to support the idea that Mrs B's awful distress linked much more to an internal state of persecution in which she felt full to bursting with unbearable feelings that had to be projected out. Her calmer state of mind came about when the nurse returned and continued to have contact with her patient as best she could.

Conclusion

In thinking about psychodynamic observation as a contribution to the training of workers caring for people who are older, a central feature is how powerful the experience is. Here, the observer was pulled into the atmosphere and drawn into the same dynamic as everyone else in the home in the face of Mrs B's screaming, which was to look away and become involved in watching the television. The experience of undertaking an observation allows the participant to fully understand how powerful the pull is for staff and carers working on an everyday basis in such intensely charged situations to enact and react without the protection of the observer role. M. J. Rustin (1989) and Hinshelwood and Skogstad (2000) emphasize that observation is a research tool as well as a training method. It allows a very particular way of coming close to the disturbance for patients and for staff that the deterioration of mental and physical capacities can arouse, and it also points out how important an understanding of such disturbance is for containing the situation.

Psychodynamic observation is also important in thinking about what it means to be really seen. Just as the eye can be an agent of projection as well as perception, so the receptive eye can provide a means of perceiving and understanding the unconscious communications and atmosphere inhabited by staff and patient. One of the core aims of psychodynamic observation is to enable the observer both to be in a powerful emotional context and to retain some capacity to think about what he or she sees going on inside him/herself as a reflection of what is going on around him or her. To gloss over the degree of difficulty, at an unconscious level, that workers may be confronted with in their daily contact with patients who are older is dangerous and can lead to an osteoporosis of thinking—a crumbling and fragmentation of thinking in the individual worker and the institutional atmosphere within which they operate. While there is no easy solution to such unconscious pressures, we would suggest that the integrative impact of undertaking a psychodynamic observation as one component of both pre- and post-qualification training for all professionals working with older people "brings the possibility of observation leading to intervention one step nearer" (Obholzer, 2000, p. x).

CHAPTER 9

Consultation at work

Maxine Dennis and David Armstrong

In this chapter we offer an example of the contribution that psychodynamically informed consultancy can make to supporting staff teams in thinking through and creatively managing the inevitable and intrinsic emotional wear and tear of working in the area of mental health and old age. This emotional undertow could be regarded as simply an occupational hazard, associated with the feelings aroused in caring for, and nursing, patients who may themselves be experiencing distress, confusion, feelings of isolation, or uncertainty or loss and may also at times be demanding, resentful, forgetful, and easily hurt. In contrast to this, the approach to consultancy to staff groups underlying the example we are offering here views the emotional undercurrents of the work and of staff's experience, both overt and covert, not simply as an occupational hazard but as an occupational "occasion"—that is, as an opportunity to extend and deepen our understanding of and response to what is happening, consciously and unconsciously, in our interactions with patients, with colleagues, and with the wider system of interdisciplinary and inter-group relations in which these interactions are embedded. The basic framework of the consultation approach we describe aims to afford staff a space in which to share and give value to the undercurrents of their experience and their meaning: to transform a hazard into an occasion.

The consultation in question arose from a request, by the manager of a unidisciplinary team working within a psychiatric hospital, to the hospital's psychotherapy department where one of us (Maxine Dennis) was working. The team worked in long-stay wards, in a day hospital, and in the community. The manager was looking for consultancy to a staff support group that would draw on psychoanalytic input and provide a place in which team members could bring and discuss the feelings being aroused in them by their work with patients who were older. Maxine had previously worked as a consultant in a similar way with an external staff group; this had gone well, and the head of department suggested she might take on this potential new assignment. The contract was to run for a year, with weekly meetings held on site. The group was made up of eight members, seven of whom were women and one a man. During the year the composition of the group changed, with one member, a student on placement, leaving; it was some time before she could be replaced.

Throughout the year the two of us met on a regular basis to discuss the work and, in particular, to provide an opportunity to reflect on and process Maxine's own transference and countertransference feelings arising out of the group experience.

What follows are Maxine's reflections on and account of her own and the group's experience as this evolved over the year. Our intention is to let the material stand for itself without, as it were, glossing over it after the event.

THE STORY OF THE CONSULTATION
by Maxine Dennis

Setting up

The initial request for consultation predated the actual start of the group by a year. It was only then that I was asked specifically for, and was able to offer, a weekly consultation to the team. I met initially with the manager of the team to discuss the request and following that I met with all the staff. In our first two meetings, I explored whether staff would be able to make the necessary time commitment to attend meetings, and I also wanted to clarify that the focus of the group would meet their requirements—specifically, to provide support for and examine their work with patients by enabling staff to make use of their transference and countertransference feelings.

The room we met in was in a fairly new part of the hospital, although the room itself was rather shabby. It was often too hot or too noisy when the window was opened. The fax machine was housed within the room, and at times we had the intrusion of incoming faxes, together with other professionals mistakenly convening for meetings in this room. The room itself seemed to reflect some of the difficulties around boundaries and the fragmentation that can often be apparent when working with older people with mental health needs as they struggle to look after themselves in the face of, at times, very frightening processes of deterioration in terms of body and mind.

In telling the story of the consultation I shall focus on and describe a number of the staff support group sessions and the themes that arose from the work presentations. In each case I present only key pieces of information in order that the material remains anonymous. I show a link between the lifecycle of the group, the material (i.e., work with patients brought by group members), and the consultation process. The cycle of the group can be separated into three phases—beginning, middle, and end—each of which had its own particular themes and dynamics.

Beginnings

The group were an established staff team who came across as warm, friendly, and open but had few opportunities to come together. I became aware that they wanted to have a time to meet, but having that time also became a challenge to them. On the one hand, there was a willingness to engage in a "new" way of thinking, which may have been facilitated by there being two members of the group who were knowledgeable about psychoanalytic ideas and seemed to represent a benign presence in the group. On the other hand, there were others for whom the way of thinking represented by the group was unfamiliar, different, and puzzling.

After having waited for a year, staff seemed uncertain about how to use the group during their first meeting. As we spoke, I had an image of a hungry baby, uncertain when first faced with the nipple—both overwhelmed by the full breast to which it is attached and yet having to suck in order to obtain the nourishment desired. I found myself interested in that analogy. There was the obvious link with the start of life and the start of a group, but also perhaps an attempt to relinquish some of the despair that might lie ahead, specifically related to this area of work, as "in old age we mourn the loss of energy and functions and the end of our own life. Facing the finiteness of our personal life and that of our loved ones is the most painful of the many processes of mourning that we have to encounter" (Salzberger Wittenberg, 1970, p. 89). I was pleased that overall the group seemed keen to have input but I was also daunted by the needs of the group. The burden of these needs was to surface sharply in the first presentation.

> The patient, Mr A, was brought for discussion by Jo, the only male staff member in a predominantly female team. Jo said that Mr A had suffered from diabetes and was becoming increasingly unable to care for himself. Jo felt that he had to coax the patient into hospital. As a day patient he had accompanied him home to do a home assessment. They were both to return to the hospital by taxi after the assessment. While in the taxi going to the patient's flat, Jo said "You're on your way to your house." The patient took offence at the use of the word "house" instead of the flat where he lived, and Jo felt that this exchange of words/misunderstanding had triggered the patient's paranoid ideas—that everyone was in league against him, was trying to harm him, and could not be trusted. Mr A refused to take part in the assessment or to return when the taxi arrived, so Jo returned without him.

> Mr A had been deteriorating at home and was finding it difficult to look after himself. Intense concern had been expressed about him as he had been carrying out some quite dangerous practices —for example, trying to boil a kettle using an electric ring upside down, and consuming a diet only of chocolate biscuits when he was diabetic. However, Mr A refused to be admitted to hospital so was still living at home.

The first staff group discussion centred on the basis for hospitalization and whether there were clear criteria for this. The group explored their feelings of failure when a patient was hospitalized, as well as the relief, especially if he or she had been living in precarious circumstances in the community. The urgency to get things right was discussed, especially without access to such a "tool" as a mental state examination that might help their decisions to be more fluid. The issue of the taxi appeared to be a useful metaphor. The worker and patient had taken a taxi, and this was going to take them back to the hospital after an allotted period of time. However, the patient's refusal to leave his home meant that the worker had to leave without him. The taxi appeared to represent both the pressure from within them and other professions to get it right and the anxiety about getting it wrong, including feeling responsible and being blamed if the patient's risky behaviour led to any serious self-harm or death. There was a real issue about the patient's "safety", which it was important to acknowledge in terms of the external situation being brought for discussion. But alongside this, what arose was a theme for the staff group of feeling violently intruded into by the patient, mobilized by and in turn mobilizing many issues of guilt. Where were the limits of the responsibility they needed to carry?

The patient was in the early stages of dementia, and his confusion appeared to be projected onto others. The paranoid organization of the patient was echoed in the session as the group discussed their own position as staff and their feeling that their own opinions were easily discredited by other professionals. The question was whether the worker felt he had the professional authority and expertise to make any clear recommendations when left on his own. There was a link between this material and another staff member's association, of a forthcoming visit to a patient who had been homicidal in the past. The discussion centred on bits of the patient's history being lost within the service, the members of the service acting rather like someone with early dementia themselves. The material of the homicidal patient also reflected the dangerous place they as a group might feel that they were left in as the group ended. They were beginning to think about areas of their work as a team that they had not had a space to do for some time, areas that were foregrounding both the ambiguity and the vulnerability of their own situation.

It was, perhaps, this dawning realization that explained why over the next few sessions there was some drifting, a difficulty in getting started or settling on a topic. The next staff meeting I describe echoed this drifting. It had been difficult to begin the group because a male staff member was accompanying a patient to the ward, another staff member had arrived late back from a computer course, and the group was informed that the student would be leaving. So the group was starting with a number of disruptions, abrupt endings, a need for guidance, together with uncertainty about who would and would not be there. The patient group experience, I felt, was now being reflected and mirrored within the here-and-now of the staff group.

At this time I became aware in myself of an uncertainty about the shape of the group and concerned about possible disintegration.

I discussed with the group the issue of starting and ending on time and preserving group space. This was difficult as some members were based on site, others in the community. The group took place at lunchtime for some, and the room was used for other meetings, so at times other people wandered in. The attention to the boundaries was important, as it appeared to enable the group to feel that there was a safe space for thinking. This was done in a very concrete way—when anybody tried to enter the room, I had to inform them that a group was in progress. It was as if the difficulties around boundaries were an expression of ambivalence about really sharing experiences together. They wanted on the one hand to do it, but their anxiety about it kept the space for thinking precarious.

Issues around the boundaries of their authority as staff members, and the struggles with their professional confidence and sense of identity in engaging with patients, were to colour much of the next few weeks. There were two presentations in particular that appeared both to clarify and to challenge the thinking of the group.

> Mrs Z was a Scottish woman nearing the anniversary of the death of her husband. She was described as having had a complicated bereavement reaction. The staff member who started to talk about Mrs Z in the staff group said the patient had dominated a talking group with dramatic stories about her husband during the Second World War, together with talk about the circumstances surrounding his death. He had been hospitalized and came out three days later. He was then rushed back into hospital, and she did not get a chance to say goodbye to him, as he never regained consciousness. She recalled the doctor saying that "he is going now", and she thought her husband was being moved to another ward, rather than her being told he was dying. The patient felt very angry with professionals for the way that they had dealt with her husband and herself. She emphasized all the losses that she had lived through—the Second World War, a miscarriage, and then her husband's death.

In the staff support group, other team members were able to highlight how Mrs Z presented in a similar way in their groups and how difficult they found it to intervene. It was as if she had experienced a trauma that she had been unable to work through and was continually repeating or rehearsing along with an accompanying projection of feelings of guilt onto the professionals, who had "let her down". In the countertransference response, because the staff member felt the guilt, it had become increasingly difficult to interpret or offer anything back because of the constant abreaction. There was an anxiety or fear of the possible impact on the patient, and of the other group members having sight of that, which hindered the presenter's response, her wish to make things safe, and her fear of disintegration. At the same time, the withholding of a response did not allow a space for others and not just one individual, so that the group risked becoming inert and lifeless. The discussion of this material led to further talk about how they saw themselves as professionals in the work and the tendency to be led by others, or by the patient's and their individual needs, at the expense of their own experience and judgement. I was aware of an implicit request that I should lead them and tell them what to do. I should be their "organizing mind".

Within the group it was as if staff felt they could take no risks for fear that they might leave the patient exposed. There was anger at not being able to face the patient's anger and help her to "know about it". The value of the group at this point was in ensuring that there was space to talk through these feelings. It seemed that they were beginning to feel less overwhelmed, and it may be that my response—taking things up actively with them, trying to make connections, and not allowing them to drift, but without offering "solutions"—was offering a clue as to how they could respond to others. I felt that the dynamic operating was one of "how we can value and use the team differently and how we can value each other differently". There was a stronger sense of the group trying to create a skin around itself, which in turn could release a new thinking about themselves and their relationships with others in a more differentiated way.

Shortly after this session, and perhaps indicating an increasing confidence in their being able to share experiences together, a student member of the staff group made a presentation. This concerned an English patient, Ms B, who lived at home and was depressed.

Ms B was living surrounded by books. She had so many that they limited access to her kitchen, and books encased her bath. The presence of so many books meant that Ms B had barely any space around her. The "care" plan currently in place was to get rid of the books. A worker from the mental health organization MIND was going to help the patient with this, but it was felt that the task was not being taken seriously. When we examined Ms B's history, we found that her mother had stopped her from reading books as a child; her sister was derogatory and critical of her; and the patient had been raped fifteen years previously. There was a query about the perpetrator of the rape being a mental health professional or a member of her family. Ms B had been a nurse at a London hospital, and she was diagnosed as being "ill" (myalgic encephalitis, ME, from which she eventually discovered she suffered, not being recognized at that time).

The patient had spoken to the student about the concrete floor in her flat not being right, saying that the floorboards were defective and that a book had fallen down. She also tended to bring up issues near the end of their meetings. I commented on the way this did not provide time for the patient's issues to be processed, merely leaving the presenter with the information. The focus of the intervention seemed primarily to be on two levels of concern: the patient's self-care/hygiene and her access to entertainment. But this risked blotting out the meaning of the patient's behaviour, her "encasement". I raised the question of her different past experiences, which she might want to keep in place, embodied in the surrounding books. The reference to concrete floor and defective floorboards I felt related to her foundations not being right to cope with the myriad of things that had happened to her. It was as if all aspects of herself had been projected into her books, with any volume being removed representing a part of herself. The patient often spoke about intrusive figures. These were both the intrusive figures from her past but also perhaps from the present, in terms of how she might perceive the role of the MIND worker.

In the next presentation made by the student into the staff support group, the discussion centred on the patient's lack of identity and, in turn, her lack of self-confidence. As with the previous presentation, there was a link with uncertainty in terms of the presenter's own role. She stated that she was not a counsellor and found it difficult to deal with what Ms B had to say and equally wondered whether she should be encouraging the MIND worker with her task. (Perhaps the MIND worker's not taking this task seriously reflected some sensed awareness of the meaning of Ms B's situation.) The two positions—attending to the meaning and addressing the manifest concerns—felt to be in conflict for her.

It seemed that Ms B had no room for "me/the self", the cluster of books representing this restricted space. Her mother had stopped her from accumulating books, so her hoarding was an attack on what mother did. She had projected herself onto the books, so one book fewer felt as though a part of her was missing. She felt that there was no foundation in herself—"*me*". The only way she seemed to keep her sense of self was to identify with the objects around her. The books represented aspects of her past that she wanted to keep ordered and in place. To remove them was, from the patient's perspective, to remove parts of her life.

This loss of the sense of "me" seemed to echo for the staff group, as well as for the student presenter, the struggle to find and keep hold of the professional "me" in their own work. Without this they could be drawn into a disabling identification with patients and an over-dependency on others (e.g., seeing me as "the expert").

In the middle

The middle phase of the group heralded an oncoming break, following which the staff team had requested that the staff support group be continued. By now, the group was more cohesive, thinking together about their identity in relation to their work in old age, as well as themselves as a staff team in relation to other professionals. Members were now bringing detailed notes about their cases and were less concerned about "getting it right". The sense of embarrassment about sharing work experiences had lessened. Prior to the break the members were made aware that the student was about to leave. They spoke about her having been with them for six months and having made a valuable contribution. She would be missed. Less consciously, and perhaps stimulated by the approaching break, I sensed that there was an awareness that the group, too, would be coming to an end, when for many it seemed that it had only just got started.

The next meeting I am about to describe was the first time the only untrained member of the group, Mary, had spoken. She talked about her work with women from a ward of chronically disabled, long-term patients. These ward-bound patients found it difficult to move out of their chairs, which they sat in for most of the day, creating an image of "patients alive in their tombs". When Mary and her colleague were asked to go to the ward, they wondered what they could do: "You feel useless going over with a pack of cards." So they ended up using music and song. They noticed the patients' eyes light up when they provided a song book with lyrics from which the patients could sing. Mary described one patient, Madge, sitting next to her, tapping her on the knee, and expressing her pleasure at the music. She also noted how "some like to be close, others clap or shed a few tears when the 'old' songs bring back memories". The discussion was about the work with patients who are severely demented and the very close bond that members of the group felt they developed between themselves and these patients. Mary seemed intuitively to have made a distinction between offering a "mindless routine"—the deadening "pack of cards"—and something more alive and creative that could afford the possibility of something happening that might be more containing.

In turn, I found myself being drawn into offering some "good food" to them, contrasting the different ways in which professionals in a hospital setting may either seek to manage and work with or avoid and defend against the pain of working with the dying. There may have been a pressure within me to give as much as I could out of concern about the break and the group's own ending. What perhaps was more important was the acknowledgement of what Mary was offering through her intuitive capacity, releasing her—and implicitly the group—from the disability of embarrassment. This session brought into focus the ability to attune to the group.

In an important session following the break, the focus was now on the ability to attune to the individual. In this session, Sarah brought notes about her talking group, which she had been running for several years with a colleague (a music therapist), in the day hospital.

The patient Sarah presented, Mr E, was a 76-year-old man from a Caribbean island with three children. He presented to the group in a flat mood and didn't know why he was in a mental health establishment. He was a thin man, often wearing oversized clothes. When entering the group he always brought a glass of milk which he would sip with a biscuit that he nibbled, while hugging onto a radiator.

In his history, Mr E had lost a plot of land to his brother, and financially things were tight. There was a phase in the talking group where he spoke about death and dying incessantly. There were only four members in the group, and the female member became exasperated with him. The patient also complained of having very little sleep. He went to bed at 8.00 p.m. and lay there rigid until his wife came to bed. She listened to the radio while he took a further two or four hours before managing to sleep. The group discussed whether they should have separate beds. Mr E was still paying off his mortgage and had been working full time. However, when he lost his job some years previously, things seemed to fall apart, including his sense of identity.

In the staff support group we spoke of the patient's sense of dislocation following his arrival in England some years back. A group member wondered about the patient being "a bit dim" and not really understanding what was said to him. He had many physical ailments and there was a question of an eating disorder. He takes a bit of the biscuit he brings with him into the group, nibbles it, and puts it back. Sarah said he reminded her of a child in oversized clothes, constantly nibbling and sipping at milk.

I felt his physical problems and eating disorder reflected both what was going on inside him (relating to a depriving object-mother) and his sense of castration. He seemed unable to take things in except as "bits of biscuit", part of him wanting to take refuge with mother but also wanting to frustrate her, a role he played out with his wife.

The patient wanted to be looked after, but he behaved in a way that invited him *not* to be looked after. Mr E, I suggested, highlighted how with ageing there may come the fear of loss of sexual potency, the threat of redundancy or displacement in work roles, anxieties arising in marital relationships, and an awareness of the inevitability of one's own death (King, 1980).

Sarah's presentation, like so many in the history of the group, raised once more the difficulty of how to respond effectively. The patient is not involved in a relationship with his wife, perhaps raising the issue of work with her also. How do staff members process what the patient is "saying", without simply getting drawn into "activity"? And with whom to share what one becomes aware of and alert to? Was this a role the group members saw themselves as having and could find the authority to voice?

Within the session I also felt the pull in the group both to acknowledge the individual experience, but also, out of uncertainty about what to do if one did, to avoid it by seeing the patient just as part of a group of old people, without his own lifelong story and attributes.

There was also one other aspect to the presentation that I was aware of and able to voice. It was the first time that the theme of ethnic and cultural differences had emerged in the material. Group members would have been aware of my own ethnic origins, similar to those of Mr E. This had never been referred to, as if I could only be seen and related to in my own professional role. In offering this material, perhaps the group, through Sarah, were acknowledging, however obliquely and ambivalently, something of my own individuality and not only my "group affiliation".

Ending

During the last few sessions of the staff group, there seemed to be a shift both in the focus of the material and in the way the group were working. The first of these sessions started off with the group talking about when an emphasis was placed on community care when there was a wish to "forget continuing care". A group member spoke of how bad this made her feel. They contrasted their sense of "keeping patients alive" with the "deathly" wards where little occurred. They spoke of their concern that going into the wards once a week (the pattern of their work in the wards) would not be enough.

The implicit reference to the life cycle of the group itself was very close to the surface. Would "continuing care" be forgotten when the group ended? Had "once a week" been enough, and what difference would the ending make in the face of the myriad different challenges they had to meet? But I also felt that, perhaps out of a difficulty in voicing angry feelings they might have about my leaving them, there was a splitting and projection of inferior treatment onto the nurses. It seemed that what could not be articulated might be the relief of only going in once a week and not having to engage in some of the daily routines.

A discussion began about the changes that were occurring in the organization. An article was mentioned that promoted "joined-up thinking" (working together). A link was made to seeing and placing their input to work as part of a bigger picture rather than as an isolated, disconnected event. This triggered a presentation from Jane.

Jane spoke about a discharged patient who kept attending the day unit and would often ask her to read certain things and help him with filling in forms. On three occasions he had brought her flowers. He had once offered her a lift home which she had refused, and he "took umbrage". She spoke about her discomfort and her difficulty in saying "No", as she was often left to deal with him. There was a silence in the group. Jane had never mentioned this patient before, and there was a feeling of her having been "left to deal with him", alone.

The patient lived on his own and had past diagnoses of schizophrenia. He appeared to have been managing in the community since his discharge from the day unit some years ago.

As the discussion continued, the group was able to work towards a team outcome in terms of how to offer this patient the support he needed in the community and how to keep the member of staff safe. It was as if, in bringing this experience to the group, Jane had tested and in turn mobilized the team's own capacity for "joined-up thinking", rather than it being isolated with one team member. What was emerging in the face of the ending was a clearer acknowledgement of the team's collective responsibility, the value of the kind of sharing they had experienced together—maybe also an acknowledgement that this responsibility would now have to be owned by them.

Conclusion

I think that over the course of a year the work discussion group offered a space where situations, dilemmas, and problems could be brought and shared over time. By paying careful attention to time and place, a setting developed in which staff members felt they could talk together about the difficulties of their work and the feelings this engendered in terms of the transference–countertransference. The group provided a containing structure within which a different and firmer sense of self and professionalism had been able to come into view, grounded in an acceptance of, and alertness to, the internal and external worlds of the older patients in their care.

Afterword

In our introduction to this chapter, we suggested that a way of thinking about what is offered in this approach to staff consultation is that it provides a setting and a space in which staff are enabled to share and give value to the emotional undertow of their experience in working with elderly patients and its meaning, and, in so doing, to transform a "hazard" into an "occasion".

How far the story of the consultation makes good this claim is for the reader to judge. There are, however, three aspects of the story we wish to highlight.

First, the account offered appears to demonstrate very powerfully the ways in which an emotional world—in this case, the emotional world of the older person in need—infects, as it were, all those who come into close contact with it. It is not only that this world evokes transferential responses in ourselves; it is also that it can elicit in us parallel emotional processes, mirroring and enacting the worlds with which we are in contact. So, in the material, it is striking how the themes of the fragility of boundaries, of fragmentation of the self and loss of identity, of failing potency and powers, loss of energy and functions, each of which can be part and parcel of the elderly patient's experience, get inside the inner worlds of staff along with an accompanying undercurrent of persecutory guilt.

Second, the material shows how this process of internal mirroring can extend beyond the boundaries of the individual member of staff into the worlds of the group or the disciplinary team and its interactions and relations with others. An example towards the end of the story is the evidence of a splitting and projection of the more persecutory elements in the work into another discipline and another setting (the nurses in the wards).

Third, this mirroring may equally characterize aspects of the wider system of organizational and inter-organizational dynamics within which any particular staff group is placed. Although this aspect is, inevitably, backgrounded in this material, it seems hinted at on more than one occasion—for example, in the discussion of what was felt to be the ambivalence surrounding community care. The process of emotional mirroring seemed to spread across the "whole system", like the ripples from a stone thrown into water. How far, then, an intervention at any one point in this system can make a difference to the whole is always to be held in question (cf. Dartington, 2004).

Nonetheless, we believe that, even if limited in its impact on the organization as a whole, the type of intervention we have described does indeed made a difference. It is not only that, in sharing their experiences of working with patients and the ways in which this was being reflected in their own feelings and responses, members of the group were better able to contain the pain of the work (and, in so doing, the pain of their patients). It is also that, in the process, they became able to enlarge the ways in which they were working, discovering, and testing new responses, both individually and collectively.

Finally, we would draw attention to the consultant's role in holding, preserving, and on occasion actively intervening to maintain the integrity of the group's boundary. We suggest that this strand in the

material may link to a conscious or unconscious organizational ambivalence, amounting at times to resistance, to the practice of reflective
thought. In a health culture increasingly being driven by the claims
of activity, of doing rather than understanding, the work of "containment"—of attention to and interpretation of experience—can easily
get neglected or sidelined, perhaps unconsciously reflecting a fear of
the limits of what can be both borne and born in so intensely charged
a world. In offering this example, we hope to have shown something
of what can take place where both the resistance and the emotional
undertow are met head on.

CHAPTER 10

Where angels fear to tread: idealism, despondency, and inhibition in thought in hospital nursing

Anna Dartington

This chapter relates to the culture and climate of nursing in Britain and how this culture is influenced by social expectation, history and tradition, institutional dynamics, professional relationships, and nurses' valuation of themselves and their task. The encounters described are from the different vantage points of tutor, student, supervisor, and work consultant.

The intervention with this key professional group raises fundamental issues in consultations to organizations with a therapeutic task. The chapter explores an initial hypothesis that nursing is being required to carry "unthinking" aspects of the hospital and health-care systems. In each of the sections evidence is gathered for the hypothesis rather in the way that a consultant gathers evidence from an accumulation of experience of her or his client group in order to make an interpretation about the dynamics of the institution.

The ideas in this chapter reflect a way of thinking shared and developed in the Tavistock Clinic Consultation to Institutions Workshop and in the Tavistock Group Relations conferences.

First published in *Winnicott Studies*, Vol. 7 (Spring 1993): 21–41.

A shortened version was included in A. Obholzer & V. Z. Roberts (Eds.), *The Unconscious at Work* (pp. 101–119). London: Routledge, 1994.

Introduction

The organization of rudimentary care systems around the processes of birth, death, injury, and disease are as old as human interest in the survival of the tribe. Indeed, it is this very fact—the inevitable social necessity of nursing, whether professional, paid, trained, or otherwise—that gives rise to such emotive and ambivalent attitudes to this work, both in society and in nurses themselves. Nurses remind us not only of our mortality as doctors also do, but of our potential vulnerability and dependency in illness.

The dualism in social attitudes to nursing, which is often referred to in the psychosocial literature as idealization and denigration, is reflected in, for example, newspaper stories of selfless heroism among nurses, set against the reality of low pay and poor working conditions. The corresponding response in nurses is, to put it crudely, flights of idealism, sometimes accompanied by illusions of omnipotence, and depths of despondency associated with a self-definition of devalued importance.

My own particular interest—and one that is a central theme of this chapter, as a mystery to be explored—is that contemporary nursing is dogged by a negative expectation that nurses should not think. By thinking, I do not mean the mental activity involved in remembering whether Mr Jones is prescribed one sleeping tablet or two, but the processes of reflection about one's own work, its efficacy and significance; the kind of approach that might evoke a response in Mr Jones such as "that nurse is so thoughtful". I mean the registering of what is observed of the patient's emotional state, the capacity to be informed by one's imagination and intuition, and the opportunity to constructively criticize and favourably influence the working environment.

This is not to say that nurses do not think, but that it seems to be an effort of both will and confidence to make the temporal and psychic space for reflection in a working life largely dominated by practical necessity, custom, tradition, habit, and even, it must be said, obedience. Putting it simply, what is usually absent is the opportunity to ask the question "why?" to someone in authority, who is not surprised by the question, who is also interested in the answer, and who can engage with it in the spirit of mutual enquiry.

In raising this issue I must briefly clarify what I am *not* talking about. First, although the expectation not to think might have some relationship to the denigration that I have spoken of, it is not, I think, simply a symptom of this. On the contrary, nurses are sometimes valued for a capacity to be passive at work, and this itself is, it seems to me, an example of the ideal of stoicism that so pervades hospital culture. The stoical ideal is something I shall return to.

Second, I do not think it can be accounted for simply in terms of a doctor–nurse polarity of functions. It is true that many doctors are unreasonably expected to have a bright idea at a moment's notice and relentlessly pressurized to come up with an answer when they have no answer to give. It is true, too, that nurses may collude in their unthinkingness, in the same way that doctors may sometimes collude in a pseudo-know-allness. Those of us who think about unconscious processes in culture and organizations are bound to look more comprehensively at the total organization for the origins of these collusive defensive patterns that are so wasteful of human resources.

We could examine the nurse's collusiveness with a non-thinking expectation in terms of women at work. Gender issues can hardly be irrelevant in the consideration of a largely female workforce, powerful by virtue of its necessity to society, but also inhibited by that same necessity, a good example being the impossibility of large-scale industrial action. Although it would be foolhardy to dismiss the potential helpfulness of a feminist critique of the contemporary nursing role, it has not been my experience that nurses feel themselves to be oppressed by men per se, more that they are suppressed by social systems and oppressed by their own unthinking collusion with their suppression. Of course, the fact that general nurses work so consistently in a "maternal" role is highly significant in many ways, and I shall be taking this into consideration. What is of most interest here is what societal or institutional dynamics can be observed that would explain the necessity for an unthinking workforce that operates at the interface between the patient and the institution. In this chapter I give some illustrations of this and related phenomena that I have observed and experienced, not as an organizational consultant but in the course of my own work with nurses and nursing. All of these illustrations relate to hospital-based nursing, mainly in general hospitals but also, where stated, in psychiatric hospitals.

Miss Nightingale—the thinking nurses' nurse-manager

"Such a head! I wish we had her at the War Office."

Queen Victoria's comment on Florence Nightingale

According to Cecil Woodham-Smith (1950), Miss Nightingale's biographer,

> It was not as an angel of mercy that she was asked to go to Scutari—relieving the sufferings of the troops was scarcely mentioned. The consideration of overwhelming importance was the opportunity offered to advance the cause of nursing. Were nurses capable of being employed with success to nurse men under such conditions? The eyes of the nation were fixed on Scutari. If the nurses acquitted themselves creditably, never again would they be despised.

Florence Nightingale was no romantic heroine; she was a feminist of her time, wanting "the eyes of the nation" to see what women could do. She was probably the first nurse-manager in the sense that we use the term today, and she was a remarkably good manager, paying close attention to the details of the patient's emotional response to his environment.

> I have often been surprised at the thoughtlessness (resulting in cruelty, quite unintentionally) of friends or of doctors who will hold a long conversation just in the room or adjoining to the room of the patient, who is either every moment expecting them to come in, or who has just seen them and knows they are talking about him. [Nightingale, 1860]

Miss Nightingale expected her nurses to think. She encouraged them not only to be observant, but to make contact with what they had observed in the patients—their need for some physical comfort, or perhaps some conversation. In fact, she urged her nurses to talk to their patients, not, she stressed, of "chattering hopes"—by which I think she meant that brittle cheeriness that one associates with air stewardesses (and some nurses, it has to be said)—but of events in the outside world:

> You have no idea what the craving of the sick, with undiminished power of thinking, but little power of doing, is to hear of good practical action, when they can no longer partake in it . . . they like you to be fresh and active and interested but they cannot bear absence of mind and they are so tired of the advice and preaching they receive from everybody. [Nightingale, 1860]

I cannot help comparing this somewhat at random with the opening sentence of an article on health care in a newspaper that happens to be here on my desk as I write this:

> When a child falls over and grazes her knee our first instinct is to pick her up and cuddle her. When an adult has a car accident and ends up in intensive care, the only human touch she is likely to feel, apart from a squeeze of the hand, is the insertion of drips, catheters and tubes. [Kingman, 1991]

If you survived the hospital at Scutari, it would have been almost entirely because of Miss Nightingale's management of an improved hygienic environment plus thoughtful and attentive bedside nursing. Today, it is biochemistry and medical technology that saves lives. The nurse is having to redefine not only her role, but the nature of her job satisfaction. Miss Nightingale wrote "but they [patients] cannot bear absence of mind". Is there a danger that the nurse might evacuate her mind into the machinery? The electricity may be running, but if the nurse is "switched off" the patient will know that he or she is alone.

The impact of the hospital culture

Most people who have spent time in hospital either as patients or employees will remember the initial impact of the hospital—the sights, sounds, and smells that assailed them as they left the world behind. The memories linger because they were and are associated with fear. It is perfectly understandable to feel afraid when we are putting our bodies and possibly our lives in the hands of strangers. It is more difficult for staff to admit their corresponding fear that because strangers are prepared to trust them with their bodies, even their lives, the burden of responsibility and its attendant dependency might prove overwhelming.

I would like to think about the impact of a new institution from two different vantage points of my own, separated in time: one as a nurse student, the other, twenty-five years later, as a group-work consultant to nurse tutors. Both hospitals were large London teaching hospitals.

Some personal recollections

I joined the nurse training school one month after my eighteenth birthday. There were about twenty of us in the group, all women (there were very few men in general nursing in those days. Currently there are around ten percent of male students.) Most of the students were middle class, mainly privately educated. The vast majority had three good A levels and had chosen nurse training as an alternative to university. Several were devout Christians and viewed nursing quite sincerely, and not at all pompously, as a form of religious vocation. It was a very different world from my previous one, the more aggressive hurly-burly of a London grammar school. Although, as time went on, girlish pranks were not entirely ruled out, the culture remained by and large serious, committed, and inhibited.

There were three months of college work before we started on the wards. We sat through lecture after lecture on anatomy and physiology; we were introduced to a working skeleton called George and gave injections to life-size plastic dummies. Occasionally, for a change, we practised emergency resuscitation procedures on each other. I obtained Miss Nightingale's *Notes on Nursing*, a model of manners that I read as I had read Jane Austen at school, morally chastened but with unqualified admiration.

When talking to my friends who were at university, I realized that, in comparison, we were being given very little opportunity to question our teachers. Certainly we had not encountered those things called seminars where, apparently, teaching and learning took place via the medium of group discussions. The nursing school seemed to pride itself in being able to recruit intelligent young women but then seemed uninterested and incurious about what was going on in our minds. Our teachers were pleasant but consistently distant, and the expectations were clearly that we would not be curious either. We asked questions about facts, of course, but we lacked both the innocence and the ruthlessness of any free-thinking 3-year-old who would insist on pushing an impossible question about death, sex, or God despite the parents' obvious discomfort. We remained in quietude, possibly experiencing the teachers as rather fragile. We had yet to learn that we, too, were fragile and afraid of all the horrors the hospital might contain.

The day arrived when we first visited the wards. I was with a party of six nurses visiting a surgical ward. I stood at the end of the bed of someone who seemed to have tubes coming out of every orifice. One tube led to a bag of urine, another to a bag of blood. He was gripping so tightly to the bed frame that his knuckles were white. I felt myself becoming giddy. In my imagination this man was being tortured, and the thought was so terrible that I could not even voice it to my friend, who, in any case, was asking the nurse in charge sensible questions about the temperature chart. I looked at the door and wondered if I would make it out of the ward before I passed out. Later, as I sat recovering in the cool corridor, I felt foolish. It occurred to me that the new patients arriving on the ward with their small suitcases might have similar waking nightmares and, like me, feel ashamed of themselves. From this relatively insignificant experience, I had learned something that I was not able to put into words at that time: that hospitals are bursting with intense primitive anxieties, largely about potential sadistic abuse of the absolute power that staff inevitably have over inpatients and that everybody has these dreadful thoughts but nobody ever speaks about them. As far as these thoughts are concerned, the staff must lie (especially to themselves) and the patients must exercise stoicism and repression.

I found that when I started working on the wards, these fears lessened. I could have a conversation with the man who had clung to his bed. He might ask me the results of a football match, or I might change his urine bag. In this way I was reassured and, in the course of these ordinary and practical exchanges, so was he. It is easier to be a participant than an observer in hospital, which is the same as saying it is easier to be busy than to have time on your hands.

The other abiding recollection is from my second week on my first ward, a male medical ward. Most of the patients were at least fifteen years older than the new nurses, but there was a boy aged 19 who was pleased to have other young people to talk to, and for me he represented a link with the more light-hearted world of my friends outside the hospital. In those days, at least in London teaching hospitals, the wards were well staffed and there were opportunities to talk to patients when we were not exceptionally busy. David had been admitted for some blood tests and investigations for anaemia. He looked strong, healthy, and handsome and quite out of place among the bronchitic elderly gentlemen and the overweight coronary patients.

One afternoon my friend Kate, a fellow student, seemed to erupt into the ward kitchen where I was preparing a tea trolley. She had overheard a conversation between the consultant and the ward sister—they had been discussing David's imminent death. I wanted to disbelieve her, but at the same time I knew from Kate's distracted earnestness that it must be true. "It's leukaemia", she added. I continued with my afternoon duties, leaden with preoccupation and anger—angry for David, for myself, and for all of us who had only just begun to live our lives. Shamefully, I avoided David, but after supper he called me over. "I was wondering", he said, "if you'd like this box of chocolates. I can't eat them, I've got too many." Like a flash, and without thinking, I remonstrated, "no you keep them, you'll enjoy them when you're better". I don't know how long the silence lasted, but David looked at me with what I can only describe with hindsight as a mixture of exasperation and pity. "I'd like you to have them" was all he said. I accepted the chocolates and he accepted the weight of my apology. David died three days later, with his girlfriend and his parents at his side.

Nightingale (1860) had written "I would appeal most seriously all friends, visitors and attendants of the sick to leave of this practice of attempting to 'cheer' the sick by making light of their danger and by exaggerating their probabilities of recovery", but I needed more than Nightingale's wise words this time. I had to talk to the ward sister. I wanted her to explain why David died. I liked her, and she seemed personally approachable but always busy. I caught her in the office—she said she had ten minutes. She talked about leukaemia, how quickly it could develop, how there was nothing to be done, that David had known the danger, that she too was sad. "You'll get used to it", she said. It was meant kindly, but what did getting "used to it" actually mean? On the face of it, her invitation was to the world of experience, of greater objectivity, but without personal supervision—without the opportunity for renewed mental digestion—it could only become an invitation to avoidance and denial. In such well-intentioned and innocent ways does the system perpetuate its defensive organization against anxiety.

Four years earlier, in 1960, Isabel Menzies had published her now famous paper "A Case Study in The Functioning of Social Systems as a Defence Against Anxiety", a report on a study of a nursing service of a general hospital. She says:

> The training system is mainly orientated to the communication of essential facts and techniques and pays minimal attention to teaching events orientated to personal maturation within the professional setting. There is no individual supervision of student nurses and no small group teaching event concerned specifically to help student nurses work over the impact of their first essays in nursing practice and handle more effectively their relations with patients and their own emotional reactions. [Menzies, 1960]

This is later related to the problem of the thirty- to fifty-percent wastage of student nurses, which Menzies goes on to suggest is in itself an "essential element in the social defence system" because while a large number of "semi-skilled" students are needed, if they were all subsequently to qualify the profession would be flooded with trained staff for whom there were no jobs.

The student nurse group project

In 1986 I was approached by a sister tutor at a large teaching hospital. She had noticed that her students were increasingly bringing up issues to do with their feelings about patients in classroom sessions. She asked me if I would be prepared to join her in a project in which weekly time-boundaried but unstructured small groups would be offered to the new nurses during the time of their first and second ward placements. Each group would be led by a tutor, and I would be acting as a work group consultant to the tutors themselves. In this hospital the drop-out rate of nursing students remained at around one-third, more or less the same wastage level that Menzies had noted in 1960. In this instance, however, the wastage had to be considered in the context of a predictable decline in the adolescent population from the mid-1980s on into the 1990s. It was perhaps at least in part for this reason that the hospital management was prepared to support the project, which was costly in tutor time and potentially disruptive to the hospital's customary methods of dealing with anxiety.

The groups were offered to the student nurses as an optional addition to the set curriculum, and the task was described to them in writing as follows:

"The purpose of the group would be for the members to talk about their experiences on the wards and how this affects them and to support and learn from each other. The member of staff would be mainly a coordinator, commentator, and supporter rather than an information giver. The ground rules of each group would be that one could say anything, that what anyone said would be respected (which, of course does not necessarily mean agreed with) by the others, and that what was discussed within the group would be confidential to the members of that group. It is hoped that the work done in such groups would not only help the members as individuals but would also be a form of learning that would lead to improved patient care."

As I entered the nurse training school for the first of my meetings with the tutors, I immediately became immersed in a large group of students who must have suddenly emerged from a lecture hall. They seemed a confident and heterogeneous group, the mixture of styles, races, accents and the presence of several young men giving the over-all impression of any comprehensive-school sixth form. The tutors themselves were welcoming, friendly, and informal. We were imme-diately on first-name terms, as if unacquaintance might be easily dis-pensed with. They had appreciated their colleague's initiative because they thought it would be supportive of the students. The notion of support was always very much to the fore, and the groups themselves came to be known as "support groups", whereas I preferred to think of them as exploratory meetings about work. The danger, as I saw it, was that "support" in the form of reassurance would pre-empt and replace exploratory thought, which it did on a number of occasions. My impression was that I was regarded as unnecessarily fussy and even somewhat truculent (rather like a difficult patient) for taking this stance.

The initial student take-up of the groups was about sixty percent. The older the student, the more interested they seemed to be. A fair proportion of the 18-year-olds did not show any apparent interest. One hypothesis we had about this was that the more immature students were struggling with mid-adolescent identity issues and that this, together with the taking up of a new role in a new institution, would have been in itself a considerable onslaught on their psychic defence mechanisms. Any additional emotional exposure in a group could have been anticipated as intolerable. However, the non-participant students were often reported as curious about what happened in the groups, and participants sometimes experienced themselves as ambas-sadors for shy or more vulnerable friends.

The project started with four groups, with six of seven members in each. I have broadly categorized the themes of the groups. The exam-ples below are some actual observations made by the students:

- *Potential and actual abuse of power by hospital staff*—for example, giv-ing and withholding of painkillers, "forcing" unwanted treatments on a terminally ill patient, blaming a patient for incontinence, pa-tients being "made to wait" if they made too many demands, lack of respect for patients' modesty and dignity.

- *Patients who exercise independent thought*—for example, the old lady who objected to being called by her first name. The Roman Catholic patient who objected to being in a gynaecology ward where patients were being admitted for termination of pregnancy (the administra-tion refused to move her). The patient who asks the most junior nurses if he is going to die. Patients who are flirtatious and make sexual remarks.

• *Coping with one's own response to tragedy while maintaining a profession-al role*—for example, the 5-year old boy who is brought to visit his dying mother; the patient who has no visitors; the teenager, brain-damaged in an accident, who will never regain consciousness; the fear of the severely disfigured patient.

• *Shame associated with incompetence*—for example, forgetting that a patient had requested that her son should be called before her death; discovering that vital apparatus is missing from the resuscitation trolley; whether you should tell the patient that this is the first injec-tion you have ever given.

The tutors were quite shaken by some of the incidents and dilemmas described in the groups, and they sympathized with the students' distress. As a group they became preoccupied with the discrepancy between what they taught in the nursing school and the reality of busy ward practice. This was for them what Bion (1980) called "a blinding flash of the obvious", because they were forced to think about something that they had forgotten or repressed and, shockingly, they experienced as knowing it as if for the first time.

Over time the tutors had developed two active roles with their stu-dents: one as a teacher, providing information, and the other as a sup-porter, providing reassurance. They were not accustomed to working with groups in a passive way in which processes are allowed to unfold and emotional states of mind are acknowledged, and they were not particularly comfortable with it. It seemed difficult for them to think about why this was so, and for a while we attributed it to the fact that it was difficult to bear the realization that the students were often not able to practice on the wards what they had been taught in the nurs-ing school. The tutors felt the sense of disillusion and helplessness that the nurses experienced, and sometimes they felt it to be necessary to give small talks on such topics as "Care of the Dying", to inject not only some proper concern for standards but also some hope into the situation. Providing a forum for the students to think had, it seemed, pushed the pain of helplessness and of failed idealism upwards into another part of the nursing system. The tutor group became restless, and their attendance at the supervision group became erratic.

Whereas many student nurses are, as Menzies (1960) states, tacitly expected to leave during training, the tutors themselves were a highly trained and valuable hospital resource. It occurred to me at the time that a tutor's rebellion about failing standards in nursing care would be very disruptive to the hospital. The connection between opportunity for thought and anarchy had never seemed so simple or so clear.

Some of the tutors were not particularly willing to acknowledge verbally the degree of mental pain among the students, and at times I found myself feeling quite irritated at their lack of willingness to try a more interpretative approach, when it would seem to be one that would most help the students to feel contained and understood. Furthermore, the tutors repeatedly referred to me as the "facilitator" when I had never described myself as such. The word is one I have come particularly to dislike because of its dual connotations of being "facile" and of "making things easy". All in all, it seemed to me that for a while there was a wish to anaesthetize me. But why? Did I represent the anarchic threat to the hospital? This had to be dismissed as a mad and grandiose idea, and yet I felt that I was being experienced as pushing them into something dangerous. Gradually it became clearer. The consequence of an accurate and helpful interpretation is likely to be increased intimacy and increased dependency. It was as if once the students were fully aware of the extent of their distress at work, they would lay their burdens at the door of the tutors, as if to say, "ok, you have helped me to recognize this. Now what are you going to do about it?" In short, the tutors would be held responsible—or at least that was the fantasy they had—and this seemed to mirror the students' fear of the consequences of directness and openness with patients: that the patients' consequent attachment would involve impossible demands.

These insights are not original. Menzies has described rigid defences against attachment in nursing and how this actually hinders the development of an appropriate and flexible professional relationship with patients:

> There is an almost explicit "ethic" that any patient must be the same as any other patient. It must not matter to the nurse whom she nurses or what illness. Nurses find it extraordinarily difficult to express preferences even for types of patients or for men or women patients. If pressed to do so, they tend to add rather guiltily some remark like "you can't help it". Conversely, it should not matter to the patient which nurse attends him or, indeed, how many different nurses do. By implication it is the duty as well as the need and privilege of the patient to be nursed and of the nurse to nurse, regardless of the fact that a patient may greatly need to "nurse" a distressed

nurse and nurses may sometimes need to be "nursed". Outside the specific requirements of his physical illness and treatment, the way a patient is nursed is determined largely by his membership of the category patient and minimally by his idiosyncratic wants and needs. [Menzies, 1960]

All of us involved in this work—students, tutors, and myself—were experiencing at first hand the unconscious assumptions of the hospital system, which were (a) that attachment should be avoided for fear of being overwhelmed with emotional demands that will threaten competence and (b) that dependency on colleagues and superiors should be avoided. One should manage stoically, not make demands on others and be prepared to stifle one's individual response. If, for a moment, we consider the institution as the patient, we could say that emotional dependency is experienced as the most dangerous and contagious of diseases. Everyone is under suspicion as a potential carrier, and an epidemic of possible fatal proportions is at any moment likely to break out. The only known method of prevention is stoicism, which is administered by example and washed down with false reassurance. Since the patient consumer, by virtue of his institutionalized role, is already infected, he must be kept at a courteous but safe distance.

This diagnosis seems shocking even as I write it. I may be forgiven for exaggeration in the service of exploration. Certainly we all know of small-scale health-care institutions, such as hospices, where appropriate and ordinary dependency in patients and staff is acknowledged and catered for with remarkably favourable consequences in terms of human potential. The fact remains that most nurses are trained in large institutions, where psychotic institutional processes lead to a kind of madness in which dependency is simultaneously encouraged and punished.

Motivation, frustration, and satisfaction in nursing

Despite the stress and distress of institutional life, nurses continue to find pleasure and satisfaction in nursing. Job satisfaction is notoriously difficult to define because the reasons why we choose the work we do and the elements that provide satisfaction are largely unconscious and related to complicated emotional necessities of our own. However, it is possible to make the general observation that many people are drawn to the "caring professions" because they have both a wish and a need to put something right, to make reparation. The reparative wish may be partly conscious or unconscious. It arises from guilt or concern, and its aim is to heal emotional wounds—one's own and those of the damaged figures of one's imagination. It can be exercised in a socially acceptable and useful way by helping others. A reparative wish is ordinary and healthy, and one might even say that to heal ourselves while promoting healing in others is a good psychic economy. Problems can arise when the reparative wish has a manic or compulsive quality—for example, the driven motivation of the "do-gooder", who appears superior and self-satisfied, out of touch with his or her own vulnerability and common humanity, seeing problems only in others, determined to "save" people with or without their consent. Fortunately such people are so grandiose that they do not tend to last long in the "down-to-earth" world of nursing, but that is not to say that all nurses are healthily motivated. Some have serious psychosomatic problems of their own, many have experienced illness or death of a family member in childhood, and some have been responsible as children for the care of younger siblings and are strongly identified with a nursing role in life.

Whatever it is that engenders the wish to nurse, job satisfaction will depend not simply on the presence of a patient, but on the presence of a patient who needs a nurse. When things are going well, most of us tend to take job satisfaction for granted. However, when it is absent for some reason, we may become acutely aware of what is missing.

The liver unit

Recently I was asked by a trainee psychotherapist, whom I will call Jane, to give her some supervision on a difficult piece of work. She was herself a nurse and had been asked by a colleague who knew and respected her work if she could offer some support to a group of qualified nurses who worked on a liver unit in a local hospital. These nurses had, as a group, been suffering from stress: some had complained of it openly, others had taken long periods of sick-leave for apparently minor illnesses; one had given her resignation, others has asked to be transferred to another unit. The hospital administrator had been alerted, and some money had suddenly become available to provide staff support. A series of whole-day meetings were organized in which Jane planned to offer these nurses some relaxation exercises combined with an opportunity to talk in a group about their stress. Out of a total of twelve staff nurses, a group of five had volunteered to attend.

After a brief introduction Jane had planned to start with some brief relaxation exercises—lying on the floor, deep breathing, neck massage, and so on—but these nurses were unable to relax. One lay on the floor like an ironing-board, saying that it made her feel worse, another became giggly, another said surely it was all pointless, and two others said they were afraid of what might "come out". Jane encouraged them to sit in a group and just talk. And, in time, they did.

They talked, not surprisingly, about the number of deaths on the ward, the liver-transplant patients whom they lost after days or weeks of painstaking intensive care, the distress of the relatives, their own exhaustion. But the worst thing—the very worst thing and the most difficult to talk about at work—was the resentment and even hatred that they sometimes felt towards the patients, who seemed to thwart their every effort and to make a nonsense of time, concern, and care. These were the alcoholic and drug-dependent patients who returned again and again to be repaired with the single intention, or so it seemed to these nurses, to continue to connive with their own death.

These nurses may or may not have been sophisticated in their knowledge of the complexity and intransigence of addiction. Our intellectual knowledge may make very little difference when we are faced day after day with the hopelessness and helplessness in the face of persistent self-destruction. Jane could at least help these nurses to consciously recognize the realistic basis of their stress and, by understanding their hatred of their patients for (as it seemed) refusing to get better, could help them not to retaliate by avoiding or ignoring the patient's distress.

What was happening here was that these nurses felt deprived of the opportunity to make reparation. They could not experience any pleasure, gratification, or significance to their work because they could not help the patients to get better. Instead, they had to watch them deteriorate constantly and repeatedly.

In this sort of extreme situation, where work satisfactions are frustrated, the workers need opportunities to mobilize ordinary appropriate defences against pain and anger. For this to happen, there has to be someone—most helpfully, a senior colleague—available to share the burden, to listen, to understand and appreciate the genuine difficulty of the task, and to promote thinking. It may be necessary for an outsider to be called in to ask the question "why", to be a catalyst and container for thinking in a highly stressed and increasingly petrified system.

If such opportunities for thought are not forthcoming and the opportunity to mobilize appropriate defences is consistently blocked over a long period of time, there are two types of response. One is the breakdown/breakout solution. This would include the development of psychosomatic symptoms, the avoidance of work, long periods of sick leave, depression, and ultimately resignation from the job. These things get noticed, of course, as in the liver unit, when it led, rather late in the day, to an offer of support to the remaining staff.

Another less conscious solution is the evolution in the worker of a pathological psychic defence, which does not get noticed in the same way because it develops gradually over time. Sometimes people erect a shell around themselves that serves to deflect the anaesthetized emotion. It is rather like the shell that some children in residential care develop so as not to feel the pain of repeated abandonment. It is largely an unconscious development and not an act of will. Such people are often very good in an emergency or crisis because being unemotional can sometimes increase their efficiency—for example, they would be less likely to panic or be afraid. If such a shell becomes a permanent feature of the personality it is at great cost to the individual, who can no longer be fully responsive to his or her emotional environment. The resulting obliviousness is obviously very dangerous to clients, patients, or colleagues, who will sense the potential cruelty inherent in the indifference.

Appropriate defences are those that are mobilized in the recognition that a situation is wrong, painful, or downright unbearable and involve attempts to protect oneself from stress in order that the work task may be preserved if at all possible. Pathological defences are those that are mobilized in order to deny reality, to allow a really unbearable situation to continue as if it were perfectly acceptable, when in fact it needs to be challenged or confronted in order to preserve both the workers and the work task. The soft end of the pathological defence is stoicism, the hard end is manic denial, a psychotic process that attempts to obliterate despair by manufacturing excitement. In manic states of mind, people are completely oblivious to both pain and danger.

Maternal transference and countertransference

D. W. Winnicott, who helped mothers to feel that being "good enough" sometimes had to be—and indeed was—all right, extended his thoughtfulness to the predicament of those in the helping professions. In his famous paper "Hate in the Countertransference" (1949), Winnicott lists reasons why an ordinary mother at times hates her ordinary baby. Among these reasons are:

> He is ruthless, treats her as scum, an unpaid servant, a slave.
>
> She has to love him, excretions and all, at least in the beginning, till he has doubts about himself. . . .
>
> His excited love is cupboard love, so that having got what he wants he throws her away like orange peel. . . .
>
> At first he does not know at all what she does or what she sacrifices for him. Especially he cannot allow for her hate. . . .
>
> He is suspicious, refuses her good food and makes her doubt herself, but eats well with his aunt. [p. 201]

Winnicott is talking here about the care of very young infants, but he equates this experience with the professional's care of the very distressed, very disturbed, very frightened, angry, dependent patient or client. Winnicott says of himself as a psychoanalyst: "Hate is expressed by the existence of the end of the hour." Of course, Winnicott does not mean that he finishes the analytic session because he hates the patient, but that the circumscribed time permits the analyst to bear the difficulty of his work and the negative emotions that are sometimes aroused in him.

There is no doubt that appointment times, teaching timetables, staff meetings, and so forth do give professionals a welcome break from stressful patients. Nurses do not have much time away from the demands of those they help. They are like mothers in that they are in attendance and available, and this very fact can give rise to much resentment and self-denigration, rather in the way that mothers at home with children complain that they feel relegated to a low-status activity and an unthinking environment. They complain about this, despite the fact that they love their children and want to be with them. I have heard many nurses say that a move from hospital work into health visiting or teaching involved a new timetabled working day, which in itself enhanced their self-esteem. Availability seems to be associated with denigration.

To play a little with Winnicott's concept, we could say that the "good-enough" patient, like the "good-enough" baby, is the one who provides enough job satisfaction to enable the nurse or the mother to continue with her work despite the unpleasant aspects that Winnicott has described: mess, indifference, and bad temper. The "good-enough" patient senses that the nurse has a need to be needed by her patients but that she also needs some protection against excessive emotional demands.

In my experience, nurses are rather secretive, possibly due to embarrassment, about the considerable satisfactions that are obtained in their work. There are inevitably very intimate moments between nurse and patient. To be with someone at his or her death, or in his or her extremity of fear or pain, to prepare the patient for major surgery that the patient knows he or she may not survive—the list of situations is endless. The nurse knows that she will be remembered, she knows, too, that temporarily very strong feelings will be transferred onto her. She knows that if a patient wakes up after major life-risking surgery and sees her face, he will experience her as an angel, not because he is hallucinating but because she is associated at that moment with the beauty of being alive. The nurse will know how much she is giving to the patient at that moment, and each will experience the individuality of the other.

The hospital culture, as we have seen, does not encourage the nurses to be "moved" by these experiences, because attachment and its attendant emotionality is felt as such a threat to the system.

It seems that nurses often keep these moments of significance and of intense job satisfaction to themselves. One possibility is that the patient unconsciously conveys his or her embarrassment to the nurse. This embarrassment is about being an adult but feeling like an infant. The nurse holds the patient's embarrassment for him or her, does not humiliate him or her, just as the mother does not humiliate her baby by telling the neighbours about the baby's burps and farts. I am suggesting that some kind of deal is struck between nurse and patient that is not a conspiracy but seems to involve a degree of secrecy about the mutual fulfilment of the nurse's reparative and maternal instincts and the patient's appropriate dependency needs.

The fascination of the charismatic rebel patient

"Charismatic: pertaining to a favour specially vouchsafed by God,
a grace, a talent."
"Rebel: one who resists, opposes or is disobedient to someone
having authority or rule."

Shorter Oxford English Dictionary

In the last few years I have been organizing courses for general and psychiatric nurses at the Tavistock Clinic. The idea is to provide some time and space away from the working environment to think about the nursing task. Recently I have been working with a small group of psychiatric nurses who meet weekly to present and discuss aspects of their work. Not for the first time my attention has been drawn to the occasional phenomenon of the psychiatric patient who manages to become a "special" in the eyes of the hospital staff, one who is allowed to assume particular rights and privileges within the hospital, although no member of staff can remember anyone making a conscious decision that this should be so (see also Main, 1968).

These patients are often quite damaged, on the borderline of serious psychotic illness, but also intelligent and imaginative in ways that suggest or approach a vitality and achievement that evokes in the staff a poignant awareness of wasted potential. Although the total hospital system is involved in the collusion I am describing, these patients hold particular significance for the nursing staff, and it is this aspect that I wish to highlight.

Mr K, a man of 32, presents himself at an emergency psychiatric outpatient clinic, complaining of depression and claiming to drink three bottles of vodka a day. He is handsome, well dressed, drunk, and extremely agitated. The patient lives alone in a flat local to the hospital but will not give his address. He has not worked for over a year. His father has just died, and he is not in contact with his mother. His sister has a PhD, his brother is a journalist. He obtained an Oxbridge scholarship but did not take it up. He has started, but not finished, three university courses. Later he confides that he is recently divorced and that his life has become unbearable. When questioned about his depression, he attempts to engage the psychiatrist in a discussion about Rousseau's concept of the noble savage. The psychiatrist suspects a psychotic episode but feels that he cannot section this patient while he is drunk. The patient senses this, dutifully threatens suicide, and is admitted voluntarily.

On the ward, Mr K remains separate from the other patients, carrying around books of poetry and social philosophy, which he settles to read from time to time. Gradually he reveals that he had undertaken a psychiatric nurse training some years previously. He apparently left the training after nine months, then he married a friend of a patient whom he had met when she was visiting the hospital. This marriage lasted six months. These facts were later verified.

While being courteous to the other patients, Mr K paid little attention to them. He was allowed to avoid ward groups, as if he had managed to convince the staff that his mind was on higher things. Mr K behaved as if his assigned nurse had been personally chosen by him and would engage her in intense discussions about politics, art, items in the news, and all manner of interesting things. Bearing in mind that Mr K was a very attractive and presentable young man, this was sometimes experienced as seductive and somewhat overwhelming. The nurse was equally thrown when, in an agitated state, Mr K would follow her around like a lost child, and at these times she felt protective and in touch with his mental pain. Mr K clearly had the capacity to evoke an intense involvement in others, even an identification with his suffering.

Several weeks later one of the senior doctors stated that Mr K "exhibits signs of a psychopathic personality" but he "cannot be sure". The nurse who was presenting this case commented that restraint about diagnosis was unusual in this particular inpatient environment.

Mr K had stopped drinking, which encouraged the staff to feel that there was hope for his recovery. When he suggested that he should start spending nights in his own flat, this was accepted by medical and nursing staff. So this patient, who had still not given his address, who refused to take part in occupational or group therapy, who as yet defied diagnosis, was allowed to "keep" a bed on the ward while he phoned the night nurses regularly and returned in the morning to take up his hospital place.

I am not suggesting that hospitals should not admit such people, nor am I suggesting that the staff were mere fools who were tricked by this patient. It seemed to me that this patient was allowed to ignore the hospital "rules" because many of the staff, and particularly the nurses, were identified with him, not for the simple reason he had at one time started a nurse training but because he so powerfully represented untapped personal potential and frustrated intelligence. Whereas the patient had been held back by his illness, the nurses felt held back by the hospital establishment. This patient's rebellion, seen as synonymous with his return to health, was tacitly encouraged and inwardly celebrated via a process of projective identification. My evidence for this was the way in which the material was presented in the group, my observation of the group's response, and also the feelings that were evoked in me (countertransference).

> In a subsequent discussion, the nurse reported that Mr K had become less agitated and more assertive. She reported an incident in the hospital pharmacy where she and Mr K were collecting a prescription. The pharmacist was busy and rather superciliously had asked the nurse to wait. Mr K had responded, somewhat incongruously, "watch it, Buster, I pay your wages", presumably referring to his National Insurance contributions. As the nurse told us this, she blushed pink with pleasure and amusement, and the group became infected with the humour of the situation. We were not completely sure what we were laughing at, but there was clearly a sneaking admiration for Mr K who, in his obvious distaste with a predictable and po-faced hierarchy, was demonstrating an audacity that the nurse had been unable to contemplate, let alone exercise. In our discussion, we recognized that it was not beyond the bounds of possibility—in fact, it was quite likely—that nurses (and doctors) sometimes project their own unconscious anxieties and wishes into the patients. The patients in their emotionally liable state are, like adolescents in the family system, particularly prone to enact the projections of those most closely associated with them.

If at an unconscious level a patient becomes a representative of or spokesperson for staff concerns, then he may well be given tacit encouragement to remain in the hospital, and many "good" reasons will emerge to justify this situation.

Conclusion

So what conclusions may be drawn from the evidence presented in this chapter, bearing in mind my initial hypothesis that hospital nurses are accepting an unthinking role conferred on them by the institution for its own purposes? My evidence has been both objective—that of the external teacher, the interested but uninvolved observer—and also subjective, by virtue of my personal association and "inside" knowledge. Even from the observer's point of view, some degree of preconception or prejudice is inevitable, and those of us who are interested in studying unconscious processes in institutions try to make special use of our subjectivity by submitting it to critical analysis. For example, as I approach the task of conclusion, I am aware that I, too, am finding it difficult to think. This seems to be something to do with the difficulty of holding in mind all the various aspects I have identified. It occurs to me that it is possible that I may have become temporarily institutionalized in my own chapter, stuck in the detail, unable to step outside and make sense of the whole range of my experience.

Many nurses have told me that when they step outside the training environment of the hospital to take up various nursing roles in the community, they experience an acute fear of both their own professional autonomy and also the autonomy of their patients. In a recent survey of stress among community psychiatric nurses (Carson, Bartlett, & Croucher, 1991), some of the most frequently reported stress factors were:

- communication problems with other professionals
- unpredictable and resistive clients
- fears for personal safety on home visits
- anxieties about travelling in certain areas

While in no way minimizing the realistic differences and difficulties of the work they have to do, community nurses become retrospectively aware of their previous protected and even infantilized status as professionals, who were not expected to think for themselves or take initiatives. If the institutionalization has not become chronic and if the new working environment is sufficiently tolerant of the individuality, the nurse will in time rediscover her curiosity and capacity for thought.

Most of us have an unthinking area of our work where we operate on unquestioned assumptions. These assumptions are subjectively experienced as innocuous habits or customs but when challenged are felt to be absolute rules that "must be there for a good reason", despite the fact that no one is able to articulate the reasons the "rules" persist. These no-go areas of institutional life are most likely to be the areas in which the most anxiety is generated and/or held.

The areas of anxiety in society's humane institutions are inevitably identified with ways of managing the containment of crisis, suffering, death, and fear in the clients and in the workers. The intense emotionality aroused is felt to threaten not only efficiency but also, at a more primitive unconscious level, an anarchic overthrow of the institution itself.

In a vast, centralized (and therefore perhaps literally "unmanageable") organization it seems to be the fate of those who work on the staff–client boundary to be ones who carry, represent, and attempt to contain this anxiety-ridden emotionality so that the rest of the organization experiences a spurious emotion-free zone in which to operate. In order to maintain this, it follows that these front-line workers must be silenced, anaesthetized, infantilized, or otherwise rendered powerless. This is otherwise known as "being kept in your place" or "knowing your place".

Menzies (1989), in her research into recruitment in the London Fire Brigade, found that:

> the same fire-fighting activities that gave rise to pride also tended to give rise to shame and embarrassment. Firemen felt and believed the public to feel that some of the things they did and delighted in were childish or rather foolish. One fireman said: "It does sound childish but we actually love playing with water" or "The public feel we just squirt water". Firemen have a painful suspicion that they are not really wanted or valued: "Nobody thinks anything of us until they have a fire; then it's different, they can't do enough for us then." It was as though they felt the public identified them with disaster and rejected them on those grounds.

Disempowerment by infantilization is pertinent to the psychology of racism, to colonizing attitudes, and to political discourse in general. It is successful only to the extent that the recipient individual or group is available for the projections of subservience, ignorance, or naivety. The young professional is naturally vulnerable.

It is certainly true that student nurses in particular often feel that, because they are afraid but must pretend to be strong for the patients, they are merely "playing nurses". They are frequently asked, "did you always want to become a nurse?", with the implication that this career choice did or should stem from some sweet and innocent notion. As with "doctors and nurses" so with "cops and robbers"—it is a commonly expressed view that the police force are some version of criminals in uniform and that they go into the job to "drive around in fast cars", and so on. Interestingly it is not so much the criminals themselves who make this observation but the so-called thinking sector of society, who are considerably more distant from the culture of dangerous physical violence.

Nurses themselves are currently reacting to their non-thinking caricature by entering an intense period of professionalism in which an increased opportunity to take degrees and postgraduate diplomas in various aspects of health care is strongly emphasized. Student nurses, under a new system of nurse education known as "Project 2000", will spend increasing amounts of time away from the wards in institutes of higher education. The plan is that trained nurses will care for the patients supported by unqualified workers called health-care assistants. However, as my colleague Julia Fabricius, herself a nurse tutor, states in a recent paper on changes in nursing: "It is generally thought by nurses that there are not enough trained nurses to do this so in fact the Health-Care Assistants will look after the patients. So again, it seems likely that despite an outwardly large change, the only real change at the level of the nurse–patient relationship will be that the Health-Care Assistant will bear the brunt instead of the student nurses" (Fabricius, 1991).

I share my colleague's scepticism but also the hope that any major change in the morale of one socially essential profession might have disruptively creative consequences in the wider system of social-care management. If, as it seems, we belong to a society that shares some sort of basic assumption that emotionality in the work place is best managed by processes of denial, splitting, and projection, then we will continue to inhibit the functioning of society's humane institutions and continue to squander the potential thoughtfulness of those who work within them.

PART **IV**

MAINLY DEMENTIA

Dedicated to the memory of
Anna Dartington and William Utermohlen

CHAPTER 11

Only connect—
the links between early and later life

Margot Waddell

> . . . Last scene of all,
> That ends this strange eventful history,
> Is second childishness and mere oblivion,
> Sans teeth, sans eyes, sans taste, sans everything.
>
> [Shakespeare, *As You Like It*, II, vii, 163–166]

These are the final words of Jaques's disquisition on the Seven Ages of Man in *As You Like It*. His reflections are prompted by an (off-stage) encounter with Touchstone (Duke Senior's clown), a meeting that is described at the beginning of the same scene. Jaques is exceedingly taken with Touchstone. He delightedly reports to Duke Senior and the outlawed court the "motley fool['s]" pronouncements on "how the world wags":

> And so, from hour to hour, we ripe and ripe,
> And then, from hour to hour, we rot and rot;
> And thereby hangs a tale
>
> [II, vii, 26–28]

This paper was originally given as a contribution to the Room to Manoeuvre: Depression, Dementia and Later Life—Current Trends in Psychodynamic Thinking Conference at the Tavistock Clinic, February 2000. First published in *Psychoanalytic Psychotherapy*, 14 (3): 239–252. Reprinted in: *Inside Lives: Psychoanalysis and the Growth of the Personality* (2nd edition). London: Karnac, 2002.

The "tale" is the most significant of all tales—it is that of the human condition. A central theme in this play, as in many of the comedies, relates to the necessity of incorporating the reality of endings (i.e., of loss, of relinquishment, and ultimately of death) into the spirit of beginnings, and of potential beginning into the sense of an ending.

The "tale" that Shakespeare so often re-tells, explicitly and implicitly, is, at its barest, that of the importance of encompassing debility and death in any story of renewal. The straightforward statement is that "second childishness and mere oblivion" are facts of life that, at every stage and age, must be recognized and understood, not sequestered and denied, if any genuine development or understanding is to occur.

The inextricable relationship between beginnings and endings is one that I shall be tracing in quite literal terms, in order to link together the ways in which psychoanalytic theories, clinical experience, and observational work with early "childishness" may contribute very immediately, even practically, to an understanding both of "second childishness" and of how to work with impaired and enfeebled states of mind. As is made so clear in *As You Like It*, ripening and rotting are, in one sense, a straightforward matter of time, of chronological time, and although time is absolute—the next hour follows the last (Touchstone's assertion that Jaques is so taken by)—yet, as life in the Forest of Arden makes so clear, the important issue is what you *do* with those hours. In terms of development, the psychotherapist is always aware that at any age what matters is what the hours *mean*, and how they are spent, in relation to the possibility of furthering or prolonging psychic growth, or of limiting and foreclosing it. In this sense, time is *not* absolute, for the extent to which we "ripe and ripe", only to "rot and rot", is dependent on the indissoluble relationship between physiological/neurological and psychological factors—between body/brain and mind. As a person physically deteriorates, early problematic psychological constellations, if unresolved, are likely to be replayed; infantile defences, if underlying anxieties remain unmodified, are re-erected; childlike needs, if unmet, resurface. These things tend to occur the more as coping abilities fall away, and raw, even abject, dependency asserts itself.

It is a full century since Freud established that a person could become mentally, even physically, sick for emotional and not just organic reasons—an idea that prompted a furious response from the medical establishment, to be met by Freud's famous statement: "I understood that from now onwards I was one of those who have disturbed the sleep of the world" (1914d, p. 21). A hundred years later we are nowhere near as far as we should be in understanding the emotional component in what are considered the organic origins of psychiatric, developmental, and behavioural disturbances. Within psychoanalysis, perhaps the most significant of the theoretical innovations have been Wilfred Bion's elaborations of Melanie Klein's conceptual framework—in turn rooted in Freud's. Bion explicitly linked emotional and cognitive deficits and thus initiated a much more extensive and confident basis for exploring deeply troubled—indeed, psychotic and schizophrenic—adult states *and*, of especial significance, areas of developmental disturbance in infants and young children. Bion's psychoanalytic model now underlies much current thinking about the nature of troubled child and adult worlds, and their roots in the emotional deficits and traumas of infancy and young childhood. Work with children's fractured mental states (e.g., Rustin, Rhode, Dubinsky, & Dubinsky, 1997), and, in particular, areas of developmental arrest, has yielded extensive understanding not only of the puzzling conditions themselves—for example, of autistic and Asperger states—but also of the non- or *un*developed aspects of all ordinary personalities and, as I am suggesting here, of the troubling mental states of the very old.

In many areas, the draw of the organic, medical explanation for such states still remains strong, and, of course, with the very elderly the actual deterioration is real and has to be taken centrally into account. But latterly neuroscience is itself coming up with evidence that strongly supports the research and intuitions of the so-called folk psychologists, those of us who have long recognized the complex intimacy of the links between cognitive and emotional deficit, between organic impairment and affective disorders, between the functioning of the brain and of the mind. The issue is not only that the brain affects the mind, but that the mind affects the brain (e.g., see Schore, 2001).

With some important exceptions, little psychoanalytic work has been done towards a greater understanding of the predicament of the very elderly—work of a kind that might harvest the insights of those most skilled in understanding the mind's capacity to grow and develop and also its propensity to become stuck, deformed, or fragmented. Those who have worked with the more severely disturbed adult patient, and also, in particular, those involved with the disordered and arrested development of young children, will be drawing on clinical and observational skills that are centrally relevant to the present problems.

The psychoanalytic picture of middle and late life stresses the way in which a person's ability to face loss of all kinds, ultimately death, is rooted in very early capacities to bear psychic reality (e.g., see Jaques, 1965; Waddell, 1998). There is a sense—to draw on George Eliot—that

> "It is never too late to become the person you might have been."

This chapter addresses that time in life when it *is* too late, in any obvious sense, and yet when the quality of mental and emotional life may still, if only very temporarily, be rendered a lot more bearable, meaningful, even enjoyable, than is often recognized. Those same models of work with early infantile and childlike states which have contributed to an understanding of the "later years" are particularly pertinent to the last years—those of "second childishness"—especially in relation to the joinings and fracturings involved in organic impairment, whether as a result of cortical vascular trauma (strokes) or of Alzheimer's Disease, or of senile confusional states more generally. (A distinction between any or all of these different states is very hard to make.)

Case description: Mrs Brown

I shall recap on a vignette that I have recounted elsewhere (Waddell, 1998, pp. 8–10)—that of 89-year-old Mrs Brown and her husband, Eric. Basing my thoughts on detailed descriptions by their family, I shall then trace their lives further as, over the following two years, Mrs Brown steadily lost her lively, creative, and enquiring mind to the depredations of Alzheimer's.

The vignette described how Mrs Brown had become painfully jealous lest her recently widowed friend, Gladys, be simply waiting for her (Mrs Brown) to die so that Gladys could move in with her husband, Eric. The emphasis was on how swiftly Mrs Brown became beset by a persecuted certainty of betrayal and abandonment by her husband.

> This certainly bore all the hallmarks of an infant or young child's jealous belief of having been supplanted in the affections of the person who matters most. The child is forced to realise that that most beloved person also has important relationships with others, be it their partner or their children. Mrs Brown was unable to hold in mind the kind of person she knew her husband to be. She ignored the real Eric and saw only a polarised and persecuting version of what she feared. It was as if she had lost her capacity for depressive concern and had become caught up in a paranoid–schizoid state,

one that was more characteristic, in development terms, of a three-months-old baby than of an 89-year-old adult. In this state of mind, Mrs Brown could turn even the most loyal and caring figure into a fickle tormentor. [p. 9]

It may be helpful to clarify what is meant here by the Kleinian terms "depressive concern" and a "paranoid–schizoid state". Aspects of the first are characterized by the capacity to bear separateness, to understand things from the other's point of view, to tolerate another person or interest temporarily coming first. The second state, by contrast, is dominated by a persecutory fear of loss or displacement and a defensive need for omnipotent control. The seeing of things in extreme and unmodified terms—all good, or all bad—is also characteristic, often resulting in imperious and demanding, or abject and terrified, behaviour. The distinction between the two is beautifully drawn by George Eliot in *Middlemarch*, written in 1872. Eliot contrasts those who can recognize that someone may have

"an equivalent centre of self, whence the lights and shadows must always fall with a certain difference"

With those who

"take the world as an udder to feed their supreme selves." [*Middlemarch*, chap. 21]

At this point, the source of Mrs Brown's anxiety was fairly clear to any sensitive and attentive observer. She could still be reassured and given some peace of mind. Her ability, even then, to take an interest, albeit selectively, in "how the world wags" to a large extent remained. At times she would talk about death and recommend that her children be preserved from what she referred to as a "*too* ripe old age" (implicitly drawing an interesting contrast with what she clearly considered to be a reasonably positive "ripeness" in a *degree* of old age) and be allowed to rot a bit earlier than she herself, for she hated what she called "dying bit by bit".

This chapter explores that later stage, when ordinary communication had ceased to be possible for Mrs Brown and the central issue had become the struggle with an ever-recurring collapse of the characteristics of depressive-position thinking back into a much more paranoid–schizoid state. Unlike previous years, when Mrs Brown could swiftly re-emerge from a persecutory state, she was now in danger of remaining cut off from those about her by the seemingly impossible roadblocks of extreme old age—roadblocks to memory, recognition, or shared meaning. She was becoming cut off not only from others, but also from herself.

This is a poignant picture. Yet my point is that even *these* states may be much less impenetrable than they seem, as the following brief examples indicate. There is increasing evidence that the anxieties and mental disturbance of later years are often quite specifically linked to the nature of early emotional struggles (e.g., see King, 1999). As the foregoing vignette suggests, in Mrs Brown's case there seem to have been underlying oedipal difficulties that had never been resolved, despite many decades of steadfast marriage and familial devotion. Following Bion, Segal, Britton, and others, the psychoanalytically minded are especially alive to the ways in which the very early capacity to form symbols (and therefore independently to think) is rooted in the ability to bear separation, to cope with the loss of the phantasy of sole possession of the caregiver, and to tolerate being, at times, excluded from the primary pair. These are tasks of early infancy and childhood. Such capacities for "triangular" relationships—capacities that begin to develop in the first year of life—are, in turn, dependent on the relative security and mutual understanding of the primary dyadic relationship between infant and caregiver—usually the mother.

The very early managing of triangularity has much to do with later ways of negotiating oedipal constellations of whatever kind. If these earliest interactions are too disturbed, the development of thinking may itself be impaired, as well as emotional and social capacities, and a person may, for ever after, be struggling with the pains of love and loss, with fears of rejection and exclusion.

Many aspects of so-called senility offer close resemblances to early disturbances of thinking, relating, and communicating. For present purposes I shall focus on a limited number of the many relevant psychoanalytic and developmental concepts: from psychoanalysis, those of projective identification, reverie, container-contained (processes and mechanisms that, in my view, belong quite as much to the last year of someone's life as to the first), and, from the field of developmental psychology, those of, for example, "joint attention skills" and "gaze monitoring". In the first or the ninety-first year, or in any year in between, cognitive and emotional growth in the individual depends on the quality of emotional exchange between self and other. Whether in extreme youth or extreme age, a person has the impulse, one might even say necessity, to project feelings from the self into the other—be it in order to communicate those emotions or to get rid of them. Much depends on whether the person acting as "container" can tolerate the disturbing projections and still go on thinking about the meaning of the experience.

It is when verbal communication is not yet developed on the one hand, or is all but lost on the other, or when it is put in abeyance by psychological catastrophe, that a caregiver's capacity to render meaningful the raw data, or sensa, of experience can determine the difference between "ripening" and "rotting". Following Bion's model, it is the mother's mental and emotional capacity to render the raw elements of the bodily and feeling states of her infant manageable, bearable, and thus comprehensible to the infant that enables him or her mentally and emotionally to develop. This capacity of the mother's was called "reverie" by Bion. The emotional intensity about which the baby is unable to think is projected into the feeding, nurturing, caring aspect of the mother—the "breast". The taking-back-in of that passionate, disturbed emotionality now, because it is unconsciously understood and thereby rendered amenable to meaning, forms the basis in the personality of a sense not only that emotional states have a shape and a form—and are not some long, utterly bewildered, terrifying internal or external scream—but also that the function (originally the mother's of bringing about that transformation) can itself become part of the developing personality. This process, what Bion calls alpha function, is a therapeutic one. A later carer, too, can provide a setting and a mental attentiveness that renders him or her available as a thinking, containing presence whose functions can be internalized.

To return to Mrs Brown. What little her family knew of her childhood was that she suffered (like Bion and so many others) the emotional deprivation of being born in India during British Colonial rule, to be raised by others, albeit initially lovingly by her ayah, and sent off to school in that unthinkably distant place, "England". Mrs Brown scarcely knew her mentally disturbed, sadistic mother (for so she was described), nor her adored but remote, and often absent, father. Her childhood fate was to be constantly uprooted, relocated, re-disrupted, and denied any consistent care or attention. During her youth and adulthood, she had drawn on the resources of class and education to find ways of socially accommodating to what was expected. Yet she had never felt personally secure.

Mrs Brown once confided to one of her daughters the painful details of her own mother's fierce—almost delusory—jealousy of, and competition with, what she felt was too close a relationship between her husband and daughter from very early days. Soon after the husband's early death, the mother seduced her daughter's young lover.

Mrs Brown felt for ever scarred by this betrayal and by the loss of a man to whom she was, at that time, so deeply devoted. She described herself as constantly having struggled, even as a child, to conceal her terrors over exclusion and her tendency towards "self-relegation", as she put it, to the league of those who "service", by contrast with those who "exercise power".

It is certainly true that fear of abandonment and inability to bear separateness are characteristic of dementia sufferers, and that these persecutory states of mind increase with organic impairment. It is nonetheless striking that, in Mrs Brown's case, it was precisely the complexity of the triangularity, and the assaults of jealous rage and anxiety, that caused her particular distress. The horror of being pushed out and replaced had undermined her confidence since early child-hood and had never quite been laid to rest. In advanced years, as she lost her acquired social skills, it was these same old infantile insecu-rities that began to reassert themselves, with an intensity that was scarcely manageable.

I shall briefly discuss a few commonplace situations in which Mrs Brown's relatives' capacities for containment enabled them to render inchoate, or apparently random, fragments of communication not only meaningful, but also of evident support in maintaining contact, and even in re-forging old links, thus momentarily reigniting the embers of a former self.

The situations describe Mrs Brown in her ninety-first year. She had lost the capacity to remember or to think in any sustained or obvi-ously recognizable way. She was becoming averse to anything new, and often to life itself. She had long been losing words, except for the most formal or learned, habitual response. These were the last to go—the relatively mindless attention to proper enquiry and concern: "You must be so tired", "Did it take you long to get here?"—a lifetime of practice in "how-very-kind-of-you"—the *mores* of polite society. She could still take her cues for response from details of her companions' expression and intonation, based on her exceptional sight and hear-ing, which remained blessedly unimpaired. This ability of hers often obscured how little she was in fact understanding.

As has long been established in the context of infants and children, changes of surroundings or of caregiver cause anxiety, and with Mrs Brown it began to be acute. The understanding accorded to the very young over matters of separation from the loved and dependable one, or from the familiar setting, has, as yet, had little impact on the care of the elderly. For them, too, searing and destabilizing "homesickness"

for the site of psychic security can set in within an instant of any altera-
tion of context. One of Mrs Brown's much-loved daughters unexpectedly arrived to stay for the weekend. The setting was immediately
different. Mrs Brown looked at her husband with intense anxiety: "Are
we still at home, Eric?"

At some point later that day, Eric got up to leave the room. In his
turn challenged by his own forgetfulness, he paused halfway to the
door and clasped his hands behind his back, indicating self-irony as
much as frustration—his characteristic pose when having lost track of
his original purpose. Mrs Brown pointed to his hands and gazed at her
daughter with what was later described as "almost youthful delight".
Insistently she pointed at Eric's posture, her finger crooked for emphasis. Her daughter said, smilingly, "Yes, good old Dad, he's forgotten
something." Mrs Brown laughed. Eric collected himself again and left
the room, shutting the door behind him. Mrs Brown looked suddenly
terrified: "When is he coming back? Where has he gone?" "I think he's
remembered something he wants in the kitchen. He'll be back in a moment." Mrs Brown remained anxious. Her daughter wondered aloud,
"Would it help if he told you what he was doing, and where he was
going, so that you would know?" Her mother nodded.

In this simple set of interactions, one can trace the almost moment-
by-moment shifts in states of mind so characteristic of the infant or
young child. The shared, humorous understanding between mother
and daughter of the meaning of Eric's gesture of uncertainty occurred
within an assured sense of available and communicable meaning. The
daughter was able rightly to interpret her mother's mood, gesture, and
gaze and to articulate it—much as a sensitive therapist might speak to
a wordless child, or a parent to a baby. It was clear, however, that when
the door shut, Eric's unexplained absence made his wife feel utterly
cut off from her base and as terrified as any infant registering loss of
the object, and feeling, as a consequence, overwhelming abandonment
and dread: "He's gone . . . He's never coming back . . . I'm all alone in
the world . . ." and so on. What was needed, and what, as a result of
her daughter's observation, subsequently became a habit in the house-
hold, was some simple explanation of the kind that a mother might
offer a young child: "I'm just going to do X; I'll be back in a minute."
Mrs Brown's emotional state could be described as shifting from depressive to paranoid–schizoid and back to depressive again, in a way
that was exquisitely related to the psychically disturbing experience of
being, at one moment, safely held within a shared triangular psychic
structure (husband–daughter–self) and, at the next, feeling severed

from her source of safety and, as a result, in some kind of emotional free-fall.

Mrs Brown's unresolved oedipal anxieties, and the associated guilt, fear, and longing, had, despite impressive social accommodation, nonetheless persisted throughout her adult life. As her social defences—and, more importantly, her memory—fell away and actual mental impairment compounded the underlying emotional difficulties, she became anguishingly prey to her tormenting jealousy and increasingly incapable of negotiating the hazards of relating to more than one other.

Her son recounted an occasion on which, just before lunch, his mother was sitting by the fire with a glass of wine beside her, but not, as yet, her customary once-daily cigarette. Son and husband were holding an animated conversation. As so often, they included her, but only by eye contact. Her son observed his mother agitatedly reaching for a matchbox. As she struck successive matches with her right hand, her left hand moved, scarcely perceptibly, towards her mouth. She would glance at the "couple" with apparent irritation, shake the match to extinguish it, and cast it into the fire. This occurred many times over. Her son, who was observing these details while yet discoursing with his father, came over to her, smiling: "Is it that by lighting a match, you think that the cigarette you are hoping for will somehow materialize?" Mrs Brown looked uncertain, smiled, and then nodded as if in affirmation. (What he did not register was the likelihood of his mother's unconscious wish to extinguish or burn up one or other of her rivals.)

These examples particularly bring to mind a recent study, "Me, You and It" (Burhouse, 1999), looking at the significance of "joint attention skills" and of "gaze monitoring", which is effectively what was going on here between Mrs Brown and her husband and son. Anna Burhouse brings together concepts from cognitive psychology, child development research, and psychoanalysis, with her own work of observing young infants. She focuses, in particular, on impairments in the formation of triangular mental space with special reference to the severe mental difficulties characteristic of the autistic spectrum. Many aspects of this research have an important bearing on the understanding of the kinds of mental problems associated with the very elderly, as the following examples indicate:

Lost for words, Mrs Brown would characteristically point to a focus of stimulation and interest and then look to a secure companion, as if sometimes anticipating a shared response. At other times, more anxiously, she would look for confirmation or enlightenment. When she encountered an emotional presence of mind that could appreciate and engage with the substance of her communication, or when she could find a meaning where as yet there was none, she was able to make something of it—to enjoy the fact that something had been understood. This was particularly the case when she seemed to be wishing to articulate her sense of beauty—that of the sky, of birds, or of flowers—aspects of the natural world that were among her few remaining sources of interest. Almost as if holding a wand, she would wordlessly and gently sweep a wafting hand in the direction of some object that attracted her. This would be followed by an intense and often quizzical look at a companion, and back again to the bird or flower, and then, in turn, back to her companion. When she sensed that the meaning of her gestures was articulated in simple terms—"Isn't the evening sky absolutely lovely"—Mrs Brown would break into a smile, with a kind of serene pleasure.

These were, indeed, moments of intense communication between herself and one other. But when a third factor was involved, things were different. The following incident was described by her son. It occurred on a day when Mrs Brown's jealous anxiety about exclusion had already been aroused. The occasion of this disturbance was a card addressed to Eric from an elderly widow, wishing him a swift recovery following a recent medical problem. Mrs Brown was to be observed staring at the card, opening and shutting it for quite long periods of time, and repeatedly muttering to herself, "Love from Lily"—the words written in the card. She seemed to become irritable at Eric's temporary, unusual debility and was herself more physically dependent than usual. At one point, she limped across the room, leaning heavily on her frame. Eric was observing her. He looked stricken and sad but was unable to help. When he said to her, "Mind the carpet" (meaning "Don't trip over the carpet"), she commented crossly to her son, "All he can think about is the carpet." She proceeded on her way, looking back every few steps to scrutinize her husband's face—half mocking him and, it almost seemed, half jeering. Was this change of mood related to trying, as a defence against her anxiety, to gang up with her son against her unusually fragile husband?—seeking to make Eric feel useless ("He can't help"), to crow, for once, over *his* helplessness?

The next day, husband, wife, and son were in the kitchen. Mrs Brown was sitting holding a yellow checked washing-up cloth. There was a bit of rubbish lying in front of her on the table. She pointed to it questioningly, as if to say, "Where does this go?" and looked at Eric. Misunderstanding her "question", and thinking that she was referring to the rubbish, Eric replied, slightly impatiently, "Over there!", nodding towards the bin. His wife stared at him uncomprehendingly—seeming to know that something was wrong, but not being able to work out what it could be. She demurred. Fleetingly she glanced down at the cloth, and then at herself: "That's a terrible thing to say!" (clearly thinking he had meant that she herself was a piece of rubbish). Ignoring this comment, Eric insisted irritably, "In there, in the proper place!" She looked unhappy and continued to dither, arousing further irritation in her husband, who quite suddenly left the room, without, on this occasion, the emotional resources to pause and try to understand what the problem really was. Later, Eric found the yellow cloth carefully folded and placed on top of the bin. Recalling the incident, he described himself as feeling very guilty: his wife had so wanted to be obedient, to do the right thing, but had been unable to sort out the muddle between the rubbish, herself, and the cloth. She had tried to follow instructions but was mystified by her residual sense that the yellow checked cloth was *not* something that should be put in the bin and nor, indeed, was she herself—although her life-long tendency to feel like rubbish had temporarily taken on a concrete reality for her.

The following morning, Eric had to go to hospital for the day for a further check-up. Despite having been carefully prepared for his departure, Mrs Brown was intensely anxious, repeating angrily, "He didn't say he was going. He didn't tell me." There was an exceptionally strong wind blowing that day, and Mrs Brown stared into the garden, distraught at the swaying, cracking branches of the nearby trees. She turned to her daughter with an air of a terrified child and said, pleadingly, falteringly, "Home [*long pause*] . . . Where's home? [*another long pause*] Take me home . . . *please*." Instead of swiftly reassuring her ("You *are* at home, Mum. Look, here are the flowers I bought this morning!" or some such thing), her daughter tried to understand something of her mother's state of terror. She talked to her quietly about the crashing and the banging. She remembered that her mother had also been terrified on the night of the mighty 1989 storm, telling her afterwards that she had thought it wartime again. She suggested that her mother might be feeling that she was back in London, that the War was on, and that "Home" meant the Old Brompton Road flat. Mrs Brown looked momentarily puzzled and then murmured "Yes. [*pause*] . . . . But I can't see anyone with guns out there." As her daughter drew the curtains and talked to her mother about why the high wind in the trees felt so distressing, the old lady's anxiety began to subside. It was as if the room became itself again in her mind—not an alien place where she was stranded and desolate.

In their different ways, these examples show how glimmers of light can be thrown on the nature of impaired and confusional states. One facet of the picture which these glimmers reveal is the fact that, whether in infancy or in old age, development runs unevenly, that the situation is not quite as Touchstone had described it—a steady process of ripening, followed by a steady process of rotting.

From the incidents described, it is possible to see how helpful to an understanding of the opaque mental states of old age might be the skills of those who work with similarly opaque mental and emotional states in childhood. Such professionals have a very particular experience of the power of infantile transference, of the way in which a mother's unconscious registering, reflecting, and thinking gives *meaning* to the infant's world—a meaning that is communicated in her responsive care—or of how, in the language of developmental psychology, "gaze-monitoring" may yield insight into an infant's needs and intentions. By the mechanism of projective identification the baby/child/elderly person who cannot understand, think, or talk about his or her fragmentary or fragmenting experience may nonetheless be able to engender in the caregiver some version of that basic experience. If, as we have seen, the caregiver can offer a mentally receptive state of mind, conscious or unconscious, the communication can be received, modified if it is one of pain and rage, appreciated if one of love and pleasure, and re-communicated, whether in more manageable or in reciprocal mode. The caregiver's mind functions as a container for, and a sorter of, the projected emotional fragments, which, as a consequence, become "the contained". Care of the elderly—those so often lacking the capacity to speak, yet so intensely riven by extreme emotional states—requires a painful reversal of the original pattern of container–contained (the young now struggling to offer states of reverie to the old).

We are familiar with observing how the behaviour of the baby is fostered by its relationship with its primary sources of love and care, but the foregoing describes the same sort of value of receptiveness to elderly as to infantile emotional experience. The turbulence of feeling—whether of joy, frustration, hopelessness, rage, fear, pleasure, persecution—is quite as intense as in the old as in the young and tests the caregiver in equivalently extreme ways. In these situations the carers, too, have much to learn and may themselves be enriched. As Rustin and Trowell (1991) say: "The capacity to contain and observe emotionally powerful psychic phenomena is the basis for knowledge of oneself, and for that contact with psychic reality which is at the core of an authentic personality" (p. 244).

Mrs Brown was fortunate to have, in Eric, a loving, sensitive, and deeply patient husband who had an unusual "untrained" capacity to bear his wife's states of mind. She was also fortunate to have children who were, in their different ways, experienced in the so-called caring professions. They were "good enough" at knowing when her insistent pointing to an object indicated, for example, a request or a plea for enlightenment; or whether it asserted a demand; or whether, by contrast, it was a communication of affect in a situation of shared intimacy. At such times of inwardness with her specific state of mind it was possible to observe a distinctive renewal of cognitive capacities in Mrs Brown's now very limited range. That is, despite in all obvious respects "rotting", Mrs Brown was still able, however briefly, to "ripen"—to a point that could, at times, even feel like a momentary late flowering.

Each time this occurred, it was as if mental pathways that had seemed to be totally overgrown, or mysteriously to diverge where once there had been a single track, had for a moment cleared or miraculously re-joined (and doubtless this was literally the case). For her, as we have seen, the times of greatest anxiety were those of being unable to tolerate feeling at the lonely point of the oedipal triangle, fearing that two others could come together only if one, usually herself, were excluded. Unable to speak or to think clearly at such times, Mrs Brown would seek, as in the cigarette incident, primitive reassurance (as if from breast or dummy). At other times she would become angry and, on occasions, abusive. To hold mentally these latter states required immense emotional resources on the part of her carers. They had to bear their own impatience, anger, even hatred, as part of their love.

The kinds of interaction described above became more and more rare as Mrs Brown's Alzheimer's made ever more destructive claims on her mental capacities. She deteriorated physically, became wholly dependent, and was increasingly silent. Eventually, this protracted "second childishness" yielded to "mere oblivion". By the time that point was reached, the "mere" of Jaques's account seemed less stark and challenging, and more appropriate than first reading suggests. For after so long a struggle in life, Mrs Brown's death seemed, to her loved ones, and almost certainly to herself, to be a matter of lesser importance, a comparatively easy thing. She had had enough. She had lived out Jaques's "last scene of all".

CHAPTER 12

No truce with the furies: issues of containment in the provision of care for people with dementia and those who care for them

Rachael Davenhill

Geriatric

What god is proud
of this garden
of dead flowers, this underwater
grotto of humanity,
where limbs wave in invisible
currents, faces drooping
on dry stalks, voices clawing
in a last desperate effort
to retain hold? Despite withered
petals, I recognise
the species: Charcot, Ménière,
Alzheimer. There are no gardeners
here, caretakers only
of reason overgrown
by confusion. This body once,
When it was in bud,
opened to love's kisses. These eyes,
cloudy with rheum,

Parts of this chapter were first published in the *Journal of Social Work Practice,* Vol. 12, No. 2 (1998).

were clear pebbles that love's rivulet
   hurried over. Is this
the best Rabbi Ben Ezra
   promised? I come away
comforting myself, as I can,
   that there is another
garden, all dew and fragrance,
   and that these are the brambles
about it we are caught in,
   a sacrifice prepared
by a torn god to a love fiercer
   than we can understand.

R. S. Thomas, "No Truce with the Furies" (1995, p. 9)

This chapter examines some of the unconscious factors involved in the silencing of debate at a particular point during the 1980s and early 1990s regarding the provision of long-term care for people in later life suffering from dementia. Particular attention is paid to factors internal and external that led to the decimation of local authority and NHS provision in this area and to a shifting of care into the private and voluntary sector in such a way that much of the time there seemed to be a malignant mirroring of the deteriorated mental state of the very people whom such services were meant to help.

There is indeed a kind of double jeopardy for the dementia sufferer in which the person is not only having to bear losing his or her mind but is also at risk of being treated mindlessly, which this particular period of history and the issues contained within it serve to highlight . The pervasive, unremitting pressure of a stance based on the denial of need had a major impact on the area of long-term care, with its sustained denial of the reality of ageing, of death, and of distress. This denial of reality took shape in a concerted attack to decimate those structures that formally existed within the welfare state to address and deal with extreme need. This led to a destructuring of services to people in later life, with a shift in local authorities to privatize residential and nursing home services often in a precipitate and unplanned way. The jury is still out in terms of whether history can be learned from or not in the longer run, with most readers being aware that the recommendations of the Royal Commission (1999) into the provision of long-term care have still not been implemented.

The welfare state and old age

The development of the welfare state in Britain attempted to address need throughout the lifespan from "cradle to grave", with the Beveridge Report of 1948 representing hope—hope for cooperation and renewal, and of altruism and reparation, following the long nightmare of the depression in the 1930s and the Second World War. Inevitably its construction also contained within it an idyll—total care, for all, for ever—and what we know from psychoanalytic theory is that idylls don't last. However, this is quite different from holding to an ideal, and the ideal inherent within the construction of the welfare state was that there should be some equitable form of social and health care provision for all citizens in need, which would be funded by a system of national insurance throughout the span of every adult's working life.

As life expectancy increased, so too did public expectations regarding social and health care delivery systems in terms of what could be provided. Timmins, in his outstanding book *The Five Giants: A Biography of the Welfare State* (1995), highlighted the increasing difficulty for people now requiring public sector services in later life:

> Not for the ones who are relatively healthy or well provided for in terms of income and family support and have a brief illness at the end of life before dying, but . . . those who died slowly and forgetfully when first capital and then some of the next generation's income vanished into longer term care which, during the 1980s the NHS no loner provided on a sufficient scale to match the growth in the numbers of the elderly. By the 1990s the Welfare State's collective smoothing of income across the life cycle with people paying in through tax and national insurance during good times to receive in bad or at times of heavy burden—i.e. when children appear, or pensions or long-term care are needed . . . the concept of cradle to grave which many of us grew up with had begun to shrink. From the late seventies onward, Julian Grand commented that "The Welfare State had been hit first by an economic and then by an ideological blizzard". [p. 503]

The Audit Commission Report, *The Coming of Age*, pointed out "that the growth in the number of people aged over seventy-five and eighty-five in recent years has been taking place at a time of significant change in the way that continual health and social care are funded . . .". During this time, the most dramatic reduction in the areas covered by the NHS was the long-term care of older people. In the early 1980s, the bulk of care for people in later life was provided directly by the public sector, whether through the NHS, through social services, or through the housing departments.

Private nursing and residential homes started to be funded through a system of social security payments, leading to an enormous expansion of residential and nursing provision in the independent sector, with residential beds increasing by 242% from 1983 to 1996. A further shift came about with the NHS and Community Care Act in 1990, which was formally introduced in 1993. This required local authority social service departments to become lead agencies for arranging social care. However, as the Audit Commission Report pointed out, previous changes had left two knock-on legacies. First, a reduction in the role of the NHS, and second, a growth in the role of the independent sector. As the commission wrote, "Neither of these changes was planned; they happened by default as a direct result of the increase in social security payments. They represent major shifts in policy that have never been debated or agreed." In the White Paper *Social Services: Achievement and Challenge*, Stephen Dorrell moved social care policy radically further to the right by suggesting that social service departments should shift into the sort of purchaser/provider split by then familiar to those of us working in the NHS. What this meant in practice was that rather than social services themselves providing residential and home care services for older people, they should concentrate on purchasing services. This was underlined by the explicit government directive that 85% of residential care was to be moved over into the private/independent sector. There seemed to be a malignancy of thought in connection to those who were young following the war, had paid tax and insurance throughout their working lives, and who were now in need of nursing and residential care, with the non-debate on the provision of long-term care and help for people in later life as long-stay wards closed, local authority homes closed, and older people were often shunted—literally overnight, with no preparation—into private homes. The stifling and silencing of debate around long-term care seemed to me an example of the death instinct in action, with silence, inertia, and inaction replacing thought. During this period, mortality rates among the very old in this country rose as a direct result of the precipitate movement of frail older people, and these rates highlighted the deadliness underlying the blind eye of a policy that impacted on the most vulnerable.

Dementia and the relocation effect

In thinking about the unconscious factors that may be involved in the sudden movement of vulnerable older people, I want to draw an analogy with gardening. What would lead a gardener to uproot the most vulnerable shoots and transplant them into another part of the garden, when all the gardening books indicate that such plants do not transplant well, adapt poorly to new conditions, and usually die? And for "vulnerable shoots" in the area of later life, research would indicate the most vulnerable to be people over the age of 80 with severe dementia (Bourestom & Pastalan, 1981; Robertson, Warrington, & Eagles, 1993). This research resides in the exploration of what has been referred to as the "relocation effect"—a relatively benign description—or "transplantation shock", which perhaps conveys more realistically the experience of older people who find themselves suddenly being moved from one form of long-term care to another without preparation. I shall not go into these studies in detail, but in summary they show that advanced age, poor prognosis, and confusional mental state are strong predictors of mortality following any move, and that intensive preparation before, during, and after any move can have a significant impact on the mortality rate (Danermark & Ekstrom, 1990; Novick, 1967; Schulz & Brenner, 1977).

The first three months following any move are the most dangerous in terms of increased mortality rates in those patients with dementia who are over the age of 80, and the human cost of precipitate closure is immense. In Britain, examples have included the deaths of eight of twenty-four elderly mentally infirm patients following their transfer from Park Prewitt Hospital to nursing homes in 1994. Five died within twenty-two days of the move (*The Guardian*, 12 March 1997). In 1995, three elderly women with learning disabilities died within eighteen months of being moved from Dovenby Hall in Cumbria to private nursing homes. Some of these women had lived in the hospital for the previous forty years. Everyone was clear that in this case there was no criticism of the quality or care at the nursing homes; it was the impact of removing the women from a stable environment which had led to the deaths. Staff were not allowed to accompany the women into the new homes to ease the transition of leaving (*Independent on Sunday*, 19 March 1995).

Research in this area shows that where a closure involves disruption to staff and residents, with minimal awareness or sensitivity as to the impact such a closure and move may have, then mortality rates among residents increase. Research also gives clear evidence as to how closures, if unavoidable, can be handled effectively. This involves both residents and staff taking part in extensive before and after resettlement programmes and in them both being moved as an intact unit (Novick, 1967; Robertson, Warrington, & Eagles, 1993). The continuity of care that familiar staff provide is extremely important for people with dementia. Each staff member carries a huge store of knowledge and, hopefully, understanding of each individual resident's needs, which may been learned through experience over many years. To move residents without any continuity of staff care is akin to kicking the crutch away from someone who cannot walk very well. That is why sudden relocation to a new setting, with new staff and insufficient preparation, is both dangerous and life threatening for people with dementia.

The external pressures leading to the political undercutting of integrated service provision in the public sector have been excellently delineated in the 1997 *Coming of Age* Audit Commission report. Throughout the 1980s and 1990s a policy of individualism was taken to its logical extreme, with the area of long-term care experiencing the way in which "Service interests are pursued in isolation, one service pursuing its own aims quite separate to the other, and often forced into competition both within the service itself and also across other sectors. Some area of policy change have led to benefit in one sector at cost to another" (Timmins, 1995). This policy held within it an attack on anything that was weak, needed constant monitoring, care, and attention, or was at constant risk of deterioration and death—and it is possible to recognize the older person in the later stages of dementia in such a description. It seemed that the welfare state and all it represented had been subject to an unconscious and at times quite conscious attack based on a denial of need and dependency. The politics of individualism, taken to the extreme and pushed into national long-term planning, ultimately held within it an omnipotent phantasy. This phantasy took the form of a belief that the individual is self-made, can provide all, and is in a position to make use of free choice at all times. Both the British Psychological Society and the Royal College of Psychiatrists were clear in their response to the previous government's document *A New Partnership for Care in Old Age* (DOH, 1996) that most proposals seemed to take no account of the fact that people making immediate choices about residential care are often at their most vulnerable point in the life cycle and are quite likely to have a degree of cognitive impairment or some form of mental distress and/or physical illness.

The more deadly response to being aware of need is to get rid of it. Steiner draws attention to this in his introduction to Hanna Segal's book *Psychoanalysis, Literature and War*:

> This hatred of reality and its replacement by omnipotent phantasy is clarified by Hanna Segal in her discussion of the two possible reactions to states of need. One is life seeking and object seeking, leading to an attempt to satisfy those needs in the real world, even when necessary, by aggressive striving. The other has as its aim to annihilate the experience of need and the mental pain which goes with it, hence the self or the part of the self capable of experiencing pain is attacked along with the object which gives arise to the awareness of need. . . . Segal emphasises that both types of reaction to need are present in all of us but the balance varies and represents to her the conflict between the life and death instincts. [Steiner, 1997, p. 5]

If "self" and "parts of self" are replaced with "patient" or "society", then it is possible to see pretty clearly why the most vulnerable individuals—those with dementia, for example—get dislodged so quickly from the social mind's eye and why those in contact with such individuals within the NHS or social services, or carers, who attempted to articulate the problem of need have also had such a rough handling.

Issues of containment in dementia

The crisis in the area of long-term care for older people in this country arose in a climate within which the then prime minister, Margaret Thatcher, could say as a matter of course that "there is no such thing as society, only individuals . . .". Contrast this with Joan Riviere, addressing the impact of loss and death on the psyche in a 1952 paper striking in its humanity: "there is no such thing as a single human being pure and simple, unmixed with other human beings; each personality is a world in himself, the company of many. . . . " Before this, in what could be a searingly accurate account of the meaning of the dementing process to the individual and to those who care for him or her (although she was not addressing the area of old age specifically in this paper), she writes:

> It is true that people as well as animals are known to pine away and die when their loved ones vanish. We are not concerned here with material realities only; death is not only a matter of whether the breath leaves the body and the heart ceases to beat. That is one item of the experience of death, it is true; but is that all that death means

to us? It is probably the most important factor in death because it is irrevocable, and thus all else that death means becomes irrevocable: namely, the cessation, the disappearance, so comparatively sudden, of a living existence, an entity, a person, a personality, a most complex and composite structure of attributes, tendencies, experiences, memories, idiosyncrasies good and bad, as well as the body they belong to. It is all this which disappears; from one moment to the next it was here and it is gone. So when one fears one's own death, it is all this which one will lose, one's "life"—in both senses—one's present breath of life and one's "past life" out of which one's identity is constituted. [Riviere, 1952, pp. 316]

Kitwood (1990b) suggested that the area of working with people suffering from dementia includes confronting organic impairment and the great difficulties there may be in consciously articulating any psychological conflicts. He thought that in dementia,

the problem . . . is not simply that of damaged brain cells, but also of damage to the psychological self and the good feeling that would sustain it. It is, I believe, quite correct to regard unattended dementia as a semi-psychotic state. . . . Dementia is envisaged as a break in cohesive awareness, a failure of the process of consistent symbolisation, so that the person has lost his or her bearing in the world, and is invaded by feelings from within. . . . [p. 49]

He observed that when organic deterioration occurs there may also be a breaking down of the individual's lifelong defences that leaves the person exposed and vulnerable to episodes of catastrophic anxiety and rage.

Dementia will always have a deeply tragic aspect, both for those who are affected and for those who are close to them. There is, however, a vast difference between a tragedy in which persons are actively involved and morally committed, and a blind and hopeless submission to fate. [Kitwood, 1997, p. 69]

Caregivers, whether immediate family or staff in residential or nursing homes, have a crucial function in containing those split off and deteriorated aspects of the person they are with, often at great cost to themselves. Why at such cost? Because, on the one hand, there is the need to mourn the loss of, in many cases, a lifelong partner. But, on the other, the process is complicated because it is not a loss in the more usual way, through physical death, but having to witness over time the incremental loss of self-awareness in the person he or she knew and who knew him or her. Clare, Baddeley, Moniz-Cook, and Woods (2003) refer to the "quiet revolution" that has taken place in dementia care in recent years with research providing strong evidence that early interventions individualized for the person with dementia and their families are effective in the short and long term, and there is a growing body of work on early-stage dementia indicating that psychotherapy can be helpful (Cheston, 1998; Husband, 2000).

Sinason (1992) described working with a man in late middle age with an early dementia whom she saw for psychotherapy sessions at home, drawing on her long experience in the field of learning disabilities. She thought that the facticity of the organic deterioration had to be acknowledged and that, while this was not transformable, the emotionally caused impairment remained open for change. When organic deterioration is severe with a resultant loss of capacity in the individual to mentalize internal objects, then there is a clear limit to the role that formal psychotherapy can play. However, psychoanalytic ideas can continue to inform a detailed understanding in thinking about the challenges of developing structures for intervention that will contain both the patient and those who care for them. Hildebrand (1982) described the way in which the carer eventually takes on the role of "auxiliary ego" for the older person with dementia, in which the care may be involved in a daily struggle to translate and make sense of the individual's distressed and at times bizarre communications, often conveyed through projective identification, which tends to replace ordinary language (see Waddell, chapter 11).

While, at the very end, the person with dementia may have very little or no awareness, those left behind are still having to live with something very painful. At the very beginning and the very end of life there is an immense dependence on the main caretaker, and this is more acute in the advanced stages of dementia. At the beginning of life there is a fragile and developing ego that has the potential to develop and be worked with. In severe dementia, there is not even that advantage, and survival does then depend on the capacity of the caretaker to remain in ongoing contact with and support humanely the older person in what carers have often described as a living death. This is often spoken about by people in the early stages of dementia following diagnosis, where the individual may retain, for quite some time, ongoing levels of self-awareness and a capacity to reflect on past, present, and future, including the painful knowledge that one's own self-awareness will diminish over time as the mind becomes irreparably damaged.

The difficulty in the later stages of dementia is that, in terms of internal containment, no robust mental structure, in a dynamic sense, with a sustained capacity for self-awareness and thought, is left. The immediate care of the person with dementia is with the family or professional carers, such as nurses, doctors, and health and social care staff, the latter often poorly paid and unsupported, who are then left holding those elements of the person they care for in memory—the person he or she once were, and yet are in daily contact with the person he or she is now, which is "not their old self—not themselves at all". Given that the basic mental apparatus no longer holds firm, the ego is emptied out—there is a weakening, a draining out of the ability to process, to articulate, to think, to understand. A reversion eventually takes place to a reliance on basic instinctual rhythms—to do with voice, taste, touch, movement, smell, and so on. That is why the maintenance of a live, consistent rhythm of routine with well-supported carers is so important. The current fragmentation of services, which I explore in more detail at the end of this chapter, means that caretakers are often left alone in a dyad with the older person, with an inadequate "third" in terms of a containing institutional or service structure that can take in the needs of the caretaker as well as the older person. If the emotional needs of staff and family members are not actively attended to, we know there can be terrible miscarriages when abuse, both physical and mental, of older people takes place, as we know it does with babies whose parents do not have sufficient internal or external resources.[1]

Conceptual overview

The development of psychoanalysis in Britain in recent years has particularly concerned itself with the impact of very early experiences and anxieties on the formation and development of personality. I want now to consider the psychoanalytic concepts of projective identification, containment, and countertransference, which are linked in important and complex ways. Building on Freud and Klein's work, Bion further developed the concept of projective identification, and this has contributed greatly in terms of our capacity to understand "the nature and vicissitudes of inter-personal, inter-group, inter-institutional and international relationships" (Obholzer, 1989, p. 58).

Projective identification describes a psychic mechanism, occurring in very early infancy, that can be a defence against and a communication about very frightening and disturbing anxieties and feelings that the infant is unable to express through language (Bion, 1962; Klein, 1946). The instinctual response of the infant to a bad experience is to try to get rid of it by projecting it out into a person in the real world (specifically the mother or main caretaker). The mother then has the possibility of experiencing some of her baby's feelings and anxieties in a very immediate way. Here projective identification can be seen both as a form of unconscious communication and also as a means of getting rid of something that the infant finds difficult to bear. How, or whether, the projections are received and responded to by the mother depends on many factors.

Bion (1962) suggested that in order to respond to the baby's distress, the adult has to be able to take in, experience, and transform (or "detoxify") the distress so that the baby is enabled to reincorporate the feelings in a benign form. The baby senses that its needs have been understood; it has the experience of being contained and feels that its distress has been alleviated. This is an active interaction between infant and mother that is ongoing. However, if the infant experiences the mother as unwilling or unable, for whatever reason, to receive, assimilate, and transform its projections, then this can lead either to the infant making ever more frenetic and violent attempts to "get through" to the mother, through an increase in projective identification, or, alternatively, giving up in despair.

The capacity to sense needs accurately, to experience within oneself the anxieties and feelings of someone else, and to understand these and respond to them in an appropriate way finds its prototype in a good-enough relationship between a mother and her baby, but this relationship is potentially present in every human relationship. This process is an important aspect of what is known as countertransference (Heimann, 1950) and can be an extremely useful tool in helping us to understand the subtle communication that can occur in the therapeutic and other relationships. The next section gives examples of the importance of containment for those who care for the person with dementia, whether family or staff member.

Carers

The role of caregiving is an enormous challenge and strain, particularly where there are preceding ambivalences in the relationship. Increasingly there is recognition of the support that those caring for a family member with dementia need, which will include everyday support and keeping the structures of the carer's everyday life in place where possible, with consistent periods of respite care. As longevity increases, it is no longer uncommon for people in their sixties and seventies to be the young old caring for parents in their nineties. A brief consultation over two or three meetings can sometimes be extremely effective for caregivers where the everyday strain of taking care of their relative may affect the capacity to take care of their own internal needs, The consultation gives an opportunity for the internal dynamics of the presenting situation to be understood and thought about in more depth:

> Mrs Y came for an extended consultation and said she felt depressed and exhausted with the day-to-day pressures of caring for her 80-year-old mother, who suffered from dementia. She was in her sixties and had enlisted her daughter, then in her forties with a young family of her own, to help her with the care of her mother. As Mrs Y described her daily life caring for her demented mother, it was easy to understand how exhausting the sheer physicality of the task was for her. Part of the work of the consultation was to try to understand more about why she felt driven to provide all the care herself, and also driven to ensure that her daughter did the same. Mrs Y said that her depression had escalated at the point her mother started to refuse food, either knocking it off the tray or spitting it out. My patient conveyed an intensity of complaint and grievance about this, which we were able eventually to link to her experience of severe postnatal depression following the birth of her daughter, when she felt invaded at times by both suicidal thoughts and thoughts of wanting to kill her baby. It transpired that the baby had refused to take the breast in the first few weeks of life, and no help had been forthcoming to support the mother–infant couple. Her focus of complaint was connected to her deep resentment of her own mother, who at that point had been highly involved in her own career midlife, whom she felt had not been available. I was eventually able to take up the phantasy of a mother who was allegedly reparative, in terms of the way Mrs Y felt she had to take on all the care of her mother but was, in fact, imprisoning her own daughter with guilt in enlisting her to take part in the duty of care, as she felt imprisoned and persecuted by an internal mother for whom nothing was good enough, however dutifully carried out.

Through this brief example I want to highlight the importance of the consultation for containing the patient's own hatred towards her mother, who, she felt, had abandoned her again. In her mother's spitting out of meals, an earlier trauma had been revived for Mrs Y of her daughter as a baby refusing to feed. Mrs Y was having to try to contain her mother's increasingly fragmented state of mind, as well as her own. She had come for the consultation at the point that she had found herself wanting to hold a pillow over her mother's face, in the same way she had once found herself in a very depressed state wanting to suffocate her own daughter as a tiny baby.

* * *

The following detailed observation undertaken by a member of the old age course at the Tavistock highlights the strains for both residents and staff in a dementia unit:

> The observation took place in a specialist unit for people with severe dementia. Nearly all the residents had lost their capacity to speak and were physically unable to do things for themselves. The observer arrived at the unit and sat at a table where there was a clear view of the main lounge. Mrs G was lying on a big sofa in a foetal-like position with her back facing away from the room, wearing an old cardigan, brown tights, and slippers. She was asleep and breathing heavily. Her hair was messy. A table with a newspaper on it was next to the sofa where she was lying. A nurse told the observer that Mrs G had only moderate dementia, and was unable to walk independently and talk, but had been moved into this unit as she had been very disturbing to the other residents in the next-door unit where there were no, or very early onset, dementia patients.
>
> Mrs G woke up briefly and turned round to face the room. She shut her eyes again. Meanwhile, another resident from the dementia unit came in and asked if there was a spare newspaper. The nurse said yes and gave her the newspaper on Mrs G's table.
>
> Mrs G immediately opened her eyes, looked at the table, and shouted:
>
> "I haven't got a paper now!"
>
> Then she shouted, "What a noise!"
>
> Her face was screwed up, and she looked very unhappy. A nurse went and sat next to her and asked if she was OK. Mrs G screwed her face up and tutted. The nurse went to get up, but Mrs G grabbed her and said, "Don't leave me—it's lonely."

The nurse said she would sit a while if that is what Mrs G wanted. She sat with her for about thirty minutes, and Mrs G slowly relaxed, closed her eyes, and went back to sleep. When the old lady was asleep, the nurse got up to start getting dinner ready. After about ten minutes, she said to the care assistant, "You had better wake Mrs G up so that she can get ready for lunch."

The care assistant woke up Mrs G and told her it was dinner time.

Mrs G said "Dinner time, is it? What are we having?" She was trying to sit herself into an upright position.

"Beef stew."

Mrs G said, "Disgusting."

She went back to lying down again and looked unhappy. Suddenly she became very anxious and said, "Where's the toilet, I'm going to do it . . . I can't stand up, my legs have gone."

The nurse went over and said her legs were tired because they'd been up all morning, and they would be OK once Mrs G started walking.

"Will you go with me?" Mrs G said.

She seemed terribly anxious, and the nurse replied, "Yes of course." She helped Mrs G to stand, and they walked slowly to the toilet together, the nurse talking quietly with her as they went. Mrs G seemed to become more stable on her feet and calmer in herself.

After going to the toilet, the nurse brought Mrs G back to her chair and then went to get her dinner from the kitchen. On her return, she put it in front of Mrs G, who looked at it and said, "That looks like a pile of shit. I'm not eating that shit!"

She pushed the plate away, and it nearly fell on the floor. Mrs G kept repeating, "It's bloody rubbish, shit it is, shit!"

She lay back down again. The nurse came over and asked her to sit up and she would get her something else. How about a sandwich? Mrs G did not answer. The nurse took away the plate of stew and bought a sandwich over. Mrs G looked at it and said

"What's this? More of your shit?"

The nurse said that it was an egg sandwich, at which point Mrs G threw it on the floor.

The nurse asked her if she wanted any rice pudding.

Mrs G said, "What, does it not have jam?"

"It can do", the nurse replied.

"OK", said Mrs G.

When she was given the rice pudding, she moved her spoon up and down in it, then crashed it down and said, "It's shit."

She looked very unhappy and went to put her head back on the pillow on the sofa. The nurse asked her if she would like a cup of tea, and Mrs G looked at her for a while. The nurse paused, then asked for a care assistant to carry on distributing tea to the other residents. She then sat down next to the old lady and gently took her hand. Mrs G started to cry. She closed her eyes and kept crying.

At one level we can see in this observation the difficulties of mixing different levels of disturbance. Mrs G's real distress seemed to start when the newspaper was removed—the newspaper connecting her to the world of no or only mild deterioration. She was then left perhaps full of an indigestible awareness of being surrounded by what she may become—silent and immobile, like so many of the other residents in this unit for severe dementia. It is possible to see the nurse's concern and kindness in her contact with Mrs G, but this is not enough. The nurse also needs knowledge. This cannot come from within; as she, like any nurse or care assistant working in this setting, is bombarded with shit and despair and resorts to the concrete solution of feeding and toileting. The shouting starts again when Mrs G is woken up and offered dinner. Mrs G asks to go to the toilet, but everything is still shit. She seems to feel persecuted by something awful being aroused in her yet again and makes it clear she wants to get rid of something by asking to to the toilet. What she actually needed was for something to be returned in the form of her newspaper. The newspaper that was taken away served to represent the less deteriorated world Mrs G was still capable of inhabiting, which was stolen away from her when she was moved prematurely to the unit with more deteriorated residents. When the newspaper was taken away, she rightly complained that this was shit.

The truth of the matter is that she was in a very shitty situation and had to close her eyes in despair as the only way of protecting herself from having to perceive again the situation she now finds herself and over which she has no control. Through close observation it could be seen that Mrs G's escalation of distress followed the removal of the newspaper that connected her to the world of more normal functioning. Just as something had settled, she was then offered food again. But it was not this sort of food that sustained her at this point. What she needed was a mind capable of taking her in and thinking about her state of mind as well as body. The observer was able to think this through with the support of a supervision group after the observation itself had taken place. However, not unusually on the unit being observed, there was no forum at all in which the nurse could talk about and process her experiences, and the opportunity for a real understanding of what had occurred with Mrs G was lost.

In her paper "Mourning and Its Relation to Manic-Depressive States" (1940), Klein commented that "Through tears, which in the unconscious mind are equated to excrement, the mourner not only expresses his feelings and thus eases tension, but also expels his 'bad' feelings and his 'bad' objects, and this adds to the relief obtained through crying" (p. 359). In the observation of Mrs G, what is immediately striking seems to be her verbal defecation—everything, she says, is shit. However, this isn't a meaningless evacuation but is accurate in terms of the situation she finds herself in, and it needs a receptive container to take in and make sense of what she is protesting about. Klein thought there was a continual oscillation and interplay between the external world and the internal world. The above example serves to illustrate one of the extreme external circumstances affecting an unseen percentage of older people who are moved into residential or nursing homes in an unplanned way. By the very nature of an unplanned admission, the person being admitted is often unknown. It is still extremely common to find that very little attempt is made to get to know the individual, to the degree that even the most basic of histories do not appear in the case notes kept by many nursing homes.

Often very primitive psychic processes occur in settings where staff are working with patients with severe psychological disturbances. If people, functioning psychologically at an infantile level, sense that their feelings have not been "taken in", experienced, understood, and responded to satisfactorily, then they may feel aggressive and destructive and may react to others around them in such a way. Staff who are involved with people experiencing such disturbances are themselves likely to experience similar aggressive feelings, since the people they are working with often find their state of mind too unbearable to tolerate and, through the mechanism of projective identification, project the unwanted feelings into the member of staff. Whether these painful and potentially destructive feelings are acted out, or are transformed by the staff member, is central to the quality of care that can be given. However, the power of such unconscious projections mean they are sometimes particularly difficult to contain. If there is some capacity to experience, understand the meaning of, and respond to these projections constructively, then it may be possible to avoid acting out feelings of, for example, hatred, cruelty, or hopelessness in a destructive way.

Whether working with individuals, groups of patients, or staff, workers are often in the "front line" in trying to make sense of complicated forms of communication. For the person in the later stages of dementia, symbolic or verbal communication may be difficult, and the more primitive preverbal mechanism of projective identification will operate more forcefully. If there is no forum in the individual or the institution in which countertransference feeling can be processed and understood, then a valuable source of information with regard to the patient will be lost. There is also a very real danger that the worker will become overwhelmed by the level of projection and will become therapeutically less effective or will act in some punitive way towards the older person. The cost—in terms of burn-out, resignations resulting in a high vacancy rate and turnover of staff, and the concomitant reduction in quality of care for the patient—can be enormous.

Menzies (1959) carried out extensive investigations as to the function of institutions in containing anxiety. She thought that organizations, in the struggle against anxiety, developed socially structured defence mechanisms, the characteristics of which help the individual avoid the experience of anxiety, guilt, doubt, and uncertainty. What is known for certain from her work is that the structure within which the staff and the individuals they care for find themselves either can fail or can help to support the everyday work and struggle to contain the projections of more disturbed states of mind. While there is an emphasis on person-centred care for people with dementia, the lived experience of many older people and their carers is the way in which dementia seems to obliterate the possibility of real thought being given to the individual as a person. I would suggest that, in part, this is due to the projection of intolerably fragmented states of mind into the carer, whether family member or clinician. From my experience and that of other colleagues working directly with older people and running work discussion groups for staff working in old age services, it is clear that a knowledge of the individual's history and past, present, and current relationships can be extremely containing for the carer in enabling him or her to take in and make sense of otherwise inexplicable communications. Person-centred care for patients has, in my view, to be yoked to person-centred care for staff, whereby their experience in working in old age settings can be taken seriously.

The next example describes the problem of faecal smearing and incontinence in a patient suffering from a psychotic depression. It highlights the importance of ensuring that, as part of the working day, sufficient time is provided in which staff can really talk to each other about the challenges of the work and the feelings that are induced:

> A mental health worker described the dread of all the staff who had to look after Mr X, an 82-year-old man who had come in as an emergency admission. Every night he would defecate and smear himself, his bed, and the walls of the room. The staff were beside themselves with rage and had taken to sedating him heavily and avoiding entering the room at night. When we went further into this in the supervision group, it transpired that none of the staff knew anything about the old man. As is very common with sudden admissions, no history had been taken, and there was nothing at all in the case notes beyond the date of admission. Slowly, over a number of highly charged discussions, the staff group were able to think about the possible meaning of the incontinence as a concretization of failed mourning. They agreed to take turns sitting with Mr X after supper, trying to articulate some of his inarticulate distress about the shitty situation he found himself in, overwhelmed by the sudden move from his home, but also overwhelmed by the rapid movement in the onset of the loss of his mind, where he found himself unable to communicate verbally. He remained a challenging resident to care for, but with a consistent approach by the staff group, particularly through the night, an approach that emphasized regular and reliable contact with Mr X, although he remained occasionally incontinent the faecal smearing eventually stopped. It seemed to me that the level of intolerable internal persecutory anxiety experienced by Mr X diminished to some extent, and that, in turn, lessened the degree of violent projections into

staff and rendered more manageable their feelings of sadism in the countertransference.

This example looks at one of the external hazards of old age: the difficulty of being catapulted suddenly from one environment to another, a problem that we saw above in both in Mrs G's move and in Mr X's unplanned admission to the nursing home. It also touches on one of the internal hazards of old age, in terms of the dementing process, that hooks into one of the most primitive annihilatory anxieties of infancy—the fear of falling into the abyss of "nameless dread" and never ultimately returning from it.

The role of the visiting consultant

In working with staff in nursing and residential homes, old age psychiatrists or clinical psychologists are often called in to see particular "problem patients" at the point at which staff in the home feel they can no longer care and wish to discharge the resident. The task of the visiting clinician then is certainly to see the older person as requested but, just as importantly, to see, listen to, take in, and think with the staff about both their own and the patient's distress.

> Dr P said that she had received a telephone call and urgent letter of referral asking her to see a 79-year-old man, Mr L, because of his "demanding and aggressive behaviour". The complaint was that he constantly rang the bell next to his bed and was bed-bound through his own choice. The last straw had come when he had lashed out and kicked a young member of staff who was pregnant, after which the home issued him with an eviction order, but there was nowhere for him to go. Mr L had been in and out of hospital a number of times and had been diagnosed as having chronic obstructive pulmonary disease. His wife had died two years previously, and he had found it increasingly difficult to cope. Mr L said that he agreed with the view of his two daughters, who said that he had always been difficult and over-dependent on his wife and that it would be best for him to move into residential accommodation. He had sold the house and moved almost immediately after his wife's death, but he now expressed confusion as to what had happened to the house and its contents. His wife had collected little china figurines, and he repeatedly said, "I don't know what happened to all the figures."

When she arrived at the home, Dr P said that the staff greeted her with enormous relief and said that they needed something to be done urgently and that unless she, the doctor, could sort Mr L out, he would lose his place in the home. Dr P was taken immediately to the side room where Mr L sat up in bed with an oxygen mask covering his face. The room was bare other than the bed, a commode, and an oxygen cylinder, and Mr L had a neglected appearance. He took the mask off and told Dr P that he thought the home was OK and that he particularly liked the food. He said he had always been a bit anxious and found it difficult to breathe sometimes. He'd been in hospital with the heart problem for six months before moving back into the home. He thought the staff sometimes stole things, and he commented that if they came when he called then he wouldn't use the bell all the time. After fifteen minutes, Mr L said he felt breathless, and Dr P said she felt dismissed when he put the oxygen mask back over his face and turned away. Dr P visited him again and learned more of his history. His early memories were dominated by the Second World War, in which he recalled hiding under the table during the blitz and his mother taking in an elderly neighbour whose home had been shattered. He thought his mother had been too charitable and that people took advantage of her. He married in his early twenties, and his wife died after their marriage of over forty years.

Here we can see that both the staff and the patient are right. The staff are right in feeling that the doctor needs to do something urgently. Dr L felt under enormous pressure to come up with some magical goods and cure Mr L in some way. In fact, what the staff needed was someone to take in the urgent pressure they felt under. Part of Dr P's role was to balance the needs of the staff and the needs of the patient, to feel confident in working with the staff group as well as seeing the patient. The patient is right, to some degree, in believing that the staff are stealing. While there was no evidence at all that they were actually stealing the patient's possessions, it was true that his dignity had been stolen and, in his neglected appearance, it was clear that he was being robbed of being taken in by another person. This was confirmed when the doctor subsequently discovered that although Mr L used the oxygen mask regularly, the cylinder had in fact been standing empty for over three weeks.

A direct repetition of the earlier childhood trauma seemed to be taking place in which the patient's house had been blown away. In the residential home, Mr L was surrounded by staff who were unable to respond to his call, representing the busy mother who, Mr L felt, was preoccupied with all the neighbour's problems, not available to take in the little boy's fears and anxieties about his world shattering as the bombs dropped. The death of his wife, the pressure to sell his home quickly, and the current eviction order were all bombshells threatening to leave him homeless. As well as the external reality, his poignant query that he didn't know where all the "figurines" were also reflected the way in which he felt he had lost contact with any good internal object. The challenge for the doctor was to think about how she could give a home to so many uncontained feelings both in the patient and in the staff, and for that she, too, needed room to think the situation through in supervision.

Note

1. A 2004 survey of 700 nurses by the Community and District Nursing Association, *Responding to Elder Abuse*, found that 88% had encountered elder abuse at work. Verbal abuse was most common (67%), followed by emotional (51%), physical (49%), financial (34%), and sexual (8%). The person carrying out the abuse was most likely to be a partner (45%), son (32%), daughter or other family member (29%), paid carer (26%), nurse (5%), or other (4%).

CHAPTER 13

Facts, phenomenology, and psychoanalytic contributions to dementia care

Andrew Balfour

It is a terrifying prospect to contemplate the progressive loss of mental capacities. Just as we all will one day be old, so it is difficult to distance ourselves from the possibility that we may eventually develop dementia ourselves. We are faced not only with the limits of our current understanding, but with a challenge to our very capacity to understand what it may be like for a person to move into a world of encroaching incomprehension. How do we think about something that we may rather not know about? With this in mind, how might the psychoanalytic approach help us in our attempts to think about dementia? In this chapter, I look first at the "facts" of dementia and current research relevant to the experience of the person with dementia for colleagues who may not be working in old age services. I then look at the contribution that a psychoanalytic approach can make to the area of dementia care.

As awareness of the dementias touches more lives, it is well known that they bring continued deterioration of mental functioning, loss of memory and language, and increasing difficulty in performing the ordinary tasks of daily life. One man in the early stages of dementia put it to me like this: "my mind's boggled, to put it in a rough term . . . it's boggled and I can't express myself very straightforwardly as I used to be able to. I have to fight my mind to get it to work, or express a word, to carry what understanding I've got." He tried to tell me about something else, but lost the words. I asked if this was an example of the feeling of being "boggled" that he had told me about. He said, "Yes, yes, I am boggled at it. It's blotchy, blotchy . . . it's a feeling that I don't know. Don't know anything about that. I don't want to appear as though I am so far away from everything, and everybody . . . it's gone right out, the subject I spoke about . . . it's gone right out of my mind." This man lost his thoughts but was able to talk about what was happening. What about those who are not able to do so, or those who recover their thoughts but know that it will not be an improving picture—they have found them again this time, but next time they may not? Think of the old adage, "at least you always have your memories". Yet, in later life, when other losses prevail, the individual may face the loss of even his or her memories of earlier times. This is a prospect that may haunt our view of old age, whether or not it is our fate to experience dementia. Until Alzheimer identified the disease, it was thought to be synonymous with old age itself. Nowadays dementia is no longer seen as a disease purely of old age, as more is known about early-onset dementia in younger people. While it is not inevitable and may not be seen as identical with old age, dementia does remain a possibility for any of us in later life.

The facts of dementia

The risk of developing dementia grows with age, rising to a one in five chance over the age of 80. There are four identified types of dementia, the most common being Alzheimer's Disease, characterized by short-term memory loss and difficulties with language in the early stages, gradually becoming more severe over time. Vascular dementia is the consequence of strokes and insufficient blood supply to the brain. It has a varied clinical picture, depending on which parts of the brain are most affected. Dementia with Lewy bodies is associated both with some of the symptoms of Alzheimer's Disease as well as symptoms that are similar to Parkinson's Disease (such as slowness, muscle stiffness, and trembling of the limbs). In addition, people may experience hallucinations and a tendency to faint or fall. Fronto-temporal dementia covers a range of conditions, associated with diverse symptoms, which may include impairments in semantic memory (the person's stored knowledge about the world), and the earliest changes are often felt in the area of personality and behaviour. Estimates vary, but approximately 700,000 people in the UK have dementia (NICE, 2004). As the proportion of older people in society continues to grow, the greatest increase in the next decade will be among those over 80 (Frampton, 2003). Over recent years there have been new ways of thinking about dementia, with a current climate of potential change, a "quiet revolution" (Clare et al., 2003), offering the opportunity of re-evaluating how to help people with dementia and those who care for them. This will be further driven with the publication of the National Institute of Clinical Excellence guidelines for the treatment and care of people with dementia.

There have been an increasing number of accounts, in the clinical and research literature, of psychotherapeutic approaches to people with dementia. These reflect a broad diversity, from counselling (La-Barge, 1981), reminiscence work (Mills & Coleman, 1994), "valida-tion therapy" (Feil, 2003), to psychodynamic approaches (Cheston, 1998; Grosclaude, 1987; Hausman, 1992; Schmid, 1990; Sinason, 1992; Weiner, 1988). Although diverse, these clinical accounts share some key essential features that focus on the emotional content and personal meaning of the communications of the person with dementia. Those describing such work comment upon modifications in technique that may need to be made as the disease progresses. These amount to an attempt to respond sensitively to the constraints of organic deteriora-tion upon factors such as the frequency of sessions, the setting, and the length and termination of the therapy (Cheston, 1998; Garner, 2004).

The phenomenological level:
the experience of the person with dementia

What is the impact of lesions, on the level of the brain, on the mind of the dementia sufferer? There is great difficulty in knowing, from the outside, what might be happening in the internal world of a person with dementia as the disease progresses. Froggatt (1988) suggests that it is because the experience of dementia is so difficult to communicate that it remains an unknown one. Weiner (1988) asks, "What observer could describe the inner lived experiences of dementia? Yet it is pre-cisely these inner lived experiences that are fundamental to one's understanding of the disease." The span of the experience, from the beginning to the later stages, is vast. As Sinason (1992) points out: "The difference between someone at the start of Alzheimer's Disease and someone who is near the end is as large as someone who is normal and someone who is profoundly handicapped. The total continuum is experienced in the mind and heart of a single being."

Early-stage dementia

The most common form of dementia, Alzheimer's Disease, is associated with "insidious onset", meaning that the changes affecting the individual happen gradually and so may not be brought to medical attention until the disease process is already well established. With improved diagnostic procedures and greater awareness of the disease among health professionals and others, its detection may be increasingly likely to happen earlier. Now we have a group of people diagnosed in the early stages of dementia, who are more likely to be aware of the diagnosis and what is facing them. What is it like to be nearer the beginning and receiving a diagnosis of dementia? Bryden (2005) writes from her experience:

> Many of us have heard at diagnosis what we now refer to as the standard dementia script: "You have about five years till you become demented, then you will probably die about three years later". No wonder we often suffer depression and despair. Dementia and Alzheimer's are both words that create fear and dread. Many of us wish we had cancer. At least then there is talk of treatment, of chemotherapy, of possible remission. There is none of that with a diagnosis of dementia.

What is conveyed is that the person diagnosed with dementia is entering a world of tremendous terror and helplessness. Bryden (2005) goes on to add: "We feel as if we are hanging onto a high cliff above a lurking black hole. Daily tasks are complex, nothing is automatic any more."

As the disease progresses, many people with Alzheimer's are found to be unaware of their illness and the impairments in functioning that it has caused. This lack of knowledge, awareness, or recognition of disease on the part of the sufferer is known as anosognosia and has traditionally been seen as a symptom of organic deterioration in which clearly organic factors are important. However, Clare (2002, 2004) and others have pointed out the important role of psychological and social factors in determining whether individuals express awareness. Bryden (2005) commented: "Don't assume that we lack insight, for we might simply be in denial—a perfectly normal response to the shock of diagnosis." In a sense, we may all share a tendency to wish to deny something felt to be so unbearable. The difficulty in thinking about the experience of the person with dementia may reflect an understandable tendency to "turn a blind eye" to such frightening and disturbing states of loss and diminution of functioning. We may much rather believe that, if we were to enter such a world ourselves, we would not know anything about it.

In my research into the experience of self-awareness in people with Alzheimer's Disease, results indicated that early on in the illness people may have a high degree of insight into what is happening (Balfour, 1995). This can be seen in the following extract from an exploratory interview conducted with Mr A, who was in the earlier stages of Alzheimer's Disease:

> "I need to feel better than I am, mind-wise. When it started to get me, I wouldn't believe it. It started when I was in the shed. I put a hammer down and wondered where it was gone. It wasn't clicking there [indicates head] like it ought to. When I went to remember where it was, there was a kind of blank".

In response to a question about what this feeling of blankness was like, he said:

> "It is nauseating really. My wife says, 'Stop and think a little while'. I say, 'It's stopping and thinking that's worrying me, because there ain't nothing coming back from the thinking'."

He then distanced himself from this, saying:

> "But normally I am quite OK. But there was a time when it seemed there was a blankness."

He went on to describe his experience as a child of having problems with his ear and being "poked about with". The doctors, however, couldn't actually do anything to help him. When I said that he might also be telling me about his experience now, he agreed and spoke of his distress, how nothing could be done, but he hoped that a cure would be found.

In recent years, there has been more research into the experience of dementia (Clare, 2004), and the current state of our knowledge suggests that at least in many cases, the early stages are characterized by an extremely painful awareness of the situation. What level of awareness may be retained as the disease progresses is unclear, and the prevailing view has been that, for many people, there will be a progress into "anosognosia" or lack of awareness. Recent studies indicate (Clare, 2004) that we need to think not just in terms of insight being present or absent, but, instead, of different levels of awareness. Disturbing states of mind, and unconscious fears or anxieties, will be experienced by individuals with dementia both early on in the illness, when fears may be more easily put into words, and also later, when communication may be operating at predominantly a nonverbal level. In this regard, the quality of caregiving—including the psychological as well as the physical dimensions of care—remains of crucial importance throughout, and this is explored in depth in the final part of the chapter.

Later-stage dementia

What is the lived experience in end-stage dementia? Richard Eyre, director of the National Theatre, wrote about his experience of his mother when she had Alzheimer's Disease:

> "The personality starts to disappear, and with it the humanity and soul, leaving as if in mockery only the body to breathe and be fed."
> [*The Times*, 3 June 1996, pp. 17]

This echoes the view that the earlier stages of dementia, associated with a painful beginning, are followed, as the disease advances, by the loss of awareness of what is happening to the self. In a guide for carers, published on the internet, a neurologist observed that the people in advanced stages of the illness did not appear to have any awareness of what was happening, commenting that at this point, "it is really the carers that [he] feels sorry for". Others, however, have written of the need to be careful about making assumptions about the absence of awareness in later-stage dementia, given the limits of our current knowledge and the risk of underestimating remaining capacities. Indeed, we may prefer to believe that there is no awareness left for the individual in such a state of neurological decline; to think otherwise may be too painful. However, it does seem that it is not a question so much of a linear progression, from awareness to unawareness, but more that people may move in and out of these states of mind, with recent research indicating that awareness may not be an all-or-nothing phenomenon (Phinney, 2002).

My interest in self-awareness and dementia started at an early point in my career after two incidents that took place while I was involved in therapeutic group work with people with dementia. In the first incident, I was observing a "reality-orientation" group, where three older men were being asked to take it in turns to turn over cards on which there was a picture of an everyday consumer item. The top of the table was taken up with piles of these cards, arranged according to which shop you would purchase them in. They had to decide which pile each card belonged to. One man turned over his card, hesitated, and clearly did not know where it belonged. He was aware of my presence as an observer and turned to me with an urbane "Noel Coward" expression, pulling a wry face. I had the inescapable conviction that this man knew that he didn't know. My impression was that he was most definitely aware of his cognitive difficulties. The second incident occurred when I took part as a visiting clinician in a group for people in the later stages of dementia, who were long-term residents in a large psychiatric hospital. The group was on a ward in the hospital, now long closed, known at the time as a "back ward". This term conveyed the hopelessness of the situation, the sense that these people had always been there and would never leave, living out of sight of the main hospital, "stowed out of conscience, as unpopular baggage" (Auden, 1968).

During the group, I found it difficult to endure the shouting and high-pitched screaming from most of the participants. It was difficult for anyone to be heard because of the disturbing noise, and the nurse who was running it was taken up mostly with trying to encourage people to stay long enough in their chairs for her to show them old pictures of London as a means of memory stimulation, which was the purpose of the group. Some members of the group were slumped in their chairs, while others were trying to get out of theirs. One woman in particular kept standing up and screaming, long piercing screams that grated on me and after a while made me feel irritated and angry, wishing I could make her be quiet. She seemed more energetic and stronger than other members of the group, and each time she was encouraged to sit down, she stood up again and screamed in a loud and forceful way. Feeling foolish to be offering what felt like a lame comment, I said to her, at a moment when she was standing up but had stopped to draw breath between her screams, that I thought she was very angry. She looked at me directly and seemed to take me in for the first time. Then she said, very clearly, "I feel frustrated, fucked up and far from home." Minutes later, she was screaming again and what speech there was seemed incoherent. This moment when she spoke clearly and looked at me so directly made an impact on me and has stayed with me over the years.

In order to explore this further, my research aimed to assess evidence of awareness in individuals across the range of disability, including people in the later stages of dementia (Balfour, 1995). I asked people with dementia to look at pictures from the Thematic Apperception Test (Murray, 1943) and then describe what they saw. The approach of using pictures to stimulate responses arose from initial difficulties that were encountered in asking people with dementia questions about their experience. While some responses were insightful and evocative, others tended either to be bland or else were very difficult to interpret. The use of pictures elicited responses even in those people who were in the advanced stages of dementia, provided that attention was paid to "snatches" of lucidity in otherwise disconnected narratives.

The responses featured a preoccupation with damage and disability when people in the advanced stage of dementia were shown a picture of a boy contemplating a violin on a table in front of him (a matched control group, who had no cognitive impairment, did not make reference to this theme):

—"There are tears in the violin. He is not very keen on the violin. He has probably been practising it and it hasn't gone quite right. . . . He's in despair over his violin."

—"He looks blind. There is something wrong with him. . . . I don't know whether he thinks at all, he is thinking about the violin and wishing for better health."

Many of these comments were contained within mostly incoherent material.

—"The violin is upside down, I think there is something wrong with it."

This was said by a woman who, according to the results of cognitive testing, was the most impaired of the group. Interestingly, it was interjected into almost wholly disconnected speech—most of what she had said had seemed to be entirely unrelated to the picture. Another woman, also at a later stage of dementia, commented:

—"It's a boy. He's got a violin. . . . He's gone deaf, very deaf. Gone very deaf. He is playing the violin, he's gone very deaf. . . . He's in despair over his violin, he can't get it to do the thing he wants. He's despondent about what he's been able to take in."

A further theme that emerged related to anger and withdrawal (defined as a retreat from the world, giving up on or disengaging from activities or other people in their responses to the pictures), as in the following:

> —"I think I would give up on the violin. I love music but I can't stand the squeely motions. . . . I should say he's fed up. He's had the violin and he finds it's not coming out with the tunes. . . . They're not how he wants them to be any more. . . . He's given up, or he wants to give up after finding he's not playing as he thinks he should."

Current perspectives

Historically, the question of what meaning can be accorded to the communication and behaviour of people with dementia as the disease progresses has been a central one. While in the past there had been little sustained interest in the experiences of people with dementia, this has begun to change in a striking way over the past decade. Previously, accounts of dementia emphasized the cognitive losses, particularly of memory and language, and this has been central to definition and diagnosis (Berrios, 1989). However, in recent years there has been a growing focus upon the wider picture, the "non-cognitive symptoms" (Berrios, 1989; Burns, 1990; Cheston & Bender, 1996). This has been associated with a developing interest in psychotherapeutic approaches to the care of people with dementia. Pioneers in this field (such as Bender, 2003; Gubrium, 1987; Kitwood, 1988, 1989, 1990a, 1990b; Lyman, 1989; Meacher, 1972; Miessen, 1993; Schmid, 1990) tended to base their contributions on a critique of the medical model of the dementias as diseases, with their own natural histories of inevitable decline. This reflects their view that organic factors have been emphasized to the neglect of psychological, and social ones, in the recent history of thinking in this area. Fertzinger (1988) echoes this position, describing a tendency towards what he calls a "monist" view of dementia, an emphasis upon diseased brain states and organic factors as the only points of relevance to our understanding of the disease.

These authors' point is a poignant one: that the individual's behaviour may be seen as simply symptomatic of disease stage, rather than as having meaning that might be understood. If the potential meaningfulness of the actions and experiences of individuals is neglected, then, they argue, there is a "death of meaning", which mirrors the end point of the dementing process. A man in the earlier stages of dementia commented: "The bit that hurts you really is that you know in your mind's eye that your are not a symptom, but in my actions I feel that I am, you know." This echoes the comments in the literature about the tendency to see disturbed behaviour as symptomatic, rather than having meaning. Kitwood (1997), whose work has had a profound influence, was interested in what he termed the "malignant social psychology" often surrounding the individual with dementia. He described how a premature foreclosure of meaning in the social and treatment context may, for the individual concerned, overlay and compound the disabling effects of the disease itself. Kitwood, whose work continues to be developed (Brooker, Edwards, & Benson, 2004), emphasized the importance of what he termed "person-centred" care for people with dementia, based upon psychotherapeutic principles

In taking a historical perspective we can see a pendulum swing from an overly-deterministic view of the role of organic factors and the neglect of psychological and social ones to a strong attack on the organic model and claims for the aetiological role of psychological and social factors. In the history of the care of people with dementia, there is a particular intensity to what is often a polarized issue in health care: the relative privileging of the mind or the body. Yet the close link between physical and psychological events, the mind and body, is particularly clear with older adults—confused states of mind can often follow disturbances in physical functioning, to take a commonly observed example. It can be difficult to carve out a space for the psychological, to think about the meaning of particular events, as well as attending to organic deterioration and social issues, recognizing that in dementia as in other areas of life it is important to attend to both external and internal realities. It is a struggle to maintain thinking about the internal world alongside the external and the physical, and the pressure can be to foreclose in one direction or another. The recent history of dementia reflects a reassertion of the importance of the person in the disease and presents a challenge to researchers and clinicians alike in the care and conceptualization of dementia.

Dementia: a psychoanalytic approach

What do psychoanalytic approaches have to offer in attempting to understand what may be going on internally for the person with dementia? The psychoanalytic approach emphasizes the importance of unconscious mental processes, with a developmental model of the mind linking early development to later life. It has sometimes been misunderstood as infantomorphic, which, of course, is not the case.

Psychoanalytic thinking does not reduce older adults to babies, but it does aim to help in understanding that some of the adverse reactions to the losses or changes associated with old age, in terms of the developmental issues specific to old age, will in part be determined by the individual's underlying psychological constellations.

Following on from Freud, the psychoanalyst Melanie Klein, writing in the 1930s and 1940s, offered a view of infantile development in which the baby is, from the earliest moments of life, involved in primitive modes of relating. Klein described two fundamental positions, two ways of being in the world. Developmentally, one precedes the other with a constant oscillation from one to another throughout life. They are essentially two different states of mind, each composed of a particular constellation of anxieties, defences, and other feelings. The first of these is the "paranoid–schizoid" position. Here, in response to primitive anxieties, the infantile mind creates various splits, the most important being between its own loving and aggressive impulses. The world is divided between idealized objects and bad ones that are felt to be persecuting and are located outside the self, in the object, often the mother. In this state of mind, there is a lack of capacity to experience loss as the absence of a good object; instead, there is felt to be a present bad object, responsible for the feelings of loss and frustration. The leading anxiety is with the survival of the self. The second position is called the depressive position where, when development proceeds normally, the infant moves to a more integrated state, in which objects are no longer experienced as all good or all bad, but as containing a more realistic mixture of qualities. There is the experience of love and hatred for the same person, leading to feelings of concern and remorse for the loved one, because of the realization that the object that is hated and attacked is also the loved object upon whom the individual depends. This leads to feelings of loss and guilt, which enables mourning to take place.

Development proceeds from the very early vulnerability of a tiny baby to greater autonomy and independence in younger adulthood, followed by a "return" in later life to similar situations faced in early life. Fortunately, for many people, the gradual "return" is not too traumatic. From a psychoanalytic perspective, the way in which this will be experienced will depend on the extent to which paranoid–schizoid or depressive anxieties are uppermost. If there have been early difficulties in facing depressive feelings, then there will be problems in facing loss later in life. If the depressive position has not been securely worked through, then unconsciously death will be viewed in terms of the persecutory anxieties of the paranoid–schizoid position (Jacques, 1965). In this state of mind, the fear of loss and loneliness may be experienced as the fear of being reduced to the level of a terrified, disorganized, and uncontained infant. Sometimes patients will describe this as, for example, falling into a black hole. The fear of loneliness can be a fear of being left alone with what are felt to be bad and unintegrated parts of the self. The "catastrophes" of old age, such as dementia, carry the threat of being abandoned to a state of utter helplessness, which may also at an unconscious level carry fears of a traumatic return to earlier states of dependency. How one manages such fears, or faces and tolerates such dependency, will depend on the internal legacy of earlier times. For the individual with dementia, the ego's resources and defences are progressively diminished and less available, and emotional difficulties such as depression, anxiety, and paranoid states may develop. In the later stages in particular, these may take a psychotic, delusional form. Our current understanding is that earlier problematic emotional constellations do not "grow old" in the sense of diminishing or fading away, but persist and become more powerful as dependency increases and adult coping falls away, "because the unconscious does not participate in the process of growing older" (Grotjahn, 1940). Miessen (1993) made a poignant observation in describing what he termed "parent fixation", whereby many people in the more advanced stages of dementia experience the delusion that their parents are alive. In a fictional account, Ian McEwan describes a man visiting his mother, in an institutional setting, who has dementia:

> [His mother, Lily, says] "I'm waiting to go home. I'm getting the bus."
> It pains him whenever she says that, even though he knows she's referring to her childhood home where she thinks her mother is waiting for her. . . . Lily says: "I was there last week . . . on the bus and my mum was in the garden. I said to her, You can walk down there, see what you're going to get and the next thing is the balancing of everything you've got. She's not well. Her feet. I'll go along there in a minute and I can't help losing her a jersey." How strange it would have been for Lily's mother, an aloof, unmaternal woman, to have known that the little girl at her skirts would one day, in a remote future, a science fiction date in the next century, talk of her all the time and long to be home with her. Would that have softened her? Now Lily is set, she'll talk for as long as he sits there. It's hard to tell if she's actually happy. Sometimes she laughs, at others she describes shadowy disputes and grievances, and her voice becomes indignant. . . . [McEwan, 2005]

At the other end of the lifespan, the infant's psychological legacy will, in part, be determined by the unresolved emotional issues of the parents, evocatively described as the presence of "ghosts in the nursery": "visitors from the unremembered pasts of the parents; the uninvited guests at the christening . . . the intruders . . . may break through . . . taking up residence in the nursery claiming tradition and rights of ownership" (Fraiberg, Adelson, & Shapiro, 1975). At the other end of life, in dementia, we see how there can be a breaking-through of earlier unresolved emotional constellations, appearing now as phantoms in the mind, the return of the long-ago-ghosts of the nursery. Current experience, even in the profound psychic disruptions of dementia, is shaped and coloured by earlier times, and even the unremembered past may now make its presence felt as "ghosts" in the care setting.

Clinical illustration: Work discussion group

A psychiatrist working in a multidisciplinary team described to members of the work discussion group a referral he'd received of a patient whom staff in a residential setting had been finding increasingly difficult to manage. This patient, Mrs Jones, had made a number of accusations about thefts from her room. Each time, there had been some investigation, but no evidence of any actual theft was found. In any case, staff were used to this: it was not an uncommon complaint from residents that things were going missing or being taken from them. On one occasion, she had become very distressed indeed, about the theft from her of a calendar. She also regularly complained that the TV and the remote control were not working properly. Staff would respond wearily to familiar complaints that they felt were to do with their resident's cognitive impairment, her loss of judgement and understanding.

When the psychiatrist found out more history, from colleagues who had also been involved in her care, he learnt about what had led to her residential placement. She had been seen by his colleagues, some months earlier, when she had complained about intruders who, she believed, had moved in to the upstairs part of her house. In fact, there was no upstairs in her house, which was a bungalow. But the psychiatrist was very affected by her conviction that there was. He found himself checking and then double-checking when he was outside the building, having to sort out for himself what was real and what was not. He temporarily lost his bearings. This can often be a confusing experience for staff, when they find that their own reality sense is being challenged or powerfully affected by close contact with such disturbed states of mind. For some time, Mrs Jones had not seemed to be too disturbed by this delusion, and she seemed to be managing at home. However, she said that she did not like their intrusive noise, and things had worsened for her when, she believed, the intruders had brought a little child to live with them, who cried in distress at night. One day, living at home, she had had a fall. She had lain on the floor for several hours before help came. When the doctor interviewed her, she had complained bitterly that these intruders, who she had tolerated for so long, had not offered her any help when she was on the floor and unable to get up or raise help. It was this incident that had led to her leaving her home and moving into residential care.

A little time before the development of her delusion about the "intruders" moving in, Mrs Jones had lost her husband of many years. He had looked after her at their home for some while following her diagnosis of dementia. What had been striking at the time was how she experienced his death. She became convinced that he was not dead at all: he was alive, but he was seeing another woman instead of her. Although the evidence was that he had been faithful to her throughout a long married life, her husband's absence was filled by a preoccupation that he was off having an affair. She expressed anger and betrayal—he was not gone but was actively withholding himself from her and excluding her by being with someone else. Instead of experiencing the loss as absence, it was filled with persecuting thoughts, to do with exclusion and betrayal, anxieties that may be linked to our earliest experiences, encountered in our first relationships. She remained for some time at home, living, as far as she was concerned, with "the intruders". After her fall, her concerned family felt that she was no longer able to live at home, and she was moved into residential care. It was, in many ways, a nice place, well equipped, and modern. But it was not her home. Without her familiar bearings, she seemed quickly to grow more confused. Waking up in the night, unsure of her surroundings, she tended to wander the corridors. In confusion and frustration, angry and lost, deserted by her familiar objects, both external and internal ones, she smashed things, possibly conveying the violent shattering of her internal world that she was experiencing. Wandering up and down, and pacing, is common in extreme states of grief or of agitation and loss. For her, an internal dislocation was met by the actual displacement of being moved out of a familiar environment. This is likely to be very important indeed, as her internal experience seems to have been of moving into states of unknowing and confusion and now her external environment, known for so many years, had gone too. External reality overlapped internal experience in such a way as to dramatically throw her capacity to find any bearings. Shortly after her admission, she again had a fall.

We can only guess at what the experience was like for this woman, whose ego functioning (i.e. the executive functioning of the mind, to do with memory, perception, judgement) was diminished, whose conscious sense of time passing, of knowing that certain predictable things happen at predictable times and could be anticipated, was lost. Although her family visited every Saturday, she complained bitterly that she was completely abandoned and left alone. Lacking fixed reference points, the knowledge about a future visit to hold on to, she seemed to experience a sense of endless, timeless, abandonment, left alone in unbearable states of mind with little internal or external support.

Are Mrs Jones's complaints and delusional beliefs to be seen only as the product of a diseased mind, and symptomatic only of organic deterioration? A psychoanalytic approach would suggest otherwise. In thinking about her internal experience, the work discussion group and her psychiatrist started to digest and make sense of that which could not be articulated at a conscious level. Her husband's death seems to have been linked to a further breakdown in her capacities, with the development of her delusional beliefs about a cohabiting intruder, living "upstairs". This may convey the breaking through "upstairs", in her mind, of intrusive and disturbing thoughts. The situation became even more intolerable for her when she felt she was confronted by the intruders' distressed young child, which might express the distressed infantile part of her, now breaking through. The trauma of her fall, and the experience of lying on the ground without help for some time, was vividly conveyed in her sense of abandonment: her bitter complaint that the intruders who lived in the house did nothing to help her. In terms of her internal experience, she made it clear that she has been abandoned by good and helpful internal figures and left in the hands of bad and persecuting ones responsible for the experience of loss and trauma.

For Mrs Jones, the loss of her husband did not appear to be experienced in terms of a sense of loss and mourning, but in a state of mind where she feels herself to be in the presence of an alive, persecuting object. The delusion that he is still alive, but betraying her with another woman, might be seen as reflective of unresolved early oedipal infantile emotional struggles to tolerate exclusion from the separate relationship of the parental couple, underlying difficulties that re-emerge as her adult cognitive capacities desert her (Waddell, 1998). In this way, her mental and physical deterioration seems to return her to earlier problematic emotional constellations, which may increasingly dominate her mind. Once in the residential home, Mrs Jones wandered about at night-time, occasionally smashing things. At such times, relatives felt that she was a long way from being the shy and sensitive woman, concerned to behave politely, that she had always been. Her accusations of theft of money and of her calendar, and complaints about the non-functioning TV, resulted in a lot of staff activity, in having to check that things had not in reality been stolen. She conveyed that what internally gave her a sense of order, symbolized by the loss of her calendar, had gone, as one capacity after another was lost. Accusations of theft were not unusual in this setting, and the staff were weary and frustrated at hearing them again and again. Just as the psychiatrist had been able to think about Mrs Jones in the work discussion group, so, over time, he was able to think with the staff team about the meaning of Mrs Jones's accusations. It became clear that these were not simply the misguided complaints of someone whose cognitive impairments made them unable to judge what was happening. Staff came to understand that the accusations conveyed how one capacity after another was being lost and how persecutory this was. Mrs Jones seemed to indicate that parts of herself, of her functioning mind, were being stolen from her and that she was left, like the TV, not working properly.

The more a mind is lost, the more it falls to the carers of people with dementia to provide a thinking mind, a container for their increasingly fragmented experience. Here there is an ongoing task: "[to] struggle to translate and make sense of the individual's distressed and at times bizarre communications, often conveyed through projective identification, which tends to replace ordinary language" (Davenhill, chapter 12). Increasingly the carer becomes the witness: the mind whose capacity to think and register what is happening to the person with dementia when his or her own capacities are progressively eroded is ever more crucial.

Waddell (1998) points out that windows of clarity, of a briefly more integrated state, may be opened for the person with dementia when emotional contact is made through finding some way, in words or action, of conveying that understanding. Weiner (1988) asks, "Does tuning in to the patient's innermost world . . . lead to a stronger sense of self? Conversely, does tuning out lead to further confusion?"

The concept of containment is important in thinking about how to respond to the attachment needs of the individual with dementia. Miessen (1993), in a series of large-scale studies, reports a high incidence of attachment-seeking behaviour in people across the range of early- to later-stage dementia. In brief, he drew on Bowlby's theory of attachment and conceptualizes the disease process as instigating a situation where it is difficult for the individual to have a secure base/ sense of attachment because links to external and internal objects are disrupted by the disease process. Miessen's studies used a version of the "strange situation" paradigm, from infancy research, to study the attachment or "proximity seeking" behaviour in old people with dementia.[1] His studies indicate the importance of understanding the attachment losses of people with dementia and the insecurity felt by such people as their links to others are progressively more threatened by the disease process. In this sense, Alzheimer's Disease is seen as a "strange situation" that keeps getting stranger.

Cheston and Bender (1996) emphasize the need for innovative practice to attend to the attachment needs of older people with dementia. There have been attempts to address these needs— for example, by giving something concretely, like the carer's voice on a tape recorder, to reassure the person with dementia (Woods & Ashley, 1995). One major innovation in terms of thinking about how to respond to such attachment needs in the caregiving situation would be to use the important link with psychoanalytic research into the other end of the lifespan to influence policy and practice. Research into infant attachment finds that the strength of the bond between the infant and their carers is linked to parental sensitivity to, and understanding of, the infant's mental world. The infant needs to encounter a mind, a mindfulness of its own internal state, in its primary caregivers: "it is not gratification of need that is at the heart of bonding, rather, it is the caregiver's capacity to create in her mind the infant's mental state" (Fonagy, Steele, Moran, Steele, & Higgitt, 1993). If we transpose this to the latter part of the lifespan, this has profound implications for our understanding of the challenges facing the carers of the individual with dementia, the difficulties of the task they face, and what supports may be needed to survive an experience that does not contain the hope of the carer—cared-for relationship in early life. At the beginning of life, the "cared-for" infant will grow and eventually become independent of the carer, whereas, for the person who is older with dementia and his or her carer, the opposite is the case.

Caring for the person with dementia within a couple or family setting

The care of the person with dementia is frequently carried out by a family member, unseen and often unacknowledged. There are six million carers in the UK looking after someone who is ill or disabled, one million of whom provide fifty or more hours a week of care. Many of these are husbands or wives.

In chapter 5, on couples psychotherapy, we saw the way in which in a relatively healthy adult relationship where projections are not fixed but fluid, partners may be able to act as containers of difficult feeling for one another in a flexible way. In a relationship where one partner has a dementia, the burden will increasingly shift to the partner without dementia to act as container for the other:

> "For my mother, the losses of Alzheimer's both amplified and reversed long-standing patterns in her marriage. My father had always refused to open himself to her, and now increasingly, he couldn't open himself . . . living with a man who mistook her for her mother, forgot every fact he had ever known about her and finally ceased to speak her name. He who had always insisted on being the boss in the marriage, the maker of decisions, the adult protector of the childlike wife, couldn't help behaving like the child. . . . Task by task, she slowly took over their life." [Jonathan Franzen, *The Guardian*, 15 December 2001]

If we are mindful of the tremendous challenge that this can present, then a focus of attention has to be given to the importance of the state of mind of the carer and to the need for support and containment. Carers may have all kinds of feelings towards the individual with dementia in their care. As well as compassion or concern, there may also be feelings of disgust or revulsion, resentment or hatred. Such feelings can arouse tremendous guilt or anxiety.

This is conveyed vividly in the responses made by carers when asked to tell the story that they thought might underlie a picture, presented to them from the Thematic Apperception Test, which showed a man in a chair and a woman standing nearby (Balfour, 1993). When asked to describe the picture, one man said:

"She's looking for the door and sees that her husband is slumped in the chair and to all intents and purposes has departed this world. She is just dusting and thinking, 'a woman's lot is never done'. I can endorse that, having had to do everything for my wife for a couple of years."

A woman whose husband was in the later stages of dementia said:

"Her husband has been an invalid for the last four years and she's nursed him for three years and he's been dead for three years. This is the first man since to ask her to marry him. She is not sure about another commitment that may turn out to be a burden in years to come. Or else she just said, 'I've been married for thirty years, and I've just got fed up and put arsenic in your tea' [claps hands]."

Another woman, whose husband with dementia had recently had a fall, commented:

"I don't know if someone is ill—possibly she's afraid or shocked because of what she's seen. It could be someone is ill on the floor. It is an illness or something. I think she will end up very shaken. And if she has seen something which upset her, she won't forget it."

Research and clinical evidence indicate how important are the environment of caregiving and the relational world of the individual with dementia (Clare & Shakespeare, 2004; Pratt & Wilkinson, 2003). There is evidence that the maintenance of the person with dementia in the community has more to do with the attitudes and well-being of the spouse-carer than factors such as severity of the disease itself. Indeed, the tremendous importance of the quality of the caregiving relationship is underscored by the finding that low levels of interaction between the partners in the marriages of people with dementia predict the move to hospital care, even the mortality of the individual with dementia two years later (Wright, 1991, 1994). This has powerful implications, and it shows the clinical significance of work that aims to support and provide containment for carers. What else does research in this area have to tell us?

In 1858 William Farr of the English General Registrar's Office wrote: "if unmarried people suffer from disease in undue proportion, the have-been-married suffer still more. . . . Marriage is a healthy estate." Murphy, Glaser, and Grundy (1997) find evidence, more than a century later, to support this association between marriage and better health. However, for spouses of people with Alzheimer's Disease dementia, marriage seems to be an "unhealthy estate" associated with chronic stress and difficulty. Fengler and Goodrich (1979) described such spouses as "hidden patients". Of all caregivers, it is the spouses of people with dementia who are shown to be the most at-risk group (Cantor, 1983; Morris, Morris, & Britton, 1988a. 1988b). Loss of intimacy is associated with spouse-carer depression (Morris, Morris, & Britton, 1988a, 1998b), and studies have found that a central difficulty for such spouses is in the area of their emotional experience, rather than other, more practical issues. Those most at risk are those who have had the poorest relationships premorbidly, as might be expected, but also those who have experienced the greatest sense of loss of intimacy as a consequence of the disease (Morris, Morris, & Britton, 1998b). The spouse's experience of a loss of understanding of the partner with dementia may be one factor in the loss of intimacy. In a study of the experiences of spouse-carers, Bull (1998) comments that "the feeling of the loss of the partner is associated with the loss of sharing or interaction with the partner. Some carers expressed this loss of communication as: 'if only I knew what he/she was thinking'." Another study describes the carer's experience of feeling out of touch with his or her partner's experience: "Some people talked of their frustration, guilt and feelings of inadequacy at not being able to understand their spouse's interactions" (Lewis, 1998).

Overall, therefore, research indicates that the quality of the relationship, particularly the level of intimacy that can be maintained, is associated with the level of emotional strain experienced by the caregiver, which is itself associated with outcomes such as the move to institutional care and even the death of the partner with dementia. It is striking that research highlights the overriding importance of the emotional impact on the caregiver of looking after the spouse, as well as the importance of the intimacy of the relationship. The experience of loss of understanding of his or her partner is very difficult for the carer, as is the sense that the partner does not have awareness or insight into the situation. Woods, Phibbs, and Steele (2000) found in their study of stressed carers, for example, that as a way of coping they were more likely to depersonalize the individual that they were looking after.

Using the concept of projective identification, we might recognize how difficult the task of sustaining emotional contact can be under such circumstances. Having emotional contact with fragmented experience is very difficult, and it is understandable that carers with little support may be less able to tolerate emotional contact with the person with dementia. The importance of trying to provide this cannot any more be ignored when there is clear research evidence indicating that whether people with dementia go into institutional care or not (and even how long they live) is linked quite specifically to the quality of the relationship with carers, which is itself affected by factors such as carer strain. In a recent article, this was expressed clearly by a residential careworker in the Midlands: "The only way someone with dementia gets one-to-one care is if they are at home, and looking after someone with dementia 24 hours a day is a killer. I know many cases in which the care caused the deaths of the partners" (McFadyean, 2005).

While there is a great deal of publicity now in terms of the needs of mothers with newborn babies for help and support early on in combating postnatal depression, there is relatively little media interest in the needs of the caring relationship at the other end of the lifespan. In the situation of caring for someone with dementia, this might be informal support from the wider family or social network, or formal support from statutory services. The key issue here is the recognition of the importance of the relationship between the person with dementia and his or her carer. The "unit of care" may be the husband with a wife with dementia, or the son or daughter with a parent, or other family members. In the interview with Mr A, that I described earlier, he went on to convey the importance for him of the containing function of the relationship with his wife. During the interview, while expressing his fears of what it meant that he now attended the "nut hatch" (the local day hospital, situated in a psychiatric hospital), he expressed his sense that his family might lose him:

> "I said to my missus, I am going to the 'nut hatch'—you are going to lose me."
>
> She cried her eyes out and said, "Don't talk like that."

He conveyed his need of his wife. Her role in serving as a memory aid, as a reassurance of his continuance and maintenance of identity, was eloquently expressed by him. For example:

"My wife will come back with what I've lost . . . then I'll carry on because I know I musn't let it get hold of me. . . . I've got a good wife, and she's a good thinker for me. I feel dodgy sometimes that I should be like I am, that she has to suffer, but she says, "I don't suffer you, you are the same old C_____ that I married years ago", she says,

"You're the same one . . . well that helps me."

When thinking about the enormous emotional and physical demands within the caring relationship, it is remarkable that care of great quality does go on; many caring relationships survive for a long time, enabling the person with dementia to remain out of institutional care and in his or her familiar environment for considerable time. This area is extremely important in terms of thinking of the future demands likely to be faced in increasing numbers by older couples and families. In the work of Bowlby (1969, 1973); Robertson and Robertson (1967–1971); Menzies (1973), and others on the care of children in institutional settings, the publication of their findings of the attachment needs of children in these circumstances led to a sea change of attitudes. There was a new perception that the "unit of care" was no longer the child in isolation, but the child and his or her mother or the family with its child patient, accompanied by a clear move in health and social policy based on psychological research that they should be cared for together, and as a whole. This has clear implications for a similar shift at the other end of life, where one of the most crucial "units of care" may be the couple where one partner has a dementia, or the family who are looking after someone with dementia.

Organizational consultation to a staff team caring for people with dementia

From thinking about informal, family carers, I now move on to consider the role of consultation in the professional care setting. Health and social care professionals who work with frail older people with dementia often, when given the opportunity to do so, convey the depth of the pain of their work and ambivalence of their feelings. These feelings, in turn, can arouse anxiety. In order for the environment of caregiving to be a containing one, staff carers themselves need containment. There is a growing body of literature supporting the value of psychotherapeutic approaches to service-level interventions with staff working with people with dementia (Arden, Garner, & Porter, 1998; Ashburner, Meyer, Johnson, & Smith, 2004; Davenhill, 1998; Holman & Jackson, 2001; Stern & Lovestone, 2000; Terry, 1997). The negative consequences of inadequate containment and support for carers can be seen particularly clearly in the case of the institutional setting. What are staff in such situations facing? Individuals with dementia at the more advanced stages are less able to communicate with language. They are also more likely to be in residential care than those in the earlier stages. Staff in contact with them are faced with patients whose capacities to express themselves verbally are fading and whose inner states are increasingly conveyed through projective processes. An account by the poet Tony Harrison that appeared in the *Guardian* newspaper some time ago, describing a visit to a day hospital for people with dementia, conveys something of the quality of the anxiety of close contact with such frailty and diminished capacities:

> "You recoil at their clutching, momentarily in ignorant fear that somehow it might transfer their terrible confusion to you. You fear too that their disabled personality might be so fragile that a false move, the wrong physical contact, could make what little control they have disintegrate before you, creating some horrendous embarrassment." [Tony Harrison, *The Guardian*, 14 April 1993]

In a consultation with a staff supervision group in a hospital setting, staff started to describe to me a difficult experience where there had been an investigation after a patient had "wandered" off the unit at night-time and was missing for 24 hours before he was found. This had been a traumatic experience for them, and they had spent an anxious day or so, waiting for news. The ensuing investigation started to have the atmosphere of a witch-hunt, as an initial mood of guilt and concern seemed to give way to a culture of blame. The case discussion group, which involved a large, multidisciplinary group of staff, became increasingly heated. The staff group were normally very thoughtful, but accusations began to fly, with comments to the effect that there were some staff who were too negligent, who did not really bother themselves with patients. Before long, there were similar comments, to the effect that others in the team were too intrusive or controlling of patients. These accusations were not exactly personal, insofar as individuals did not name other individuals. Initially, in fact, the targets of the comments were unclear. and they were kept as more or less impersonal observations. Gradually, however, it was "nursing staff" who behaved in this way, or "care managers" or "doctors" who behaved in that way. Soon, it became clear that it was the different professional groups who became the identified targets. At one point, there was a comment that a patient had been virtually "strapped down" to keep him or her quiet; at other points, staff were said to be too busy and so were neglectful of the patients. One person commented that some staff were too busy ever to think about the minds of their patients. As the consultant to the group, I felt similarly "strapped down", metaphorically speaking, constrained in terms of what could freely be put into words, and I found it very difficult to think. Complaints were also made about the "mayhem" that periodically erupted on the ward.

Later on, after the meeting, I became interested in their use of this word "mayhem", and I looked it up. Among other definitions, *Collins Dictionary* offers, "violent maiming". This seemed to convey the violent attack upon psychic movement, on freedom of thought, the "maiming" of the capacity to think and reflect in this atmosphere. Within the group, I had started to feel increasingly hopeless about making any improvement in what was happening in the room, as every avenue seemed to be shot down. After a while, it did become possible to think about whether these were some of the feelings that were difficult to face, feelings of hopelessness in the staff group, the sense that whatever they did, made little difference. In terms of repair, or cure for their patients, the situation was indeed hopeless. Often, their own feelings were turned away from, and projected into the "mindless" organization they claimed to work in, which they often attacked in this way. They described the tremendous painfulness of the work, that good work often meant helping people to die. There was the sense of their potentially being overwhelmed by something deathly, reflected in the "dying institution, decaying NHS", which they often referred to: "people come here to die . . . it's a death sentence. They come in alive and they leave, dead."

The staff conveyed the sense that if they found words for their feelings, there was a fear of what would emerge, particularly if this entailed negative feelings rather than compassionate ones. We may be drawn to this area of work in part because of an internal, unconscious motivation to repair damage. In situations where there is no hope of cure, and where the situation is one of progressive deterioration, as in dementia, the failure of such reparative wishes may be hard to bear. The primitive, persecutory guilt that can be felt by staff in such circumstances is very powerful and can be projected around the system. The persecutory elements of their experience were split off and projected into different, rival professional groups. The other groups then became the lodging point for feelings that were unbearable for individual staff members to know about in themselves. One of the consequences was that staff showed an increasing division of labour, at a point where there was a need for more integration within the service and a preoccupation with disputes within the multiprofessional team over issues of role and identity. In such conditions, the emotional atmosphere of the care setting became one of schism and fragmentation, at worst a malignant mirroring of the internal fragmentation of the individuals with dementia in their care.

Two particular features of the descriptions of life on the unit stood out: the "mayhem" that periodically erupted, which was linked to the "too-busy-ness" of the staff to think about the minds of their patients. This can often be observed in the defences utilized by professionals dealing with people experiencing such profound loss: a maiming of the capacity to think, and a retreat into "busy-ness", which avoids a direct contact with such disturbed states of mind. If we consider the level of anxiety that may be felt by such patients, and projected into the professionals involved, it is possible to see how it may lead to fragmentation of thinking in them—mayhem, so to speak—and strongly negative feelings may be felt towards those in their care. If this is not contained, if professionals do not have a forum for thinking about such experience, then important sources of information about the patients' state of mind may be neglected and there is the danger that such feelings may be acted out by staff, with all the risks that go along with this. Staff can find themselves acting in ways that echo the difficulties of their patients. In this way, the emotional world of older people with dementia can "infect" those around them, creating a parallel emotional process that, particularly in less contained settings, may be mirrored and enacted by staff.

The question of what happens to our capacity to bear witness when faced with such states of disturbance and deterioration in our patients runs through this chapter. None of us is immune in such circumstances from the difficulty of maintaining an emotional engagement and a capacity to think. For the carer of the person with dementia, there is a constant struggle to hold on to a reflective position in the work, when thinking about the meaning of one's experiences can so often seem to be swimming against the tide.

I have described the contribution that psychoanalytic thinking can make for different "units of care" in attempting to understand some of the anxieties and states of mind of the individual with dementia, the carer, and the wider unit of the professional caregiving team in organizational settings. I have tried to show how important, at all of these levels, such attempts at understanding are when the internal situation of the individual with dementia is an inexorable move towards progressive loss of understanding. This is profoundly painful to witness, and the challenges facing carers in maintaining an emotional availability in such circumstances cannot be underestimated. Both clinical experience and research indicate the crucial importance of "containing the container": the importance of providing the opportunity for carers to process and think about their experience, in order that they are, in turn, helped to take in and think about the experience of those in their care.

Note

1. The "strange situation" (Ainsworth & Witting, 1969) assesses the security of mother–infant attachment through the infant's reactions towards the mother during a series of brief separations and reunions. Miessen's (1993) "strange visiting procedure" aims to facilitate the exploration of attachment behaviour of people with dementia, under similarly controlled conditions.

CHAPTER 14

The pink ribbon

A. S. Byatt

He held the mass of hair—long, coarse, iron-grey—over his left hand, and brushed it firmly and vigorously with his right. It was greasy to the touch, despite the effort he and Mrs. Bright had put into washing it. He used an old-fashioned brush, with black bristles in a soft, coral-coloured rubber pad, in a lacquered black frame. He brushed and brushed. Mrs. Bright's black face smiled approval. Mrs. Bright would have liked him to call her Deanna, which was her name, but he could not. It would have showed a lack of respect, and he respected and needed Mrs. Bright. And the name had inappropriate associations, nothing to do with a massively overweight Jamaican home help. He separated the hair deftly into three strips. Mrs. Bright remarked, as she frequently remarked, that it was very *strong* hair, it must have been lovely when Mado was young. "Maddy Mad Mado," said the person in the wing-chair in a kind of growl. She was staring at the television screen, which was dead and grey and sprinkled with dust particles. Her face was dimly reflected in it, a heavy grey face with an angry mouth and dark eye-caverns. James began to plait the hair, pulling it tightly into a long serpent. He said, as he often said, that hairs thickened with age, they got stronger. Hairs in the nostrils, hairs on the heavy chin, grasses on a rock-face.

Mrs. Bright, who knew the answer, asked what colour it had been, and was told that it had been fine, and coal-black. Blacker than yours, said James Ennis to Deanna Bright. Black as night. He combed and twisted. So deft he was, for a man, indeed for anyone, said Mrs. Bright. I was trained to do for myself, said James. In the Air Force, in the War. He came to the tail of the plait, and twisted an elastic band round it, three times. The woman in the chair winced and wriggled. James patted her shoulder. She was wearing a towelling gown, pinned at the neck with a nappy-pin for safety. It was white, which, although it showed every mark, was convenient to boil, in case of accidents, which happened constantly, of every description.

Mrs. Bright watched James with approval, as he came to the end of the hair dressing. The pinning up of the fat coil, the precise insertion of thick steel hair-pins. And finally, the attachment of the crisp pink ribbon. A really pretty pink ribbon. A sweet colour, fresh. A lovely colour, she said, as she always said.

"Yes," said James.

"You are a real kind man," said Deanna Bright. The person in the chair plucked at the ribbon.

"No, love," said Deanna Bright. "Have this." She handed her a silk scarf, which Mado fingered dubiously. "They like to touch soft things. I give a lot of them soft toys. They take comfort in them. Some folk will tell you it's because they're in their second childhood, but that's not it. This is an end not a beginning, best to keep things straight. But it calms them to hold on, to stroke, to touch, isn't it?"

This was the day when Mrs. Bright took over whilst James "slipped out" to go to the library and do a little personal shopping. They took care to "settle" Mado before he left. James turned the television on, to distract her gaze and cover the sound of the door opening and shutting. There was a picture of childish flower-drawings and regulated grassy hummocks. There was smiley music. There were portly coloured creatures, purple, green, yellow, scarlet, titupping and trotting. Look at the little fairies and elves, said James, more or less without expression. "Burr," said mad Mado, and then suddenly clearly, in a human voice, "They try to get her to dance, but she won't." "Look, there's a scooter," James persisted.

Mrs. Bright said, "Where does she wander, I ask myself."

"Nowhere," said James. "She sits here. Except when she tries to get out. When she rattles the door."

"We are all raised in glory," said Deanna Bright. "When she's raised, she'll be a singing soul. So where is she wandering now?"

"Her poor brain is a mass of thick plaques and tangles of meaning-less stuff. Like moth-eaten knitting. There's no one there, Mrs. Bright. Or not much of anyone."

"They took her into a dark a dark darkness and lost her," said Mado.

"Took who, dear?"

"They don't know", said Mado vaguely. "Not much they don't."

"Who's 'they'?"

"Who's they," Mado repeated dully.

"It's no good," said James. "She doesn't know the meaning of words."

"You have to keep trying," said Deanna Bright. "Go out now, Mr. Ennis, now she's watching them. I'll put her lunch together while you're gone."

He went out, carrying his red shopping-bag, and once he was in the street he straightened his back, as he always did, breathing the outside air in great gulps, like a man who has been suffocating or drowning. He walked down streets of identical grey houses to the High Street, waited for his pension in the Post Office, bought sausages, mince and a small chicken in the butcher's and vegetables from the amiable Turk on the corner. These were the people he talked to, the blood-stained butcher, the soft-voiced greengrocer, but never for long, for Mrs. Bright's time was ticking away. They asked after his wife and he said she was as well as could be expected. She was full of life, al-ways one for a joke, said the butcher, recalling someone James barely remembered and could not mourn. A kind lady, said the Turk. Yes, said James, as he always did when he didn't want to argue. He would have liked to go into the bookshop, but there was no time, since he needed to go to Boots, and get his prescriptions, and hers. Things to calm two people whose calm lives were a form of frenzy.

She used to do their shopping. She was the one who went out, as she was the one who had a network of friends and acquaintances, some of them known to him, many of them not. She had not liked to tell him—no, she had liked not to tell him—where she was going or for how long. He hadn't minded. He was good company for himself. Then one day a stranger had knocked at his door and shepherded his wife into the room, saying that he had found her wandering, that she had seemed to be lost. She was recovered by then, she threw her head back and shrilled with laughter. "Just think, James, I had got so *abstracted*, I'd gone back to Mecklenburgh Square, as if we'd just been out on one of our little outings to survey the damage, after the, after the—" "After the bombing," said James.

"Yes," she said. "But there was no smoke without fire this time."

"I think she needs a nice cup of tea," said the friendly stranger. It was a moment when James could have *known*, and he had chosen not to. She had always been eccentric.

The queue for prescriptions in Boots was long, and he was sent away for twenty minutes—not long enough for the bookshop, long enough to impinge on Deanna Bright. He wandered around the shop, an old man with a shock of white hair, in a crumpled macintosh. He didn't want to stop near the nursing counter, and found himself aimlessly and unexpectedly in the baby department, amongst different packets of pads and animal-headed toothbrushes. There was a high, shining chrome gibbet hung with the plump, staggering television dolls, purple, green, yellow and red, smiling with black eyes and dark mouths in puppet-mask faces. They were all encased in suffocating polythene. They can't breathe in there, James caught himself thinking, but this was not a sign of madness, no, but a sign of super-sanity, for he had been brooding, as anyone in his position occasionally must brood, he supposed, on what could be done, swiftly, with a plastic bag. They looked benign and inane. He came closer, checking his watch, and read their names, Tinky-Wink, Dipsy, Laa-Laa and Po. They had greyish shiny screens pinned on their round bellies, and antennae on their hooded heads. A symbiosis of a television and a one-year-old infant. Ingenious, after all,

The woman behind the counter—busty, hennaed, bespectacled, smiley—said the Teletubbies were very popular, very popular. "They really *love* them." Could she show him one?

"Why not?" said James.

She took Tinky-Wink and Po out of their shimmery sheaths and pressed their little bellies briskly, which caused them to chirp meaningless little songs. "They each have their own, you know, their signature song, easy to remember, for very little kids. They like remembering things, they like to hear them over and over."

"Do they?" said James vaguely.

"Oh yes. And look how soft they are, and made of sensible towelling, you can get them really clean in a washing machine in no time, if there's any sort of an accident. Durable, they are."

He had a vision of ragged bodies flailing, in a spin cycle. Not the circles of Heaven and Purgatory and Hell, but rag dolls flailing in a spin cycle.

"I'll take one."

"Which one would you like? Is it for a little girl or a little boy? A grandchild? Tinky-Wink is a boy—even though he has a handbag—and so is Dipsy. Laa-Laa and Po are girls. You can't *see* the difference of course. Is it a grandson or granddaughter?"

"No," said James. He said. "I don't have children. It's for someone else. I'll take the green one. It's a slightly bilious green and the name's appropriate."

Dipsy was detached from his meat-hook and an identical Dipsy slid into view from behind him.

"Shall I gift-wrap him, sir?"

"Yes", said James. That would precisely exhaust the twenty minutes.

They had waited to start the child, until the War was over. And then, after the War, when he had been demobbed, and gone back to teaching classics to schoolboys, the conjured child had refused to enter the circle. It had had names—Camilla, Julius, when they were romantic, Blob and Tiny Tim when they were upset or annoyed. It answered to no name, it refused to be. Hitler took it, she used to say. He shook the parcel, covered with woolly lambs on a flue field. "Dipsy," he said to it. "Dipsy fits the case, we're all dipsy." He wondered if he had been talking aloud in Boots. He looked around. No one was staring. Probably he had not.

He always had to stiffen himself against opening his own front door. He was a self-disciplined man, who had been a good teacher, and a good officer in the Air Force, partly because he was equable. He believed, in a classical way, in good temper and reason. He knew that he himself was a vessel of seething rage, against fate, against age, against, God help him (but there was no God) mad Mado himself, who was not *responsible* for his plight, or for hers, though she felt her own baffled bad temper from time to time, and was ready to blame him. He did not want to go into that captivity, with its sick smell and its lurching violence. As he always did, he took out his keys and let himself in. He even found a grim little smile for Deanna Bright.

Mrs. Bright had given Mado her lunch—spooned soup, fingers of toast, a supermarket custard in a plastic cup. Mado fought being fed, but enough went down, Mrs. Bright said. Before Mrs. Bright, he had left Mado little meals in the fridge. This had ceased when he came home and found her at the table with a meal she had put together. In consisted of a conical heap of ground coffee and a puddle of damp flour, which she was attempting to spoon up with a dry avocado stone. He was still intellectually curious enough at that stage to wonder whether the form of the stone had recalled some primitive memory of the shape of a spoon.

"No, dear," he had said. "That won't do, that's all wrong." And she had struck at him with the pointed end, bruising his cheek, and had swept coffee, flour, and plate, away onto the carpet. This then, was a tale of strangeness he could just about tell to a friend in a pub. It had an aesthetic horror to it that was pleasing. He was past that now, there was nothing left in him that wanted to tell anything to anyone, in a pub of anywhere else.

"How has she been?" he asked Deanna Bright.

"Not difficult. Complaining a bit about too many visitors."

"Ah," said James. He tried a joke. "I wish I knew who they were. I could do with someone to talk to."

"She says they're spies. She says she sent them out on mission and they pretended to have been killed, but secretly they have got back."

"Spies," said James.

Deanna Bright's face was alive with pity and concern.

"It's surprising how many of them talk about spies, and secret services, and that. I suppose they get distrustful."

"She did send out spies, in the War," said James. "She was in the Intelligence Service. She sent them out to France and Norway and Holland, in boats and parachutes. Most of them didn't come back."

"They hid," said Mado loudly. "They are angry, they mean bad, they mean danger, they want—"

"They want?" said Deanna.

"Lamb cutlets," said mad Mado. "Cold cutlets. Very cold with sauce."

"She means revenge," said James. "A dish best eaten cold. It's somehow encouraging, when there's any sort of a meaning. They might well want revenge."

Deanna Bright looked doubtful, possibly not knowing the saying, possibly doubting Mado's power to make sophisticated connections. She had once spoken sternly to James when he had referred to the woman in the chair as a zombie. "You don't know what you're saying," she said. "You don't *know* that word. She's a poor creature and a wandering soul. Not one of them."

Now, she crammed her woolly hat onto her springing hair, and set off to help other fraying souls and bodies.

When James was alone, alone that was with mad Mado, he unwrapped Dipsy and handed it mutely to her. She snatched at the doll, held it up, and stared at its mild little face, turned it over on her knee and fingered the towelling. She said, "They are waiting for us. We're late. We have to get to the clinic. Or maybe it's the cobbler. Sasha hasn't come *again*. They queued half the day for a bit of pork belly.

Her strong fingers kneaded the doll.

"They wired all the upstairs. They lie there and listen in and make dirty jokes. Sasha thinks it's funny.

At the very beginning he had found the sudden presence of invisible people both grotesque and fascinating. He had been married to a woman—met at university in 1939—who spoke like a radio announcer and never mentioned her family. They had married quickly—he was going into battle, they might either of them be cut off tomorrow—and she had said she had no close family, she was an independent orphan, two of their fellow students as witnesses would do for the wedding party. When her wits wandered now the staircases and cupboards filled up with people, people to be accused and berated, pleaded with and conciliated, people who threatened. To some of these she spoke in a rough Cockney voice, shrill and childish, "don't hit me any more, Ma, I'll be good, I wasn't bad, *don't*, Ma, *don't*." Never much more information. When he asked questions about her mother, she said, "I'm an orphan, I *said*." Then there was Sasha, an undependable friend, of whose existence, past or present, he knew nothing, except that she and Mado were "blood-sisters, you know, we cut our wrists and rubbed it in, rubbed it in, *mingled* the blood, Sasha is the only one and she keeps hiding—" And then there were the wartime ghosts who walked again. Friends bombed in their sleep, friends shot down over Germany, men and women sent out on missions—"Come in Akela, Akela come in—" the old voice beseeched, cracking. He himself was many people. He was Robin Binson, who he had always thought was her lover in 1942, Robin darling, give us a fag, let's try to forget it all. That to him, James, had been what she said lying naked on the counterpane, as the bombs fell. Let's try to forget it all. She had forgotten it all, and it all flew about in threads and fragments.

Before the invisible people, there had been bouts of fear connected with shadowy or inauspicious aspects of the visible. Her own face in a mirror, seen through a doorway, who's *that*, I don't want her here, she means no good. Involuntary cringing before her shadow or his, cast on walls, or shop-windows, in the days when they still went out. And there had been the endless agitated chatter about Intelligence. It was a word, he reflected in his solitude, in the presence of absence, which had always meant a lot to her. At University it had been her highest term of praise. She knows a lot, she works, but she hasn't got the essence of the thing, she's not *intelligent*. Or "I like Des. He's quick. He's *intelligent*," as though the word was interchangeable with "sexy." Which for her it was, perhaps. They had both been going to be schoolteachers, until the war came. He was a classicist, she had read French and German. When they married she had had to give up the idea of teaching, because married women were not allowed to teach, in the Depression of the 1930s, since they might take work from male breadwinners. Then, as the men volunteered, or were called up, the women had been allowed to take their jobs, even in boys' schools. They had been both delighted, at least partly because neither of them enjoyed the gloom into which she was cast by lack of intelligent occupation. He had been jealous, in his camps and billets, and later as he flew around the Mediterranean, of her colleagues in the staffroom. But she hadn't been contented. She'd applied to do real war work, and had vanished into the Ministry of Information, where her colleagues were elegant poets, shadowy foreigners, and expert linguists. Her London was burning and hectic. He had supposed that she would go back into teaching, as he did, once it was all over. But she had developed a taste for Intelligence. She stayed on, always secretive about what she actually *did*, earning more than he did, which he tried not to mind.

The grey day wore on. He gave her supper, which she whined about. He took her to the bathroom. Another landmark was when, years ago, he had said, "You just go to the bathroom and I'll get your bed ready." And she had said, staring with her now habitual suspicion,

"Where's that?"

"Where's what?"

"That room you said I'd got to go to. Where is it?"

So he took her by the hand. "Don't *pull*. Wait for Sasha. Sasha's knickers are twisted. *Wait for her.*"

He tried to talk to her still. Very occasionally, she answered. He did not know how much of the time, if any, she knew who he was.

Once or twice, waiting to attend to her washing, leaving her bedroom after tucking her in, he had a vertiginous sense that he himself did not know who he was or where he was, or where he had set out to walk to. Once for a dreadful moment he asked himself where the bathroom was, as the full rooms went round him like a carousel. At twenty he would have known he was tired and laughed. Now, he asked himself—as he asked himself every time he reassured himself that his keys and his money were safe—was it a beginning?

When she had got to bed he sat and tried to read Virgil. He thought that the effort of remembering the grammar and the metrics would in some sense exercise his own brain-cells, keep the connections in there flashing and fluent. O pater, anne aliquas ad caelum hinc ire putandum est animas. He had thought of joining an evening class, even of doing a Masters or a Doctorate, but he couldn't go out, it wasn't possible. Every time he forgot a phrase he had once known by heart, singing in the nerves, he felt a brief chill of panic. Is it beginning? I used to know what the pluperfect of "vago" was. The gruff voice complained from her bedroom and he went to unknot the sheets. He didn't like going to bed himself for he so dreaded being woken.

So he dozed over *Aeneid* V1 and heard the ruffle of his own snore. He picked up Dipsy, who had been dropped in front of the television, and with him the pink ribbon, and a few of the steel hairpins. He began abstractedly to drive the hairpins into Dipsy's silver screen in his greenish towelling tummy. He stabbed and stabbed.

It was a quiet street, at dead of night. It had a few midnight windows where the square screen lights flickered. There wasn't much music, or what there was respectably contained. People didn't come home late, or natter to each other on doorsteps. So he was surprised to hear running feet in full flight, two pairs, a pursuit. Then his doorbell shrilled. He thought, I don't go down at this time of night, it isn't safe. The bell shrilled more insistently. He heard palms, or fists, beating on the door.

He went down, mostly to prevent Mado being woken. He opened the door, on the chain.

"Let me in. O let me in. There's a huge black man, with a knife, he means to kill me, let me in."

"You could be a burglar," said James.

"I could. But if you don't let me in, I'll be dead. O quick, O *please.*"

James heard the other, heavier feet, and opened the door. She was thin, she slipped in like an eel, she leaned against the door whilst he put back the chain and turned the deadlock. They listened, in the silent stairway. The other feet hesitated, stopped. And then went on, still running, but more slowly.

James heard her panting in the shadow. He said, "Let me give you a glass of water. Come up." He lived on the first floor. He led the way. She followed. She sank, gracefully, into his armchair, and buried her face in her hands, before he could see it clearly.

She was wearing black shiny sandals with very high, slender heels. Her toenails were painted scarlet. Her legs were young and long. She wore a kind of flimsy scarlet silk shift, slit up the thigh, with narrow shoulder straps. It was a style the younger James would have identified as "tarty" but he was observant, he knew that everyone now dressed in ways he would have thought as tarty, but expected to be treated with respect. Her hands, holding her head, were long and slender, like her feet, and the nails were also painted red. Her face was hidden by a mass of fine black hair, which was escaping out of a knot on the crown of her head. He was surprised she could have run so fast, in those shoes. Her shoulders heaved; the silk moved with her panting. He padded into the kitchen and found her a glass of water.

She had a sharp lovely face, with red lips in a wide mouth, and long black lashes under lids painted to look bruised. He asked if he should call the police, and she shook her head, mutely sipping water, sitting more easily in his armchair.

"I didn't think you'd open," she said. "I thought I'd had it. I owe you."

"Anyone would . . ."

"They wouldn't. I owe you."

He could no think what to say next. It seemed ill-mannered to question her, and she sat, still shivering a little, showing no sign of elaborating her story. He usually had something a little stronger than water, as a nightcap, at this time, he said. Would she care to join him? Whisky, for instance was good for shock.

He had been a man who attracted women easily, at least in his RAF days with his gold moustache. He had long ago told himself that he must understand when it was all over and abandon it gracefully. There would have been no problem in offering her a nightcap if she had not been beautiful. He told himself that he would have asked her easily enough if she had been fat and toothy.

"Whisky is what I need," she said lightly. "On the rocks, if you don't think that's vulgar."

"Drink is drink," said James, who indeed never put ice in good whisky.

When he came back from the kitchen with the glasses, she was pacing the room, looking at his book-shelves, at the photographs on his desk, at the laundry basket in which Mado's paraphernalia was heaped at night, at the wing chair over the back of which the pink ribbon was carefully laid out for tomorrow, in the seat of which Dipsy sprawled, lime-green and softly smiling. He went across to her and handed her the clinking glass. They raised their glasses to each other. The tendrils of hair in the nape of her briefly bowed neck were still damp. She flicked a scarlet finger across Dipsy and looked a question at James. He turned away, and at the same moment a crash and a howl from Mado's room set him running along the corridor.

Mado stopped at her doorway, wound somehow in her sheets, like a toga, or grave cloths. Her teeth were chattering. Her grey hair spilled over her face and shoulders. "You crept into my room," she said, "but you don't respond, you mean to hurt me I know you are a bad man, I live with a bad man, there's no help . . ."

James said, "Hush now, let's get back to bed."

Mado became quite frantic, staring over James's shoulder, making wild signs of warding off violence, cowering and gibbering. Behind James the red silk dress ruffled. He said "My wife is ill. I'll need a moment or two."

"Get that out of here," said Mado. "That's a wicked witch, that means *bad* to us all—"

"I'm sorry," said James to his visitor.

"No need," she said, retreating.

It might have taken hours, or all night, to settle Mado, but that night the life and fight went out of her as the other woman retreated; she allowed herself to be put back into a reconstructed bed, after the necessary visit to the bathroom. James went back, feeling ashamed, for no good reason, and diminished, from civilised host to freak.

"I'm sorry," he said, apologising generally, for life, for Mado, for age, for the fusty smell of his home, for inexorable declined. "I'm sorry."

"Why? You've nothing to be sorry about for. You're kind, I can see, it's hard. How long has she been like that?"

The ease of the question drew a sigh of relief.

"Five years since she knew who I was," he said. "I do my best, but it isn't enough. We are neither of us happy, but we have to go on."

"You have friends?"

"Fewer and fewer, as much because I can't stand them as because they can't stand me, that is, her—"

"Have you any more whisky?"

She sat down again and he fetched the bottle. She asked light little questions, and he told her things, things like the avocado stone, things like the Intelligence, and she smiled but did not laugh, acknowledging with her attentive, mobile face the aesthetic comedy, and its smallness compared to the smothering bulk of the whole.

"I'm sorry" he kept saying. "I don't ever talk."

"Don't be," she said. "There's no need. No call to be *sorry.*"

After the next glass she began to roam the room again, the red silk fluttering round her thighs. He thought one compliment would not be misconstrued and told her she was wearing a very fetching dress. This caused her to throw back her head and laugh, freely, lightly, so that then they both froze and listened to hear if Mado had stirred. She went back to the wing chair and picked up the pink ribbon, running it between her long fingers, testing it.

"She doesn't like pink," she told him.

"No," he agreed. "She hates it. She always did. Babyish, she said. Wouldn't wear pink panties or a pink slip. Ivory or ice-blue, she liked. And red."

"She liked red," said the visitor, picking up Dipsy. "You could have got the red one, Po, but you got this bile-coloured one."

"I did it for myself," he said. "A harmless act of violence. It does no hurt."

The young woman swung away from the chair, leaving doll and ribbon in place.

"Dipsy's a daft word," she said.

"Po is even nastier," he said defensively. "Potties it means. Pot-bellies."

"The river Po is the River Eridanus, that goes down to the Underworld. A magical river. You could have got Po."

"What is *your* name?" he asked, as though it followed, a little drunk, mesmerised by the flow of the red silk as she paced.

"Dido. I call myself Dido, anyhow. I'm an orphan. I cast my family off and other names with it. I like Dido. I must go now."

"I'll come down with you, and make sure the coast is clear."

"Thank you," she said. "I'll be seeing you."

He wished she would, but knew she wouldn't.

AFTERWARDS, many things made him doubt that she had really been there at all. Starting with the name she had given herself, Dido, out of his reading. Though equally, she could have picked up his book whilst he was seeing to Mado, and chosen the name of the passionate queen more or less at random. She had known that Po was Eridanus, which he had forgotten, he thought, registering fear at a known fact lost, as he always did. She had some classical knowledge, unexpectedly. And why not, why should a beautiful woman in red silk not know some classical things, names of rivers, and so on? She had known that Mado hated pink, which she could not have known, which Mrs. Bright did not know, which he kept to himself. He must have invented, or at least misremembered, that part of the conversation. Maybe she existed as little—or as much—as Sasha, the imaginary blood-sister. He felt a wild sense of loss, with her departure, as though she had brought life into the room—pursued by death and the dark—and had taken it away again. What he felt for her was not sexual desire. He saw the old man he was from the outside, with what he thought was clarity. His creased face and his arthritic fingers and his cobbled teeth and his no doubt graveyard breath had nothing to do with anything so alive and lovely. What he felt was more primitive, pleasure in quickness. She was the quick, and he was the dead. She would never come again.

In bed that night he was visited—as he increasingly was—by a memory so vivid that for a time it seemed as though it was real and here and now. This happened more and more often as he slipped and lost his footing on the slopes between sleep and waking. It was as though only a membrane separated him from the life of the past, as only a caul had separated him from the open air at the moment of birth. Mostly he was a boy again, wandering amongst the intense horse-smell and daisy-bright fields of his childhood, paddling in trout-streams, hearing his parents discuss him in lowered voices, or riding donkeys on wide wet sands. But tonight he relived his first night with Madeleine.

They were students and virgins; he had half-feared and half-hoped that she might not be, for he wanted to be the first and he wanted it not to be a fiasco, or a worse kind of failure. He hadn't asked her about it until they were undressing together in the hotel room he had taken. She turned to laugh at him through the black hair she was unpinning, catching exactly both his anxieties.

"No there's no one else, and yes, you will have to work it all out from scratch, but since human beings always *have* worked it out, we'll probably manage. We've done pretty well up to now," she said, glancing under her lashes, recalling increasingly complicated and tantalising fumbles in cars, in college rooms, in the river near the roots of willows.

She had always demonstrated a sturdy, and even shocking, absence of the normal feminine reticences, or modesty or even anxiety. She loved her own body, and he worshipped it.

They went at it, she said later, tooth and claw, feather and velvet, blood and honey. This night he relived intimacies he had very slowly forgotten through years of war, and other snatched moments of bliss-ful violence, and then the effacement of habit. He remembered feeling, and then thinking, no one else has ever known what this is *really* like, no one else can ever have got this *right*, or the human race would be different. And when he said so to her, she laughed her sharp laugh, and said he was presumptuous—I *told* you, James, *everyone* does it or almost—and then she broke down and kissed him all over his body, and her eyes were hot with tears as they moved like questing insects across his belly, and her muffled voice said, don't believe me, I believe you, no one else *ever* . . .

And tonight, he didn't know—he kept rising towards like a trout in a river and submerging again—whether he was a soul in bliss, or somehow caught in the toils of torment. His hands were nervy and ag-ile and they were lumpen and groping. The woman rode him, curved in delight, and lay simultaneously like putty across him.

And his eyes which had watered but never wept, were full of tears.

The next day, he believed he might have called her up from the maze of his unconscious. But Deanna Bright, putting things away in the kitchen, rubbed away traces of scarlet lipstick from a glass he'd thought he's rinsed, and looked a question.

"Someone was being attacked in the street. I took her in."

"You want to watch out, Mr. Ennis. People aren't always what they seem."

"We need to change her sheets again," he said, changing the sub-ject.

Something had changed, however. He had changed. He was afraid of forgetting things, but now he began to be tormented by remember-ing things, with vivid precision. People and things from his past slid and hissed into reality, obscuring the stained carpet and the wing-chair in which Mado chattered to Sasha, or turned the lime-green dolly in clumsy fingers. He told himself he was like a drowning man, with his life flashing before his eyes, and stopped to wonder exactly how that would be, would you *see* the quick and the dead before your real staring under-water pupils, or would they wind on a speeded-up film inside the dark theatre of the waterlogged head? What happened to him now, was that as he woke out of a nap over his book, or stumbled into his bedroom undoing his buttons, he saw visions, heard sounds, smelled smells, long gone, but now there to be, so to speak, read and *checked*. Dead Germans in the North African desert, their caps, their water-cans. The old woman he and Madeleine had pushed under the table on the worst night of the Blitz, and revived with whisky when she seemed to be having a heart attack. She had one red felt slipper with a pom-pom and one bare foot. He saw her gnarled toes, he fitted Madeleine's sheepskin slippers to the trembling feet, he smelled—for hours together—the smell of smouldering London when they went out to survey the damage. Grit in his nose, grit in his lungs, grit of stones and explosives and cinders of flesh and bone. They had walked out after the night of May 10th and seen the damage at Westminster Abbey and the gutted House of Commons, had strolled through the parks, seeing fenced-off unexploded bombs and children sailing boats on the Round Pond. He saw now the fencing and the deck chairs, the rubble and the children.

He remembered the fear, but also the young blood in him driven by the fact of survival and the desire to survive. He had been afraid—he remembered the moan of the sirens, the bang and whine of the big bombs, the grinding drone of the bomber engines, and Madeleine's wild laughter as the crashes were elsewhere. Death was close. Friends you were meeting for dinner, who lived in your head as you set off to meet them, never came, because they were mangled meat under brick and timber. Other friends who stared in your memory as the dead stare whilst they take up the final shape your memory will give them, suddenly turned up on the doorstep in lumpen living flesh, bruised and dirty, carrying bags of salvaged belongings, and begged for a bed, for a cup of tea. Fatigue blurred everyone's vision and sharpened their senses. He remembered seeing a mother and child lying under a bench, arms wrapped round each other, and dreading to stir them, in case they were dead. But they were only homeless walkers, sleeping the sleep of the exhausted.

She did not enter these new windows on lost life, Madeleine. The sound of her laughter, that once was the nearest thing.

When "this" began, he had known that it required more courage to get up every day, to watch over Mado's wandering mind and shambling body, than anything he, or they, had faced in that past. And he had drawn himself up, like a soldier, to do his duty, deciding that it was in both their interests that he should never think of Madeleine, for his duty was here, now, to Mado, whose need was extreme.

The fact that he was unsettled unsettled Mado, who became what

James and Deanna Bright refrained from calling "naughty" for that implied the impossible second childhood. "Wild" James called it. "Restless" was Deanna Bright's word. She began to break things and to hide things. He found her dropping their silver cutlery, inherited from his parents in a plush-lined black case—piece by piece out of the window, listening to the old ring of metal on pavement. The Teletubbies had odd little meals made of pink splats of custard gurgling from a lavender machine, and "toasts" with smiley faces which cascaded from a toaster. Excess food was slurped up by an excitable vacuum cleaner called Noo-noo. They splatted custard (she hated pink) roused Mado to brief bursts of competitive energy and the carpet was covered in milk and honey, with baby cream and salad dressing. And with whisky. She poured his Glenfiddich into the hearthrug. The smell of it recalled Dido but the libation produced no spirit. James bought another bottle. The smell lingered, mixed with the ghostly smoke and ashes of burning London in 1941.

There came a night when she reappeared and reappeared after he had settled her, whining in the doorway as he tried to construe *Aeneid* V1. "I can't do it," she said, "I can't get it," but could not say what she could not do or get. For a dreadful moment James raised his hand to slap or punch the moaning creature, and she backed away, bubbling. Time for Teletubbies to go to bed, said James instead, in a jingly voice. He pushed her—gently—into her room, and pushed Dipsy into her arms. She tossed Dipsy back at him, snorting angrily, and turned her face to the wall. He picked up Dipsy by the foot and went back to the Underworld and its perpetual twilight. He found himself torturing Dipsy, winding his little wrist round, and again, driving hairpins into the terry towelling plump belly. As long as the little unkind acts were harmless, his rational mind said, stabbing.

The doorbell rang. He waited for Mado to respond—if it disturbed her, he wouldn't open, it would be unbearable. But she was still. The bell sounded again. At the third shrilling, he went down. There she was in the doorway, the dark woman, in the red silk dress, like a puppy.

"I come bearing gifts," she said. "To thank you. May I come in?"

"You may," he said, with clumsy ceremony. "You may have a glass of whisky, if you will."

He imagined the elegant nose wrinkled at the smell of his rooms.

"Here," she said, handing him a box of Black Magic chocolates, tied with a scarlet ribbon. Chocolates out of the cinemas of his youth, which had somehow persisted into the present. "And here," she said, lifting her other hand, "for her. I know she'd rather have the red one. Have Po."

He realised Dipsy and the hairpin were still in his hand. Po was done up in what he thought of as cellophane, a beautiful word, also from those earlier days, related to diaphane, although he knew really that she was smiling out of a plastic bag, also done up with a red ribbon. He put down Dipsy, accepted both presents, put them down on the table, and went to fetch whisky, large whiskies, one on the rocks, one neat.

"I didn't think you'd come back."

"Ah, but I had to. And you live so sadly, I thought you might be pleased to see me."

"O I am. But I didn't expect you."

They sat and talked. She crossed and uncrossed her long legs, and he looked at her ankles with intense pleasure and without desire. He remembered Madeleine, running away on moor land, looking back to make sure he could catch her. Dido asked him polite questions about himself, and turned away those he asked in return, so that he found himself, as the smoky spirit rose in his nostrils, telling her about his life, about the returning folk who occupied his flat, mingling with whoever or whatever mad Mado had conjured up. We are quite a crowd, quite a throng of restless spirits, he said, these days, thick as leaves and only two of us flesh and blood. I find myself in odd times and places, quite out of mind until now.

"Such as?"

"Today I remembered packing a crate of oranges and lemons in Algiers. They were lovely things—golden and yellow and shining— and we chose them carefully, the Arab and me, and packed them in wood-shavings and nailed the lid down. And a friend who was a pilot brought them back for her, as a surprise, they couldn't get citrus fruit in the War, you know, they craved for it."

"And when she opened the crate," said Dido, "she could smell the half-forgotten smell of citrus oil and juice. And she pulled away the wood-shavings and put her hand in, like someone looking for treasure in a Lucky Dip at a village fete. And her fingers came up covered with moss-green powder, a lovely colour in the abstract, the colour of lichens and mould. And she took the mouldy lemon out, in its little nest of silver paper, and looked at the orange below, and that simply dissolved into beautiful pale-green powder, like a puff-ball. And she went on, and on, getting dust everywhere, piling them up on newspaper, and there was not one good one."

"That's not true. She said it was a—treasure-chest of delights. She said they were—unbelievably delicious. She said she savoured *every-one*."

"She was always a great liar. As you always knew. It was a wonderful gift. It had rotted on airfields and in depots. It was an accident that it mouldered. She thanked you for the gift."

"How do you know?"

"Don't you know how I know?"

"I am an old man. I am going mad. You are a phantasm."

"Touch me."

"I daren't."

"I said, touch me."

He stood up unsteadily and crossed the swirling space between them. He put the tips of his fingers on the silky hair, and then he touched, chastely and with terror, the warm young skin of her arm.

"Palpable," he said, finding an arcane word from the humming in his brain.

"You see?"

"No, I don't. I believe I believe you are there." He said, "What else do you know? That I might have known, and don't know."

"Sit down and I'll tell you."

"She used to say, Hitler had destroyed the days of her youth, and the quiet days of her marriage, and the child she might have had. And given her drama—too much drama—and dissatisfaction, and external restlessness, so she could never be content. She thought these thoughts with great violence, most especially when she was living the quiet days that were simply a *semblance* of quiet days, a simulacrum of a life, so to speak. Though if a kitchen and a plate of macaroni cheese are a phantasm maybe, just maybe, they are more exciting than when they stretch before you as your settled and invariable fate."

"As it is now," he said. Thinking of custard on the floor.

The worst time—the most unreal—was his, was your, embarkation leave. Before you went where you couldn't say where you were going, where the orange groves and the lemons bloomed. So you sat both, day by day, for those two weeks, and she watched the clock ticking, and mended your shirt-collar like a wax doll housewife with her head bent over the darning mushroom in the dusty blue heels. And you went out now and then together to survey the damage—churches burst open like smashed fruit, plate glass glittering on pavements the length of Oxford Street and Knightsbridge, and you talked rather carefully of nothing much, as though there was a competition in banality. And when you left, she knew she was not pregnant, and gave you a little peck on the cheek—*acting* the little English wife—no Romeo and Juliet kissing—and off you went with your kit-bag, into the dark, temporary or permanent."

"Yes," said James.

"Yes," she said. "And then she lay on the floor and howled like an animal, rolled up and down as though she was in extreme agony. And then she got up and had a bath, and painted her toenails and fingernails with her remaining varnish, and rough-dried her hair, and turned on some soothing music, and became—someone else.

"And then the doorbell rang. And there you were—there *he* was—on the doorstep. She thought it was a ghost. The world was full of the walking dead in those days.

"The embarkation was cancelled," said James reasonably then, reasonably now.

"So she hit out, at the smiling face, with all her strength."

"And drew blood," said James. "With her wedding ring."

"And kissed the blood," said Dido, "and kissed and kissed the mark her hand had made."

"But we survived," said James. He said, "Coming back, being a revenant, was always dangerous. I remember arriving at night back in 1943 when the V-1s were falling. I remember arriving at night—I'd hitched a lift in a troop-lorry—and being put down near some depot at Waterloo. There weren't any buses or taxis to be had, and the sounds of what might have been them approaching in the blackout were sometimes those damned flying bombs, like monstrous clockwork, that ticked and then went out. And then exploded. And the sky was full of flames and smoke, colours you couldn't see now, because the sky is always red over London and you can't see the stars. Those things didn't need the full moon, like the bombers did, but we still felt uneasy when it was full. It was full moon that night. So I walked, carrying as much of my kit as I could, falling into potholes, and listening for the damned things. And when I'd walked for an hour or two, I saw I was walking in the general direction of a steady blaze. Tongues licking up, that *glow*, brick-dust in the air, walls hot to the touch. And the closer I got to home, the closer to the crater, so to speak. And I came up against the barriers, and bucket-chains, and one fire-engine feebly spraying.

And I ran. I ran up against the barriers, and the wardens tried to turn me back, and I said, "that's my house, my wife's in there. And I pushed someone over, and ran into the dust. And saw the house was a shell. The roof and the bedrooms were rubble on the downstairs rooms. I thought she must be in the shelter, and I started pulling at bricks, and burned beams, and I burned my hands. And they pulled me from behind, shouting. And I saw the pit in the living-room floor, and there was someone pulling at my collar. So I looked up, and there she was, in a nightdress shredded to ribbons by glass and a fire-man's jacket, with her hair burned to a birds nest and her face black as night with no eyebrows—and sooty hot hands with broken nails—"

"There was nothing left," said Dido. "Except each other." She said, "You said you were Aeneas looking for Creusa in burning Troy. And she said to you, "I'm not a ghost, I'm flesh and blood." And they kissed, with soot on their tongues, and the burning city in their lungs. Flesh and blood."

James began to shake. He was exceedingly tired and confused and somehow certain that all this presaged his own death, or madness at least, and if he went mad or died, what would become of mad Mado?

"Who are you?" he said, in a tired old voice. "Why are you here?"

"Don't you know?" she said kindly. "I am the Fetch."

"Fetch?"

She sat in his chair, smiling and waiting, sleek and dark in red silk.

"Madeleine?" said James.

"In a sense. You would never listen to anything about spiritual things. You always made cynical jokes, when it was a question of astrology, or clairvoyance, or the otherworld."

"Astronomy is mystery enough," said James as he always said. "A great mystery. We used to fly under the stars as thick as daisies. You can't see them now."

"There are many things in heaven and earth you can't *see* James. The etheric body can get separated from—from the clay. It can wander into churchyards. It needs to be set free. As she needs to be set free."

"I know what you are telling me," said James. "You must know I've thought about it."

"You don't do it, because you would be set free yourself, and you think that would be wrong. But you don't think of her, or you would know what she wants. What I want."

"Dido," said James, using the name for the first time." She doesn't know what she wants, she can't rightly want or not want, her skull is full of plaques and tangles-"

"You make me angry," said Dido in Madeleine's voice. "All those young Germans in the war, with their lives in front of them, and their girls and their parents, that was all right, your own young pilots on missions with wonderful brains humming with cleverness and hope and rational fear—*that* was alright. But a miserable hulk decorated with a pink ribbon—"

"You could always twist anything."

"Intelligence. O yes. I could always twist anything."

She stood up to go. James stood up to see her out. He meant not to say anything, to be strong, but he heard his own voice,

"Shall I see you again?"

Black silk hair, red silk dress, anachronistic silk stockings with perfect seams up the perfect legs.

"That depends," said Dido. "As you know. That depends."

The next day, he knew she had been there, for the signs were solid. Lipstick on the whisky glass, berib-boned chocolates, little red Po smiling at him in her polythene casing. He imagined that Deanna Bright looked at him oddly. She refused a chocolate when he offered one. She picked up Po with sturdy black fingers.

"Shall I get it out, then?"

"No," he said. "No, leave it in the bag for the present."

"I see you had company again," said Deanna Bright.

"Yes," said James.

Deanna Bright shrugged and left rather early.

On the television, in broad daylight, the Telebubbies were sitting on the end of their casket-shaped cradles, swathed in shimmering coverlets like parachute silk, or those silvery blankets wrapped around those rescued from hypothermia or drowning. They lay down to sleep like nodding ninepins, each snoring his or her differentiated snore. Nightnight Teletubbies said the mid-Atlantic motherly voice in the cathode tubing. Night, said mad Mado, more and more angrily, night, night, night, night.

"Come to bed," said James, very gently, adjusting the pink ribbon.

"Night," said Mado.

"Just a rest, for a while," said James.

CHAPTER 15

Caring for a relative with dementia— who is the sufferer?

Heather Wood

When working with people with dementia and their relatives, it is sometimes hard to know who is "the sufferer". The individual with confusion will experience increasing and severe disability, and a proportion of people, particularly in the early stages of the disease, find their situation highly distressing. Yet for some, and certainly in the later stages of the disease, the deterioration in cognitive functioning and awareness can offer a buffer, and they may seem to be sheltered from the tragedy of their condition. Their relatives, usually fully aware of what is happening, will be faced with the emotional pain of the changes that have befallen their loved one and the transformation of their previous relationship. It may seem as if the relative has become the container for the emotional suffering on behalf of both of them.

There is no doubt that caring for someone with senile dementia is a physically demanding, exhausting, and, at times, distressing task. Mace and Rabins (1985) entitled their book *The 36-Hour Day*. The task may also entail considerable psychological adaptation and carers, sometimes themselves in their eighties or nineties, may need to draw upon hitherto untapped aspects of themselves in order to meet this situation.

As the disease progresses, the afflicted person experiences progressive intellectual deterioration, with memory loss, confusion, and ultimately, perhaps, loss of all speech, continence, mobility, and comprehension. For the carer this often means a gradual and protracted death of the former relationship, with attendant processes of mourning. Some carers cannot cope with the emotional demands placed upon them and seek out a residential placement for the sufferer. However, among those who choose to persevere, it is possible to observe the emergence of a new and powerful bond, more akin to the maternal relationship to a baby.

Considerable progress has been made within services in challenging the tendency to infantilize or patronize older adults. Such attitudes threaten to deny their sexuality, their history, their achievements, and their dignity. Yet in rejecting the notion that people in later life are "just like children", it would be unfortunate to discredit maternal-type care and the role that this might have with people who are severely disoriented and confused. There are fundamental differences between older people with dementia and children, but there may be value in comparing the dynamic processes that occur between dependant and carer in both situations.

The observations that follow derive from a group run for people caring for relatives with dementia which met for two-and-a-half years. In practice, all but one of the sufferers had dementia of the Alzheimer's type; one had a multi-infarct dementia. The relatives were predominantly spouses, although two daughters attended intermittently.

All of the sufferers were clients at a day hospital, which they attended between one and three days per week. All carers were offered the opportunity to join the relatives group, so they were self-selected. The group was held fortnightly for one-and-a-quarter hours while the sufferers attended the day unit. The group was led by a clinical psychologist and a nurse from the day unit, with two trainee psychologists who co-led the group at different times.

The work was undertaken a number of years ago, and services and care practices will have undergone development since that time. Nevertheless, I assume that the psychological processes observed have some enduring applicability. The names and identities of participants has been disguised as far as possible, but should any relative recognize the descriptions included here, I hope they will feel that their family experience has been valued and respected.

Relatives' support groups are not uncommon, but what may have been unusual about this one was that, in accordance with other types of psychodynamic group work, comments were taken up as ways of expressing or displacing more unconscious feelings. For example, a recurring topic early in the group was a discussion about what type of locks or door handles would enable them to get in, even if their confused relative tried to lock them out. While this was a real practical concern, we inferred that it also reflected their frustration and desperation at not being able to get through to their spouses emotionally.

The carers

Some thumbnail sketches of the participants may serve as an introduction. Mr Andrews was a regular attender from the start. He was in his eighties and told us with pride that he had been married for fifty-six years. He was a gentle, modest man and inspired great affection in the team of staff working with his wife. She was suffering from severe dementia, had lost all speech, was incontinent at night, and paced relentlessly. When Mr Andrews could tolerate her no more he sat her on the floor, where she was immobilized until he could bear to get her up again. He was devoted to his wife, wanted no help in the home, and was determined to have her at home to the last if he possibly could.

Mr Roberts had been a high-ranking civil servant and was an organizer. Without having been asked to do so, every morning he would telephone the day unit to give them a progress report on his wife and to let them know whether she had had a bowel movement that day. He was also in his eighties and was unable to lift his wife, who was wheelchair-bound. He therefore had a district nurse calling twice daily to get his wife up and to put her to bed. At times he was at pains to distinguish himself from the other members of the group by virtue of his knowledge, life experience, or strength of character, and perhaps when he felt that the group leaders were failing in their role, he would take it upon himself to deliver diagnoses on people's relatives: "It sounds like Parkinson's as well as dementia to me." However, this blustering manner may have served to conceal his disadvantage: his wife was the most severely disabled, and she had to be fed as well as being immobile and incontinent.

Mr Roberts was particularly impatient with Mr King who was in his fifties and had had to give up work to care for his wife. Mr King seemed to have more difficulty than the others in getting anything for himself. He had the least cooperative GP and had struggled for four or five years without help. When he went to see the continence advisor, he appeared to come home with fewer supplies than the other group members, and he was the only one who had never met the Consultant for Old Age Psychiatry, thereby missing out on an important symbol of social respect and recognition. Mr King was more anxious about contributing in the group, and he seemed more overtly ambivalent towards his wife than the others. She was very confused and at times aggressive, but she retained some speech and thus was less severely disabled than some of the others. Mr King nevertheless regarded it as inevitable that she would soon have to enter continuing care, while some of the others resisted this at all costs. It was notable that Mr King and his wife were significantly younger than some of the others, and he had had to relinquish his career in order to care for her. In addition, it was striking that some of the most devoted carers were in childless couples; Mr King and his wife had adult children. Thus a number of factors may have contributed to his ambivalence and sense of burden.

The fourth of this core of regular attenders was Mr Green. He was in his late fifties and seventeen years younger than his wife who, he led us to believe, had mothered and disciplined him. Now the roles were reversed, and he found himself having to assume increasing responsibility for her care as she deteriorated rapidly. Mr Green was a working-class man and a raconteur. He was used to disability, with a physically frail father and a sister with learning disabilities, both of whom were cared for by his brother. Mr Green believed that humour was the only way to cope, and he would regale us with tales of "My Doris". When he had had enough of her, he told her that it was 11.30 and put her to bed, irrespective of the actual time. In the group his cheery tales were initially delivered in a relentless and domineering way, although, as the group progressed, he could reveal more distress.

If the women in the group have been left until last, it is because these men essentially formed the core of the group, and no women attended so consistently. Mrs Price cared for her father, but she took the opportunity of him attending the day unit to get on with her freelance work at home. As she was coping well, the pleasure of being alone at home began to outweigh any benefit she derived from the group. Mrs Stevens came when her husband went into hospital for long-term care, because she felt unable to cope with her guilt and the loss. She was in her seventies and had been married for forty-eight years. In contrast to the men in the group, she was very open about the grief evoked by the disease and the admission of her husband to hospital. Mrs O'Reilly had to bear the additional grief of a husband with early-onset dementia, but after a long struggle she was relieved when he died, and she stopped coming to the group immediately. A number of other people came to the group for limited periods and then left.

Group dynamics and the dynamics between carer and spouse

The nature of the bond between these relatives and their partners first became apparent early in the history of the group. The quality of the interaction in the group was such that it was hard to believe that anyone could benefit from it. Members seemed incapable of listening to each other. One man, Mr Thompson, appeared to be very deaf and either sat in silence or delivered a monologue, oblivious to interruptions. Others seemed to suffer from a functional deafness, which blunted their sensitivity to any expression of need or emotion by other people. They would interrupt, talk over each other, ignore others, and demand attention for their own story. We had moments of thinking that our expectations of the group had been wildly unrealistic.

We persistently commented on the distress for them of constantly being with a loved one with whom it was impossible to communicate coherently and who often did not recognize them. Over time, people's hearing recovered. Mr Roberts commented at the end of one group on how much he had got from listening to other people's stories. This man, who had seemed quite insensitive, told us how he would always respond to any verbalization his wife made as though it made sense, trying to draw her out and make conversation. Thus, rather than being closed to others, he was telling us how much of his energy he invested in trying to forge some contact with his wife. Mr Thompson retained a degree of hearing loss but began to interact more with others. However, the deafness reappeared in new members, who monopolized and bullied the group in a way that had started to become familiar to us. It seemed that what was being brought into the group were the uncomprehending patients, locked in their own worlds, unreceptive, unresponsive, but very demanding. These relatives had become containers for the cut-off, uncommunicative parts of their spouses, and we were given the opportunity to experience what it was like to be with people who never listened or acknowledged anyone else's existence.

It seemed that they had not only adapted at a practical level to the changes required of them, but had become merged with their spouses, internalizing a sense of their confusion. The relatives had become oblivious to others, absorbed in this interplay. What we were witnessing appeared to be an old age equivalent of the mother–infant relationship.

Mourning of the couple relationship

Throughout the group, the processes characteristic of this mother–infant type of relationship were interwoven with more familiar aspects of mourning (Parkes, 1972). The transition to a maternal-type relationship occurred simultaneously with a progressive loss of the marital relationship, which was at times confusing for group members and ourselves. Mrs Stevens' husband had been taken into hospital for continuing care, but, having been exhausted by caring for him for twenty-four hours a day, she was now at a loss to know what to do with herself. She explained that it was not her husband himself that she was missing, but someone who had needed her complete attention for several years. Her sons urged her to clear out his clothes and belongings, but she felt it was inappropriate while he was still alive. Apologizing for "making myself unhappy", she settled down to the task of mourning the husband she had lost, savouring old letters and photos, and allowing herself to weep. The man in hospital did not know her, but he still had a place in her life and in her home, although the man she had been married to had gone.

It is not easy for people to accept this transition. All of the rage and denial found in normal mourning were evident. The ambulance service, which ferried the sufferers to the day unit, was a convenient focus for much anger. Their inconsistent schedules, and the inaccessibility of anyone who seemed to be in charge of the system, engendered frustration and fury in the relatives. They felt as helpless faced with the ambulance service as they did faced with the disease. The former was easier to acknowledge, but making this link enabled one woman to contact her anger that, after years working as a nurse, she should be spending her retirement nursing an ill and difficult husband.

Early in the group we were quizzed about why more research was not being done. Was it possible to replace arteries to the brain? Perhaps recent advances in transplant surgery would lead to brain transplants? It was difficult to face the current level of ignorance about the disease and that, for their relatives, it was too late even for medical miracles.

The "searching and yearning" (Parkes, 1972) manifested in mourning were apparent in the search for glimpses of their partners as they had known them. Mr Roberts' wife had been a singer and would respond to Gilbert and Sullivan in a way that left him convinced that she understood every word. On one occasion a home help had brought her daughter, and his wife had spontaneously said "hello" and expressed interest in the child. Again, it seemed that he probably over-interpreted her response in his desperate need to believe that there were islands in her personality that were still quite intact, waiting to be discovered. The metaphor of doors and keys was a recurring one in the group: their spouses were seen to be potentially accessible if only they could find the right combination. Mrs Stevens reported that her husband had suddenly told her one day that she was always on the go, and that she should sit down for a while. This level of recognition was quite exceptional. "You have to keep listening out, though. Nine-tenths of what he says is rubbish. Then you get a few words of sense. You have to keep listening out or you might miss it."

As their partners lost many of their former characteristics, some lost self-control and restraint. Some relatives were shocked and disgusted when forced to confront violence, greed, and soiling. Mr Andrews' wife would eat the entire contents of the fruit bowl if left unattended. Mr King's wife had, on one occasion, appeared to try to strangle her teenage granddaughter, and the family were now afraid for her to visit. Another man, Mr Baker, would leave his wife unattended in the bathroom, but would return to find faeces smeared everywhere. With his voice full of anger and despair, he proclaimed in one group that "ours must be the only house around here where you have to wash the soap".

As the group evolved, the shock and distress diminished, and the fact of their spouses being incontinent was assimilated. Much of one group was spent discussing which incontinence pads were best for which occasions, strategies to avoid wet beds, and ways of obtaining the supplies they needed. I was reminded of comparable conversations between mothers. Mr Andrews asserted that he had married his wife for better or for worse, and there was an amused chorus from the others, "And this is the worse!"

At times there is no doubt that members of the group took pleasure in their own capacity to change and adapt, and occasionally they described feeling fortunate compared to people who had not been challenged to develop during their retirement. While this might be seen as a denial of their own loss, there were undoubtedly genuine satisfactions, particularly for the men, for whom this caring role had considerable novelty. Men in their eighties who had never done the shopping before shared amusement about the discovery that you always leave the supermarket with more than you intended to buy. They were proud of their own ingenuity in response to problems. One man was afraid that he would not wake if his wife got out of bed in the night and wandered, so he loosely tied her wrist to his, so that as she got out of bed she tugged on him. There was a sense of privilege and an awareness of their own importance in sustaining the life and identity of their partners.

The emergence of a maternal-type relationship

Primary preoccupation

Alongside these processes of mourning, denial, anger, searching, and grief, we therefore witnessed the emergence of an intense dependency relationship. Winnicott (1956, 1960) describes the state of "primary maternal preoccupation" in which the mother is not simply preoccupied with her new baby, but is given over to the care of the baby, which at first seems like part of herself. She is content if she knows that the baby is comfortable, and through her identification with the baby she can gauge what it feels and what it needs. Members of the group had similar experiences in relation to their spouses. All of their spouses were admitted to hospital for relief stays periodically, to give them a break. However, they all agreed, "It's a physical rest but not a mental rest. You are thinking all the time whether they are all right." Mr Green telephoned daily to see how his wife was, and he apologized to the ward sister for making a nuisance of himself. She reassured him that it was fine to phone—he could phone twenty times a day if he wanted. Mr Green repeated this several times to us, with dismay. It was as though, in her generosity, she had intuitively comprehended that this was indeed what he felt like doing.

Mr Andrews' wife was admitted to hospital for a relief stay, which extended as she developed a leg ulcer, lost the capacity to walk, and showed less and less recognition of her environment. He counted the weeks, knowing that he could not have her at home if she were immobile, but "longing for a miracle" that would return her to him. During this time this sprightly man slumped visibly, as though he had lost his direction and purpose.

The principal fear of members of the group was that anything should happen to them that would prevent them seeing their task through to its conclusion. Whereas a mother fears for her child if anything should happen to her, these people were afraid of dying before their spouses. During the course of the group, Mr Green had a second, and major, heart attack. He was back at the group within a fortnight, greatly subdued by the experience, and spoke about the imperative for him to survive: "Sometimes it's harder to live than to die."

After two and a half years the group had reduced in size, as some people's relatives had died and they had stopped coming. All of the sufferers had eventually been admitted to hospital. It seemed inappropriate to introduce new members to a group that had survived such painful times together, and in which death was a central theme, but inappropriate to continue to meet until the last relative had died. We agreed a date for a final meeting. On that day, Mr Andrews came to the group and told us that his brother-in-law's funeral was that same morning, but he had missed it to come. Mr Andrews had known his brother-in-law for over eighty years. I commented on his decision to come to the group, but he had no doubts about the choice that he had made: "That's about death, but so long as my wife is alive she comes first, and this is about life."

Auxiliary memory

People caring for those suffering from dementia find over time that they come to know more about the sufferers than the sufferers can tell about themselves. As the memory slowly deteriorates, the person who is closest can "catch" the memories that were recalled a month ago, but forgotten now, and can feed them back to the individual. At first the carer may prompt, remind, or supplement what is recalled, and the sufferer may recognize this familiar information. This process, whereby the carer uses his or her own memory to supplement that of the sufferer, can extend the period of awareness. In time even this fails to make an impact, and the carer must hold the knowledge of who the person was, when he or she him/herself may have no recall or recognition of events or people.

With a newborn baby, the mother or carer holds the ego functions for the infant, who is not yet able to think about, recall, explain, or anticipate events or its own experience. As the child develops, it is increasingly able to assume these functions for itself. Strachey (1934), in a seminal paper about the mode of operation of psychoanalysis, argued that the psychoanalyst becomes an "auxiliary superego" for the patient, offering a benign and realistic view to the patient in a way that ultimately enables him or her to internalize this function. The notion that the analyst serves as a container for parts of the patient, until those parts can be re-owned and safely internalized by the patient, has been developed extensively by Bion (1962) and others. In the process of caring for someone with dementia, a carer can assume the memory function for the other, remembering and reminding him or her about day-to-day events and, ultimately, holding the biographical informa-tion about the person that constitutes his or her history and identity. Unlike the analytic process or child development, this function is not "given back", but can grow until the carer holds the identity of the person when he or she can no longer speak for him/herself. In this way, the carer acts as an "auxiliary memory".

The clearest manifestation of this process is when carers preserve and communicate to staff a vivid picture of their relative in the past which may have a vitality that shapes the way in which staff be-have towards that person. Mr Roberts' wife was distinguished in our minds by her love of opera and skills as a navigator as they drove all over Europe. Mr Green's wife had been an outspoken van driver. Mr Andrews had married the girl who lived down the road, and both had lived quiet and unadventurous lives, still in the same street.

One of the most difficult things to bear is that they themselves are often forgotten or denied in this process. Mr Green's wife would demand to see "my Bert" but then deny that he was Bert. "My wife won't have her rings taken off. God, she puts up a fight. You can't get her engagement ring off her. She says 'My Bert gave this to me'. She doesn't know who I am but she says, 'Bert gave this to me'." Mrs Stevens' husband would ask whether she were married. When she replied that she was married to him he replied, "You're not my wife. My wife left me three years ago." Nevertheless, the relatives would continue to behave as though the relationship were unchanged. When his wife was in hospital for a relief stay, Mr Andrews travelled a hun-dred miles to stay with his sister. On his wife's birthday he returned by coach, visited his wife, and brought her a cake, and then returned by coach to his sister. This man was 83 and his wife showed no recogni-tion of him by this stage, but his need to sustain her identity and their bond was upheld.

Projection and projective identification as modes of communication

In addition to this equivalent to primary maternal preoccupation, and the functioning of the spouse as an auxiliary memory, the third conspicuous feature of this emerging relationship was the replacement of verbal communication with primitive methods of communication. The term "projective identification" was coined by Klein (1946) to de-scribe the way in which unwanted feelings or parts of the self may be projected into an other so that the other becomes identified with those parts. While projective identification is regarded as a mechanism of defence, its importance as a means of communication has also been stressed, particularly when, as between mother and infant, verbal communication is not available. It is questionable whether someone with dementia may be seen to be actively expelling their confusion, even at an unconscious level, and thus the term may not be strictly applicable here. Nevertheless, the way in which new members of the group seemed to have internalized the confusion of their relatives has already been described, and they did indeed behave like recipients of projected qualities. The dementia sufferers also were used as objects of the carers' projections.

Mrs Stevens felt that her husband's emotional absence had left her carrying the grief about his illness for both of them. She had been with her son to see her husband, and her husband had pointed at her and said to the son, "That woman looks a bit like your mother"; he then proceeded to ignore her for half an hour. She found consolation in the fact that if he did not know her, he could not be missing her, but she then felt left with all the sadness. Others in the group found this acknowledgement of grief hard to tolerate, and the group took off in a discussion of the physical strength of their relatives, and how they would resist being dressed or bathed with great force. Mr Green added that his sister with learning disabilities could lift items of furniture that left the men in the family feeling weak. At this point their charges were invested with the strength that they felt they needed to counteract this discussion of grief.

On one occasion Mr Green's wife was admitted to the very busy, crowded, and understaffed inpatient ward where, in those days, patients were provided with clothing from a communal collection, which was often ill-fitting and unsightly. Mr Green was extremely distressed about this degrading situation; the patients were described as roaming around like animals, looking like tramps; one group member drew an analogy with the degradation of Belsen. Observing his distress, Mr Roberts advised him, "That feeling can get put into you if you are not careful—it's as though there's a transfer of feelings from the patient to you. You have to be careful to protect yourself from that if you are going to keep going." For a man who had once seemed overbearing and insensitive in the group, the organizer and the diagnostician, it was a perceptive and empathic acknowledgment of these subtle projective processes.

After the group had been running for nearly two years, it was also possible to talk about their fear that they might have been damaged intrapsychically through this prolonged identification with someone who was progressively disabled. In one group, they had been talking about their wives, when Mr Roberts turned to me and said that as I had known them over a long period of time now, did I think that they had . . . and seemingly as one voice, the group said, "Deteriorated!". There was much laughter at this idea, but later in the group Mr Roberts told us about an incident during the war when he had gone to rescue someone who was drowning but then risked being pushed underwater and drowning himself. When we linked this to their own fear of being dragged under, they began to describe their anxiety that through caring for their wives, they had become "cabbages". Two of them had given up jobs to care for their wives and wondered what else they could be doing with their lives. They felt that they were doing nothing. When their wives were asleep, they could not read or watch television, and they felt aimless. Mr Green described a day when he got up at 4 a.m. and spent twenty hours spring cleaning before going back to bed. He conveyed that it was a vain attempt to counteract his feeling of emptiness.

Conclusions

It is a widespread assumption that increasing age is marked by a diminishing capacity to change and adapt and that this must be taken into account when attempting therapeutic interventions with older adults. Freud (1905a) left an unfortunate legacy when he discouraged analytic work with people over 50, although, since the pioneering papers of King (1974), Hildebrand (1982), and Hess (1987), this has now been extensively challenged. The members of this group demonstrated a remarkable capacity both to adapt to the demands of a relative with dementia and to use a psychodynamic approach to therapy. The men—in particular, those who had had no experience of child care or work in the caring professions—found themselves in their latter years responding with creativity and determination to the challenge of becoming a carer. None had had any prior experience of psychotherapy, but they were able to respond to interpretations and recognize that events reported as facts could be seen as metaphors for their emotional experience. There were observable changes in their ability to acknowledge, experience, and process emotion.

Members of this group were distinguished by the determination to persevere, which raises the question of why some people can tolerate this immensely difficult task, whereas others opt for residential care.

Gilhooly (1986) found that proximity of family relationship was important: the more remote the relationship, the greater the preference for institutional care. Emotional proximity also appears to be important: Morris, Morris, and Britton (1988a) found that carers who reported lower levels of marital intimacy at the time, and prior to the onset of dementia, had higher levels of perceived strain and depression. The quality of the previous relationship may be important: a person who has felt well cared for by an other when they were dependent may be more able to accept a role reversal and reciprocate this caring when the other becomes dependent. This would be consistent with impressions gained from the group. Some men described how consistently and unselfishly their wives had cared for them during their marriages—now it was their turn.

These observations also have implications for the way in which services are organized. Where this type of bond exists, a person with dementia may approach the end of his or her life recognized and valued as an individual. In turn, he or she can elicit capacities that the carer was unaware of possessing. In contrast, a person with dementia and institutionalization is perceived to be psychologically "toxic", even by his or her own relatives. The double dehumanization of the disease and the institution can be a recipe for despair.

Where close bonds exist, it seems vital to support them through the provision of flexible and domiciliary-based care. When residential care is a necessity, those staff who are able to form close bonds with people who are confused will inevitably struggle with the costs of such an identification, at times feeling confused, frustrated, or stripped of humanity themselves. The nurses in the day unit were so sceptical about the value of this group that I was led to question its worth, until I realized that the relatives were receiving more support than the nurses. I instituted a weekly support group for the nurses, in which, among other things, they planned a journal article about the difficulties of their work. I do not think the article was ever written, but they agreed on a title: "It's Uphill All the Way, and When You Get There, There Is No Hope". Once there was a forum where this level of despair among the nurses could be aired, the criticisms of the group ceased.

The casual rotation of nurses between wards, or the lack of support and low pay that can lead to a high staff turnover in residential homes, may mean that the informal knowledge of who these people with dementia are, or were, is lost forever. Very often records contain factual information about illnesses or addresses, but it is the care assistants, nurses, and ancillary staff who remember the biographical data, function as auxiliary memories, and hold the identity of their patients or residents in mind.

Finally, at the moment of death, it is important to recognize what it is that has been lost. Those who have separated themselves from their relatives may feel some relief that the process has come to an end, but Mr Roberts told us that nothing he had experienced when his wife was ill compared with his feelings after her death. He had already mourned the marriage. His experience was now more like that of a bereaved parent. Providing this type of care may also meet the carer's dependency needs; at a deeper level, his experience may have resembled that of a child who has lost an unresponsive but ever-present parent.

CHAPTER 16

My unfaithful brain—
a journey into Alzheimer's Disease

Anna Dartington and Rebekah Pratt

Introduction,
by Rebekah Pratt

"Walk with me. Hand in hand through the nightmare of narrative,
the neat sentences secret-nailed over meaning. Meaning mewed
up like an anchorite, its vision in broken pieces behind the wall.
And if we pull away the panelling, then what? Without the
surface, what hope of contact, of conversation? How will I come
to read the rawness inside?"

Jeanette Winterson, *Gut Symmetries* (1977, p. 24)

The "Unfaithful Brain" is the story of Anna, the psychotherapist,
the social worker, the nurse, the writer, the poet, and a person
with Alzheimer's Disease at 54 years of age. The progression of
Alzheimer's Disease had meant for Anna that the smooth panelling of
conversation was disrupted by lost words and fragmented sentences.
Over eight visits, spread over a number of months, I met with Anna.
My role was to act as a facilitator, to engage in conversations, taped
and transcribed, and to offer a telling of Anna's story. The account
presented in "My Unfaithful Brain" is the product of these meetings
and the process of reflection they stimulated. I shall reflect on the

process of developing the story and explore what the truth is when it comes to the retrieval and retelling of someone else's story. How can one person's narrative be extracted meaningfully when the surface of conversation changes and becomes disrupted?

When I visited Anna she was 58 years old. I taped our extensive conversations, which were a combination of connecting through our mutual likes—cats, sunshine, the garden, flowers, and colours and of each other—and reflecting on our different experiences, in particular Anna's experience of having Alzheimer's Disease. Anna wanted to share her story, so that other people could learn about what it can be like to live with Alzheimer's Disease.

> R[ebekah]: I think that you sharing your story is going to help people learn about it too. Do you think?
>
> A[nna]: Yes, that it is not some terrible awful thing in the middle of the wood, which it could feel, but actually you can bring out some diamonds too.

The part of this process that is more difficult to explain is how the story was constructed. Some of the conversation I had with Anna was very little to do with her experience of Alzheimer's Disease and much more to do with our mutual interests and likes. I felt it was important to know Anna as a person in order to have a context for her story.

> R: We talked about what it is like to have Alzheimer's.
>
> A: Yes, we had to talk about that.
>
> R: But you are obviously much more than Alzheimer's, so we talked about other things too, got to know each other a bit.
>
> A: Yes.

Our conversations about Alzheimer's Disease were extensive. At times we reflected on chronology, from the noticing of changes, assessments, getting a diagnosis, and life beyond the diagnosis. At other times we explored general areas of Anna's life, such as relationships, dealing with changes, thoughts about illness, and planning for the future. On every topic we had many conversations, each time adding a layer of meaning about that particular aspect of experience.

After our meetings I retreated to write the story. The material I had from our meetings were the tapes and the transcripts, which reflected the conversations that were frustrated by lost words and fragments of sentences. I also had Anna's earlier writing, where I could gain a sense of her style of written communication. Finally, I kept a photograph of Anna with me, to help me keep her in mind.

My role was to gather up our conversations and, where necessary, piece back together the fragments into a cohesive story. This raises the question of how accurate the story is, how much it represents the truth. When we hear a sentence that is a fragment, is this a symptom of disrupted cognition or disrupted speech? Either way, could the fragments be placed back together to make a coherent whole and represent the intention to achieve coherence, regardless of how it comes to be disrupted? In this sense my role was as a translator, a tool or vehicle used to overcome this one particular disabling aspect of Alzheimer's Disease.

When piecing Anna's story together I used her own words wherever possible. My own words were used to smooth the connections between segments of meaning. The final product is like a completed jigsaw. Anna provided most of the pieces, I fitted them back together. Learning how Anna wanted her story told was based on developing a relationship with Anna in which there would be understanding and trust.

R: What if some people come along and say, well, how do I know that's the truth? Is that Anna's story or Rebekah's writing?

A: Well, we'll have to say it is both of ours, isn't it? I should think so, that's how I was thinking of it. We talked a lot about it and around it and this is what we've come up with.

The story is written in sections to reflect some of the fragmentation of the telling of the story, the flow of focus and distraction, and to break it down into smaller units of story that Anna could study and comment on. Our conversations were fluid and would shift in and out of focus, with times of precise clarity and times when other life events would shift the focus.

I had concerns that some people may have negative assumptions about the ability of an individual with Alzheimer's Disease to express herself, which would mean my own contribution would be magnified at the cost of being able to recognize Anna in the work. Anna shared some of these concerns, and here we discuss it in an extract that is typical of the many exchanges the story has been written from:

R: Sometimes I wonder if people read it and they say, oh well, if they didn't know you, well, this is someone with Alzheimer's, how can they say these things about their life?

A: I know, but they'd be wrong, wouldn't they.

R: You know what I mean, don't you, you've seen this before.

A: You mean, they think, how could they do this if they have Alzheimer's?

R: Yes.

A: The trouble is, my Alzheimer's is a funny thing to me. I have days of being, I can do this, I can do that, yeah yeah yeah, and other days, other days, I think, I've forgotten that. And anything you're trying to write, you have that. But certainly, I think the thing that people will really be interested about, how we could get together, because we didn't know each other very much, and how it worked, and we knew what we were wanting to get to, did we?

R: More or less.

A: Well, we certainly got quite quickly into a kind of way of talking, very quickly.

R: And being able to really communicate with each other.

A: Yeah. Well you are an open person, I know, and so am I, so, you know, that is one thing.

R: Do you think that we might challenge some people's stereotypes about Alzheimer's, reading it?

A: Yes, I hate that, people have so many things about it, don't they, in their minds.

R: I think that sometimes people have quite negative things about it.

A: Yes, like they're daft or something.

R: I wonder. Do you think, have you noticed that with people?

A: Well, something with people I don't know. I mean that lady [*a carer who had just visited*], I wonder what she might think about it, not that we were talking about it with her. I think it's a bit frightening for some people actually, so I never go around, saying, sometimes I just say, I feel quite good today, or this is a good day, or we've done some good work today. I mean, that's how we go. I wouldn't go into the ins and outs of it really.

The day I emailed the first draft of the story to Anna and her husband, I felt the full burden of the respect I have for Anna and my sense of responsibility to "get it right". Her husband read the piece with Anna, and then emailed me a comment from Anna on the work that reassured me that the story offers a truth that Anna wanted to achieve:

A: It sounds like me.

It comes up like the fox, very very quietly

"The outsider is well placed to observe the world. The marginal position is a potentially creative one because the intellectual and emotional distance from familiar experience makes a space for a new viewpoint or an original thought to take shape."

Anna Dartington (1994, p. 92)

Can I tell you about the day my brain left me? My unfaithful brain left me slowly, but there were also a few exact moments that marked the start of when my brain began to leave. I know I didn't lose my brain, but my brain lost me. It lost me at a very important meeting for securing funding for research, when all of a sudden there were no words. I couldn't even say "I can't say anything"—is there anything worse than that? Maybe it left itself behind with my briefcase, full with a career built on thinking, and forgotten on an underground train. Could I have known then I was right on the cusp of moving from being somebody working well in the world to being someone who would soon not work at all? Maybe it was left with the newly begun doctoral research, now archived into boxes. It left me while playing scrabble with my family, and it left me when I needed it to guide my coordination as I walked though the world as an independent, energetic woman with a successful career and busy life.

These moments came up on me like the fox, very, very quietly. It was these series of moments, taken together, that started to build into a sense of knowing that something was wrong. One of the first times I knew that these moments were more than a series of unrelated mishaps was on holiday. I went to paint the wonderful hibiscus flowers I look forward to seeing each year in the little part of Greece we travel to. I went to paint these flowers, but I couldn't do anything. I didn't realize till then how much that things were happening with my brain, that it wasn't working. This year we went on holiday and I saw these lovely flowers again. This time I didn't try to draw them; somebody else must do it now.

It was frightening to know things were changing, to know these series of moments were accumulating into an overall sense of something really being wrong. A friend who is a doctor eventually began to notice the changes that were happening. He intervened and encouraged me to have these changes investigated. It was one thing to know in private that my brain had become unfaithful, but it was frightening to learn that my brain's private betrayal had become publicly observable.

There is science, which has to be done,
but there also has to be compassion

Finding out what was causing my difficulties was explored in a lengthy diagnostic process. This marked the start of negotiating new relationships with professionals, where I was placed in the unfamiliar role of "the patient". My mother had a series of strokes not long before I started experiencing difficulties, and the initial investigations explored the impact of depression upon my memory and speech. Once depression was ruled out, more detailed assessments were carried out during a stay in hospital.

Hospital life required me to be the patient, and to act the way a patient has to be. I was constantly available for many tests, including taking blood daily. This not only hurt, but also left me feeling like an object, a real thing, a pin cushion. The hospital was a very large and frightening place. The staff were not very good at saying what they were doing and why they were doing it. I was frightened by the changes I was experiencing, and by the tests and scans, but in a way the staff seemed frightened too. Were they frightened at being confronted by a 54-year-old woman in the process of acquiring a diagnosis of Alzheimer's Disease, or was it to do with the sometimes fiercely hierarchical medical world they were working in? Whatever it was, there was a frightening feeling throughout the ward.

In this frightening environment, people were held in the singular position of being constantly restricted to their beds. My experiences as a psychotherapist, social worker, and nurse left me feeling that holding people in such a physically immobile posture reinforced the idea of being a patient and of being ill. I desperately wanted to improve the setting and felt more could be done to encourage a feeling of wellness. The physical immobilization reflected a wider emotional immobilization, with patients—and even staff—being held in an emotional posture of fear.

Perhaps one of the most frightening things that happened during my time in hospital was having a brain biopsy. It was put to me that there would be better information about how things were through using the biopsy to look at part of my brain. When I think back, I am not longer sure why I consented to the biopsy, or even whom I did it for. Did I do it for the doctors at the hospital? For science? For me? For something? If I could make that decision again, I would probably make a different decision. Should consent for such a procedure be asked for when someone is in such a frightened position?

Some of the staff did provide compassion alongside medicine. Compassion came in small gestures. One of the doctors always made a point of sitting by me, perhaps because I was the youngest person in the ward. I found this gesture very thoughtful, providing some acknowledgement of how I was as an individual. Even when going through a difficult time, compassion can be given through the way people speak and interact with you.

An explanation of my diagnosis of Alzheimer's Disease was eventually shared with me by a young registrar. This nice young man showed me the pictures of my brain captured on the scans, explaining the dots and markings that showed the difference between what my brain should be like and what it had become. Even though I didn't always understand it, it was important for me to try to understand what was happening and what my diagnosis was. Ultimately I needed to know the truth about what was happening to me so I would know what I had to work with.

The busybodies and the mediators

The diagnosis of Alzheimer's Disease brought many changes into my life, and one of those changes was starting to have new professionals enter my life. I had been entered into a system where I receive home-care visits on a daily basis from a range of carers who provide assistance with a range of daily tasks. For me it was difficult to be put into this system of care, and it is one I didn't really want to be taking part in. I have gone along with it, but it is not something that I wanted. I wanted just to be left by myself, but, along with Alzheimer's Disease, some decisions have become no longer about my needs alone. My husband wants to know I'm alright after he goes to work. We all have our worries, and when we have different concerns it's not easy, but he worries about the way I am, and this is why the carers come.

I don't mind having someone help me, although I can still do most things on my own. Sometimes I feel that there are others who might need carers more than me. I have noticed that despite my initial objections to this system, there are times when I don't mind the carer coming, and there are times when I find the carer very difficult. The difference in the experience of the carer is connected to a number of things, but in particular some carers give the impression of being busybodies, whereas others can act as mediators who work with me to negotiate this new reality.

The busybodies leave me feeling taken down a peg. Sometimes this is because the carer is a young woman who tells me what to do. I may indeed be difficult for these carers as I can do most things, and they are focused on completing a set of tasks through instruction. I feel put down, having these people younger than me telling me what to do. When you are capable of finding your own clothes, it is very difficult to be asked "Where are your socks?" The busybodies rush through in a hurry, disrupting my desire to start my day at my own pace. Having the carers come was something I would not choose, and the busybodies reinforce the sense that my choices are becoming less my own. I don't want to be case-worked. I want to just look out of the window if I want to.

Not only is having a busybody carer hard for me, but it is hard for the carer too. Being a busybody can define the relationship between the carer and the person receiving the care. When a carer starts pushing me around, I don't like it. The extent of our relationship is, "No thanks, I can do it myself." When I think about the relationships I had with people I worked with, I knew those people and, in comparison, I don't know these people at all. If I said to one of those girls, "What is it like for you?" she would just say, "What?" They don't want me to talk to them. I suppose somehow I actually feel insulted by it all. They talk to me like a child, and I don't like it. Some people even act as if I might be contagious, a thing to be handled carefully with rubber gloves.

I have a very different experience with the carers who are mediators. The mediators work with me in negotiating the world on my own terms. The carers find different ways in which to build a relationship with me so that this can happen; with one it is the reassurance of a friendly smile, while another uses humour. Finding a way to communicate makes the way for the relationship in which we can work together to do what needs to be done. With one carer we share a joke, in that I will call her "mother" as she comes to help me along. We can share a joke like this because this carer is confident in her own authority, does not compromise my own ability to make decisions, and is caring. Sharing a joke together lightens the situation for me—and for her, as being a carer can be a difficult job.

I was thought of as a mediator in my own professional life for the adolescents I worked with, but it does not mean I know what it takes to be a mediator. It may have been easier for me to be a mediator in that I only worked with people who chose to come to me, whereas I have not chosen to have these carers working with me. One possible difference between the busybodies and the mediators is being able to have empathy. To be able to mediate, you need both to know what it might be like for another person and to have an emotional connection to your job. To have empathy for those you work with means being able to consider their experience. Perhaps the busybodies find it difficult to confront the issues of change and loss when thinking about what Alzheimer's Disease might be like for others.

I've lost so much of my autonomy

I had a career that was reliant on language, and now my language is starting to fail me. I will be in the middle of talking, knowing exactly what I want to say, and end up babbling. One of the most terrible things is just my brain saying "I'm doing something else", and this is what I feel is happening when my words fail me. That's the main thing, in some ways; once you have lost your words, there's nothing. You can say, right I'm in control of this—but you are not. It is like losing autonomy over yourself when you lose your words. I have lost the autonomy that the full command over language can give.

In my working life I had a lot of autonomy and independence, and this loss of autonomy has spread through different dimensions of my life. The loss of autonomy started with the time I spent in hospital being assessed, feeling like I was redefined as a patient and confined to my bed. Since that time, my loss of autonomy is illustrated by the things I can no longer do, the things I need to ask for help with, and my changing abilities. In this sense, the carers that visit can represent the help I would like to not need. When they help with things I can do alone, it can be an affront to my continued efforts to maintain as much of my autonomy as I can.

Autonomy in my relationship with others has also changed. I now rely on my husband to act as an extension for my own memory and thinking. This means that there are times when he makes decisions that I do not necessarily agree with, despite the overwhelming support and strength he has shown. The fact I now rely on others, be it he or one of the carers who visit, to facilitate the expression of my autonomy is a compromise in itself, compared to the independence I am used to. My husband and I are now also known as the "carer and patient", which is a new title for us. Sometimes it is as if my diagnosis has merged us into a new singular unit. We now work more as a team, and he lets me use him as an extension of my memory.

You have to be able to bear the sorrow

Facing change is hard, particularly the changes that come with a progressive illness like Alzheimer's Disease. There are a number of things I have lost that have caused me great sadness. The first of these was stopping my work, and stopping my doctoral research. It was hard to give up something that meant so much, and it continues to be hard to accept the loss of some of my own abilities. I know that words are becoming harder to find and string together into the sentences I want to use to express myself. I am finding that there are times when my thoughts work better and times when they are slower. It is becoming more difficult to speak when I am trying to express myself quickly, as well as when I am trying to talk about issues of emotional significance for me. I also know my perception has been affected by Alzheimer's Disease, causing me difficulties with vision.

It has taken time to find a way to approach abilities that are declining. My instinct is to hold on to things that are becoming difficult to do, because I might never have that particular ability again. But then, on the other side, it is sometimes so hard to hold on, and it is so easy to leave it. Somewhere in the middle there is a balance in holding on to abilities while it is productive, but also knowing when to let go. I had wanted to learn how to play the piano, but as with so many new activities, to attempt them is to risk not being able to bear the potential sorrow that will come should I not be able to succeed.

The Alzheimer's outsider

"We are all fundamentally alone with our own experience and at the same time, willingly or unwillingly, but inevitably, an integral part of human groups: at work, in families, as citizens and members of the wider society."

Anna Dartington (1994, p. 91)

To have Alzheimer's is to be on the outside of wider society. This happens in many different ways. For me, the first move to the outer edges was leaving the world of work prematurely. The world of work provided such a concrete daily reality, and to leave it unexpectedly was a difficult adjustment.

Relationships with other people highlight the outsider aspect of Alzheimer's Disease. In relation to professionals we now have contact with, there is a sense of no longer trusting me to remember important things. Carers will speak to my husband as if I am not there, in order to pass on information. At one psychiatric appointment the psychiatrist asked me, do you know why you are here? I said, Yes, I've got Alzheimer's. He then asked me what I thought that to mean, and I described how there are tangles in your brain. He then put me outside in a chair—like this little Milly Molly Mandy—so he could speak to my husband. Even though he also spent time with me alone, I felt relegated to the outside of this exchange. I have even become an outsider to discussions about me.

Sometimes you are placed on the outside when others with no knowledge of Alzheimer's Disease try to understand your difficulties. For example, my walking has been affected, and if I happen to stumble some people think I have been drinking. If I need to take a seat, or rest, people cannot see my disability and may interpret my behaviour as pushiness or being lazy. Sometimes my difficulties are pointed out by others to my husband, as if I am not there. My age may compound this sense of being an outsider, as many people's experience of Alzheimer's Disease is that of older people—fathers, mothers, uncles, aunts—and not that of wives, husbands, sisters, brothers.

Something that reinforces the idea of being an outsider is when people only visit me in pairs, as if they are worried that something may happen or go wrong during a visit. People often visit only if my husband is also there, as if my individuality has been redefined into a comfortable pair, and this makes me feel terrible. Sometimes there is a sense that people are waiting for your demise. There are only windows into knowing what others think of the experience of Alzheimer's Disease and how it may have changed my life. These windows give a sense of me being an outsider in relation to wider society.

The now, the then, and the in-between

It has been a great disappointment to have this sort of stop in a sort of halfway life. I think, I feel, I wish I could have had the whole world, my whole brain, and I wish I could have used it more, so I was, in a way, stopped from something I was doing. I'm not bitter, but I realize it could just have been easier. Some of the things that have happened to me in my life might make other people feel sorry for me, and I wouldn't particularly want that to happen. In a way I'm becoming more secretive now; otherwise, I might have to tell people about my lost abilities or that I feel I didn't finish something in my life.

When I think about the future, I think mostly about dying. In a way, when I think about dying, it is as if it is just something that happens. The only thing to think about it is how it is going to happen, and all I can do is say that I want my husband to be with me and I want to be at home. We have sorted out as much as we can really. I am adamant that I want to die at home and not in hospital, in so much as that can be; there is no reason why that shouldn't happen. I have a feeling that I will know that I am going to die, before it happens. I've always expected that I would get quite a lot of headaches before something happens; that's just because I feel it in me, nobody's told me that. Once I had a friend who was helping me but she had to go home; my husband was out and I was on my own, and I started feeling like my head was a bit funny, that I had a headache. Even though I know I am not close to dying, headaches trigger feelings of fear about dying alone. On that day when I was on my own, I felt an overwhelming sense of being alone and even of being abandoned, and that I may never see people, like my friend who had had to leave, ever again.

Between now and death, there is the in-between, and while I'm okay now, I don't know for how much longer. I plan to carry on and try to have as much fun as I can. We have holidays to take in our special place in Greece. I want to have loveliness, all sorts of cakes and fine things. I have gained a deeper appreciation for the fine things in life, for flowers, the arrangement of colours, and humour. I think about writing poetry and am trying to find a way to do this, most likely with my husband's help. I also spend time feeling sad, and sometimes

I think about death. I work with a psychoanalyst to reflect on the feelings I have and the changes I am experiencing.

I think that when I first knew I had Alzheimer's, I was probably struggling with it. I think the difference now is that I know I can still do things. You could certainly say I've grown up. Before I was busy being clever and planning to do things, but then this struck me. I have had to learn to be patient and to let myself just be. This isn't always easy for me, but I am trying to just go with it. Despite the challenges of Alzheimer's Disease, my daily life continues in some very usual and familiar ways. I think, laugh, talk, garden; we have visitors; we travel. In many ways, life continues as it always has. While I have lost some things from my life, I retain much and plan to continue making the most of that.

I spend time reflecting on metaphor as a way of exploring my experiences and feelings. I saw a stem of flowers that reminded me of how it feels to have Alzheimer's. The stem had interesting leaves, which looked a little foreboding, and a subtle beautiful flower at the tip of the stem. When the flowers are nearly indistinguishable from the leaves, it reminds me of something I feel when people come and see me. Sometimes I know they know I have this thing and sometimes they don't, and I think that's how I feel: I'm a bit of this and a bit of that. I really can sit down and talk, and I also get terribly tired. I wonder if others can distinguish the leaves from the flower when they spend time with me.

I know my story hasn't finished yet. I may now need someone to work with me, to make another voice for me, so I can continue to tell my story. Working together with someone, I can tell my story in a way in which I can still be in it. Together we have told this story, and it worked, it worked really well.

Managing frustration

[*Anna continues to tell her story, and her husband continues to be her scribe. One aspect of living with Alzheimer's Disease is the increasing need to manage frustration, and he continues to note down Anna's comments for her. Here is part of how the story continues.*]

I just try and work it out really, there isn't much I can do, except to have these pills that I have, that I think are magic and are actually keeping me alive.

There was an odd thing that happened yesterday. It was like I described before, when the fox comes quickly.

When I was in the supermarket, what you were saying to me wasn't what I saw. Suddenly there was something I could not do, I could not have, I could not get then—a special washing liquid for my clothes.

This is the killer, where everything gets scrabbled—funny, I was playing scrabble when I lost it before. It was like that this morning again. I cannot even remember it now. It may be twisted—or it may be a good insight. I think you have seen both of those.

My eyes are a part of it. They are good. But people have not seen what I have seen. You are being the scribe of that.

It is always something down to earth. I was thinking, we had gone to the supermarket, which we did—I wanted the purple washing liquid they have there. I thought I heard you say it was not there. This is the desiccated brain. It is difficult to describe. The ordinary brain is easy to understand.

It is awful for you to think about it. You said the man over the road would have it. I did not understand.

It is possible—this is my good brain thinking—that this means something. I have had a good brain: it does come forth sometimes. Can we describe this to our friends, when we see them again?

Out there I was thinking about the purple washing liquid. It is not madness. It is confusion. It could go into madness. I hope it will not. When I am mad, I know I am mad. The thing that turned in my brain was that we went to that place (the supermarket) and we did not get the thing (the washing liquid).

The actual thing that we were party to, that got in my hair, the only good that it can bring, is that if we explain, some people could understand it.

I remember being in the hospital the first time, feeling like this, dreamy, worrying what was going to happen. This is the other side of what we are saying. Why can it not all be put together? Why can we not go to the supermarket now and get what we want? It is a real mix-up. Even you get mixed up.

I got in a muddle about the supermarket like the hospital, not liking the place, about the things that I cannot have . . . if we are going to be interpretative about myself. I could see in the hospital people struggling with their words, trying to get out of the prison.

I like going to the sea. I will not be like this then.

Was I in a fugue? If I said that, I was getting uppity. But it probably is what we are talking about. You are talking to somebody and you cannot connect. In a fugue, you are trying to get rid of something frightening. We want to get to the edge of talking about it, and this will be part of the book, I hope. It is not bad to jump into the madness if you can get out of it. But it is frightening, and I do not want to get further into it. I am trying to get the other things in perspective.

Some people would like to dissect all of this. But these are ordinary things. We did not have a row. You got my new glasses. The changing of the glasses has something to do with it. I wanted the new glasses desperately, and when I got them I was changed a bit. This is an odd way of talking. Others would think I was mad, but it gives an insight into what it is like. I have the insight because I have been through it. I cannot stand up and talk like before, but I think it is worth describing.

Let's get back into the world.

* * *

Anna Dartington wrote this in 2003–2004 and died on the 18th of May, 2007.

CHAPTER 17

Conveying the experience
of Alzheimer's Disease through art:
the later paintings of William Utermohlen

Patrice Polini

The world represented by the artist is a subjective world, the result of the specific story of an individual in permanent interaction with his internal and external environment. The last works of William Utermohlen, between 1990 and 2000, constitute a rare testimony to the processes of creativity and inner life of a patient suffering from Alzheimer's Disease. In this chapter, the reader will be able to follow the changes in his technique as it becomes increasingly affected by the symptoms of dementia as they unfold. These include:

• trouble with memory and concentration

• disorganization of temporal and spatial mental representation

• difficulty in recognizing objects and in understanding their function

• inability to make decisions or anticipate movement

• the gradual dimming of clear thought and judgement

These disorders will ultimately undermine the artist's technical abilities and render painting and drawing impossible in the end. The neuropathological aspects of William Utermohlen's late works are therefore a unique clinical journal of the evolution of the cognitive disorders of his disease. However, Utermohlen's late *oeuvre* is particularly precious in our view because it also constitutes the narrative of the artist's subjective experience of his illness. The images show the gradual modification of his perception of the world, both of his external environment and of his psychic universe. Through them, we share his terrible feeling of dereliction, progressive isolation, and loss of self-control. *Anosognosia*, the almost total unawareness by the patient of his symptoms, is a clinical characteristic of the state of Alzheimer's dementia. Considered at times as a defensive mechanism against the distress caused by an eroded self-image, it is also the consequence of a neurological disorder. In our opinion, Utermohlen's last works show that an awareness of his pathological disorders appears well before the medical diagnosis of dementia was established in 1995. This awareness also persists much longer than is usually believed. We feel it is the artist's ability to depict his experience of illness visually rather than verbally—to paint words—that allowed him to continue to represent his mental and sensorial condition for such a long period (1990–2000) through his art.

Artistic creation may, for William Utermohlen, also be an attempt at self-healing. By continuing to paint, the artist tries to fight off the process of psychic disorganization by maintaining the existential bearings of the painter and his sense of identity. We witness here a relentless struggle to preserve life through the creative process. To the extreme limits of his ability, he has succeeded in preserving his world, to depict himself so as not to disappear.

The conversation pieces

Premonition . . . to get one's bearings, to mend oneself

In a series of six paintings executed between 1990 and 1993 entitled "The Conversation Pieces", William Utermohlen described his immediate environment, perhaps in an attempt to mentally fix it. By inscribing it on canvas, perhaps he is trying to stop time and to maintain his spatial and temporal bearings. In *Maida Vale* [Figure 1], the artist paints his wife, Patricia, sitting across the dining-room table from one of her students. The central foreground is taken up by an empty chair. It leans to the left as if addressing us a sign. A sign of the artist's absence?

William was 62 years old when the diagnosis of Alzheimer's was established in November 1995. However, the first difficulties began

Figure 1.   *Maida Vale* 1990. Oil on canvas.

to appear four years earlier: trouble with remembering recent events, a tendency to gradually forget one thing after another, a constant looking for his belongings. On a trip to Paris, William was unable to find his way back to the apartment he was staying in after visiting the Louvre. Later he forgot to show up at appointments or his own art classes. He frequently lost his way when using public transport. His wife noticed he could no longer knot his tie, that he had trouble finding his words, reading the time, counting change. Faced with a vanishing present and an increasing difficulty in naming things, William fulfilled a need to in some way take stock, to make a spatial and temporal inventory of his world

The artist's jacket posed on the back of a chair in the foreground of *W9* [Figure 2] underlines his presence/absence in his world in the same way that the inclining chair did in *Maida Vale*.

Figure 2.   *W9* 1990. Oil on canvas.

The frozen image

All the scenes in the "Conversation Pieces" are set in the artist's apartment in central London and define its rich atmosphere. The titles all refer to space or time: the name of the district (*W9*) or neighbourhood he lives in (*Maida Vale*), the time of day (*Night* [Figure 4]), the season of the year (*Snow* [Figure 5]), the room in the house (*Bed* [Figure 6]), the event taking place (*Conversation* [Figure 3]). These are the spatial and temporal bearings he is trying to fix on the canvas. Like a snapshot, every painting seems to freeze the instant and suspend time so that its flow can be reversed. To seize things is to re-create what was a way of resisting the inexorable deterioration, the return to nothingness. The richly decorated and detailed interiors are rendered with great care and recreate the atmosphere of the artist's domestic environment: the pictures on the walls (many by him, old and recent), the fine furniture, his familiar objects. This domestic environment is paired in the paintings with an equally familiar exterior world composed of the views from the windows: the back gardens, the ducks paddling in the canal in front of the house.

The paintings have a powerful, sensory quality: along with the intense colours and visual stimuli of *W9*, the artist also evokes the sounds of voices of the conversing figures, the smell of cigarettes, the taste of coffee and wine, tactile sensations, the warmth of the room (see also *Night* and *Snow*). The paintings also convey specific emotional moments as we are confronted by the artist's closest circle of relations and friends. His wife, Patricia, who is an art historian, is the principal heroine of the paintings and of his life. She is represented absorbed in conversation with friends or pupils (*W9*). The relationships between the figures seem intimate and are sharply rendered. Their stories are silently narrated to us, and their emotional ties defined.

We can guess at the existence of a subtle range of emotions and complex affective relations (see also *Night*) that the artist perfectly analyses and reconstitutes for us. By knotting together in his compositions images, beings, objects, emotions, and symbols, the artist creates an envelope that is filled out with his whole personal world and that helps to preserve him from the creeping confusion he feels growing within. By transcribing on canvas the events of his daily life, his routine and his bearings, he may strengthen his ties to the world and inscribe on the paintings a visible trail through which his lost memory can find him. Like echo chambers of the his senses and emotions, the "Conversation Pieces" try to maintain an overall and coherent interpretation of reality in which William can continue to represent the world to us and to himself.

Introduction of time in the image

In *Conversation* [Figure 3], what are they talking about? Are they talking about art and its history, which is the passion of the artist's wife? What might be even more essential here is the wish to stay within the flow of language, which his wife has always represented, in his

Figure 3.   *Conversation* 1990–1991. Oil on canvas.

attempt to maintain an inner discourse that helps him to interpret reality. Soon the slowing down of the thinking process and the loss of the meaning of words will make him a stranger to verbal communication. Speaking will only induce helplessness and a feeling of estrangement, as even familiar words will become indecipherable riddles. These depictions of a silent narrative describe William's struggle to keep up with language, since language is the only way to make sense of and give meaning to life. Sensing he is about to lose language, he must recount his story in the paintings as the only way to give meaning to the flow of his life. Will the black cat pawing at Patricia in *Conversation*, perhaps representing his dependent self, be noticed by his mistress? Will she respond to his appeal?

The wind of oblivion

The wind of oblivion has risen and is threatening to carry all in its path. William seems to have entered the realm of Night. The skylight is cut up into three black rectangles, suspended above the figures like guillotine blades [Figure 4]. This is the first appearance of a death symbol we will see again. For the time being, seen from without, life goes on as usual. He wonders, perhaps, have his wife and friends not noticed anything? Can't they see that for him the world will never be the

Figure 4.   *Night* 1990–91. Oil on canvas.

same again? Can't they see that he is lost? Can't she see that she will lose him? The memory disorders get worse, and the inner perception of time falls apart. At the heart of William's familiar domestic world, at first insidiously and then more and more markedly, appear signs of disorganization and a disquieting strangeness. Space is dislocated as if taken over by a whirlwind, and the artist openly expresses his sense of disorientation in time in space. Points of bearing reel as the fishbowl floats up, perspectives unwind as the table rises, we tip over as the walls incline and we're overtaken by vertigo. Objects float away in all directions as if freed from the laws of gravity, with no apparent relation to each other or the space around them. Merely perceiving and naming them is now enough, organizing them is beyond the artist's capacity. The artist seems to be trying, as we have already seen in the earlier pictures, to freeze the events of his life, to suspend passing time, to re-establish its wholeness and continuity. In weaving together past, present, and future, he has tried to patch up the torn framework of his sense of time. But nothing can resist the acceleration of fleeting time. As in a clinical diary the pictures record the gradual failure to stop the process of inescapable deterioration of memory and reason.

The crushed world

In *Snow* [Figure 5], the artists represents himself for the first time in the "Conversation Pieces", and we can consider this work as the first self-portrait of a long series that will follow. He is seated on a couch holding his cat in his arms. He is isolated as if excluded from the world of the chatting figures on the left: a stranger to their discussion, their

Figure 5.   *Snow* 1991. Oil on canvas.

thoughts, their language, their words, and their emotions. The world has been flattened into a single plane. It is difficult to define what is up and what is down, to tell apart inside from out. Perception of difference has become very crude and is limited to violent contrasts of primary colour and simplified forms. Figurative definition verges on abstraction. All becomes alike. The figures foreshortened from above are hard to identify and seem no more important than the objects and the décor. As confusion and disorientation grow, the rational translation of sense perceptions is impeded. What was familiar and intimate becomes unrecognizable, as if overcome by the empty landscape out the windows—a strange and disquieting effect. The artist is now threatened by the appearance of a new world that is deserted: white and silent, like the snow outside. As if caught in ice his thinking gradually congeals, ideas and words disappear. His figure is almost animal-like, one foot posed on the ground but the other turned up as if to leave. The present doesn't register any more, only the past bursts in in spurts: in the mirror above the mantelpiece we see the reflection of an old friend who died a few years before. The gaping [green] door in the background opens twice into another world, that of death and oblivion.

The time of dreams

The artist is asleep in bed next to his wife [Figure 6]. The outside is no longer shown: we are in the intimacy of the bedroom, in the midst of the artist's inner world. Here we see the artist penetrate into a world of dreams. A world where waking reason is asleep, a world without causality or linear time. A moving, uncontrollable world with unstable surfaces. To the artist's world of dreams is opposed the world of knowledge, language, and reason, here embodied by the artist's wife absorbed in her reading. Verbal communication has become difficult, and the artist has the premonition that words will soon be no more than sound bites and random noise, as to a man sinking into sleep. Without words the only thing left will be to paint what he feels: fragmented memories of sense impressions whose intensity and organization are no longer controllable. *Bed* is a witness to the moment when words cease to give meaning to what is felt by the body before its object—when body and object become one. The artist shows himself only through his face, which he detaches from the body and projects into the mirror at bottom left. This is the last attempt to preserve the unity of the self, to fix an image of himself when physical and psychic

Figure 6.   *Bed* 1991. Oil on canvas.

self-consciousness becomes vague. *Bed* shows the silent space in which the artist will soon be locked up, deprived of words and content like the cats dozing on the bed to lead an almost organic existence, which we cannot imagine. Is he also showing us his fear of returning to maternal dependency, the utter regression and submission to another's will? The same [green] door as in *Snow* opens like a blade that will henceforth cut him off from reality. It is an opening into the unknown, darkness, and nothingness.

* * *

In 1993–94 William Utermohlen executed a series of lithographs to illustrate a book of ten poems by Wilfred Owen, the great British poet killed at the end the First World War. This is not the artist's first attempt to treat the theme of war, which also appears in the *Dante* and *Mummers* cycles of the 1960s and the *Vietnam* paintings of the early 1970s. But at this point in his life, his art is focused on a new emergency: the threat posed by the dissolution of meaning. By illustrating a text [Figure 7], he again tries to anchor himself in the language he has lost, the language of others, through which he hopes to transcribe

Happy are men who yet before they are
    killed
Can let their veins run cold. . . .

. . . And in the happy no time of his
    sleeping,
Death took him by the heart . . .

Figure 7.   Two of the lithographs illustrating Wilfred Owen's *Ten Poems*.

his own perceptions. The interpretation of reality becomes precarious, uncertain, and unstable. The process of the loosening of life ties has truly begun. The very composition of the image comes apart. Things destruct as they are drawn. The drawing process on a lithographic stone cannot be disguised as on an oil painting or erased as on paper. It is here entirely spontaneous and often genuinely uncertain and awkward. We can follow line by line the making of the image. All of William's subsequent works will be marked by this same expressive force, whereby the power of the work will rest as much on the artist's gesture, the trace of the creative process, rather than the exactitude of his drawing.

The traumatic moment. "I was getting out!"

A long fallow period followed the Wilfred Owen project. He accepted a commission for a family portrait but was unable to go beyond the initial stages. He spent long hours facing his easel doing nothing. Every action was a burden. Every brush mark on the canvas was immediately erased. Nothing takes on form any more. The background of the picture remained blank. A doctor diagnosed depression and prescribed a treatment that had no effect. A neurological diagnosis is then undertaken. In August 1995 a magnetic resonance imaging scan reveals generalized cerebral atrophy. Formal neuropsychological assessment showed a global cognitive deterioration, and the diagnosis of Alzheimer's Disease was made.

In *Blue Skies* [Figure 8] the artist bears witness to the announcement of his illness and his deterioration. Like an explosion or an implosion, the traumatic revelation of a deadly illness shatters the self's ability to see and think. The diagnosis of this ghastly psychic death before even real death produces a deep dread: the worst is confirmed, the end is now inexorable. What is shown here is a crossroads, a key moment, and a crossing over, after which the framework of the self dissolves. The will to life tips over and freezes like the studio skylight suspended above the artist in the picture. Time has stopped. Space is laid bare. All is extinguished. Action is suspended. Words and ideas are gone. Life

Figure 8.   *Blue Skies* 1995. Oil on canvas.

opens unto the steely-blue emptiness of a dreadful future: an obliterating hole poised above ready to suck him in. In order not to be engulfed by the darkness, he hangs unto the table like a shipwrecked man unto his raft; or like a painter holding unto his canvas. In order to survive he must be able to show this catastrophic moment; he must depict the unspeakable. Never before has a painting spoken so clearly of the ending of psychic life, the traumatism and desperate effort to continue to exist by continuing to depict the world.

* * *

The diagnosis is clear. The doctors are now testing his memory. They have asked him if he still knows the day, the month, the year, the place he is in. If he can still memorize a list of words. If he can still complete a simple subtraction, name ordinary objects, copy simple geometric shapes. The humiliation of failing to answer these simple questions shatters his self-confidence. Soon, he feels, he will be unable to answer any questions at all. All hope of a cure or even a stabilization of his condition is lost. Violently confronted by his own deterioration, the fall in his self-esteem is dizzying [Figure 9]. The wound to his vanity is so fierce that everything in him has broken into pieces. The self is associated to a broken, fragmented body. The self-image is dislocated, there is no sense left of a continuous identity. The ghostly figure to the right is like the drawn contour of a fallen corpse. A part of his life has been murdered.

Figure 9.   *Self-portrait with chair and geometric figure* 1996.

Face to face

William now knows the prognosis of his disease, and he knows that its disorders are irreversible. How does one go on living when confronted daily by deterioration and the death of self? In order to maintain a sense of continuity, an identity, and also as a way of bearing witness to his experience, the artist will execute a series of self-portraits over the period of the next four years until the total loss of his manual and psycho-perceptive abilities brings all painting and drawing to an end. The self-portrait tries to fix an image of the self, and to fill the breech that from now on separates the artist from himself. To paint oneself is a way of marking continuity and the passing of time. The experience of seeing one's own image in the mirror is a key moment in the development of one's personality. Calling forth one's double through the mirror reflection is usually a way of reducing the gap between the self and that strange other, and it lays the foundation for future identity models [Figure 10]. Through the self-portrait, William attempts to regain his experience of being present, the reality of his existence, however terrifying and tragic. He bears witness to his experience, and

Figure 10.   *Self-Portrait 1* 1996. Oil on paper.

we witness the poignant truth he shares with us: the world has shrunk as if behind prison bars. He is reduced to seeing life through a loophole in the form of a cleaver. All that is left, he seems to indicate, is to wait for the hour of his death sentence.

Mourning one's self

It is with great anguish that William watches himself disappear little by little every day. The artist mourns his lost self. His look [Figure 11] is empty of all hope, the centre of his pupil a blind spot. His reflection is coming apart, and he cannot put himself back together. The double in the mirror sends back a negative, a death-carrying image that he had hoped to escape. He's become a shadow of his old self, and only the clothes floating on the ghostly body still show the bright colours of life.

Cut away from the world

The scan imagery has cut up his head into slices. From what the doctors have told him, he has retained awareness that only an autopsy will allow a true diagnosis of his condition. The truth will be known

Figure 11.   *Self-portrait* 1996. Mixed media on paper.

Figure 12.   *Self-portrait with saw* 1997. Oil on canvas.

post mortem. This notion haunts him, and he speaks of it constantly to those close to him.

The vertical saw like a guillotine blade [Figure 12] symbolizes once more the approach of the prefigured death. It also points to that other death, that of his psyche. The split between what he feels, what he would like to do or say, and that which he is actually reduced to doing is each day greater. Not able to find himself within himself, he senses a stranger lurking at the heart of his being. It is an encounter with the unknown within. His possibilities of expression are no longer adequate to the extreme nature of his experience.

* * *

Forms are blurred. Motivation, attention, memory, visual recognition are disorganized and render all tasks uncertain and awkward. The artist now paints as if groping. In these portraits [Figure 13], sadness, anxiety, resignation, the feeling of feebleness, and the shame induced by this experience are depicted with a remarkable expressive precision despite the crusty paint surfaces and the uncertain drawing. What is captured here is the image at the centre of an emotion, emotion at its purest, strongest, and most exact. We are confronted by William's reality, immediate and intense, true beyond all attempts at a manufactured "realism". Capturing through a fugitive facial expression the instant of experience of a specific emotion is another way of freezing time. If his experience of time is now nothing but a disjointed sequence of superimposed moments, it is still possible to assign to every one of

Self portrait (yellow)   *Self portrait (green*

Figure 13.   *Self portraits* 1997. Oil on canvas.

these a singular sensation. Through the portraits the artist anchors his experience of the present to what is happening, to what he is doing, and to what he feels at the very moment of painting. He must continue recognizing himself. He must continue recognizing Pat, his wife, who takes care of him and on whom he now depends for all the motions of his daily life. He will paint a last portrait of her [Figure 14]. He gives her the blue eyes of lovers. Her lipstick smears as if he had just kissed her. How long will he still be able to tell her that he loves her?

Figure 14.   *Portrait of Patricia Utermohlen (Pat)* 1997. Oil on canvas.

Même quand nous sommes loin
  l'un de l'autre
Tout nous unit
	Even when we are far from
	  each other
	Everything unites us

Fais la part de l'écho
Celle du miroir
Celle de la chambre
  celle de la ville
Celle de chaque homme de chaque
  femme
Celle de la solitude
Et c'est toujours ta part
Et c'est toujours la mienne
Nous avons partagé
Mais ta part tu me l'as
  vouée
Et la mienne je te la voue
	You playing the part of an echo
	That of a mirror
	That of the bedroom
	  that of the town
	That of each man and each
	  woman
	That of solitude
	And it is always your part
	And it is always mine
	We shared
	But your part you have
	  dedicated to me
	And mine I dedicate to you

[Paul Eluard, Untitled, in *La Vie immediate*, 1967]

* * *

For the last time the artist picks up his brushes and his palette. Alone in the studio, he wants to experience again the old motions of painting. For the last time he wants to reconstruct a likeness [Figure 15]. He uses again the pose of the oldest self-portrait he's kept [Figure 16]. He was 22 years old at the time. He already had that same great, open gaze

Figure 15. *Self-portrait (with easel)* 1998. Oil on canvas.

Figure 16. *Self-portrait* 1955. Drawing on paper.

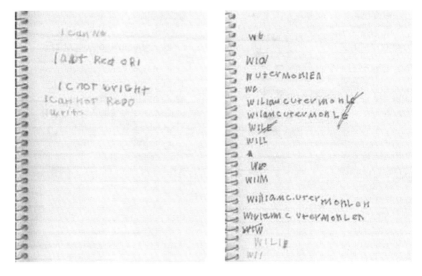

Figure 17.   Notebook of W. Utermohlen c. 1996

unto the world, that same perplexed and anxious, questioning note in facing himself and his future. But in the 1998 self-portrait, the architecture of his psyche is shot to pieces, something the artist now expresses and enshrines in the very act of portraying himself.

The artist's head is tightly framed by the rectangle of his easel. The red and yellow lines narrow into the shape of a guillotine. Let loose, the destructive forces split the space of the picture and break up this last portrayal of the self. All signs allowing the naming, the depiction, and the definition of the self disappear one by one. It will soon become impossible to sign his name at the bottom of the canvas. Very soon he will stop recognizing his name. [Figure 17.]

Effacement. The fleeting shadow

Time is no more but a sequence of instants. Time has devoured itself, and the drawing is erased as soon as it is drawn [Figures 18, 19]. The image changes and is dismantled as it is being structured. Neither totally present nor totally absent, the subject of the image is like a fleeting form constantly redrawn. The artist has assimilated his drawing method to his destiny: to subsist while disappearing. Perception can still call forth a primal image. But what emerges is also foreign and threatening to the artist's sense of self. A self-destructing construction: to preserve the self, the artist must constantly reconstruct it as he is tak-

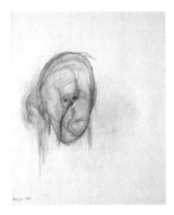 

Figure 18. *Self-portrait. 08. 30. 2000.*   Figure 19. *Erased Self-portrait* 2000.
                  Drawing on paper.   Oil on canvas.

ing it apart. He must constantly become an object that, by the nature of its condition, is vowed to disappear.

*   *   *

"Dust in the air is suspended
marks the place where a story ended."

T. S. Eliot, "Little Gidding"

These last coloured traces [Figures 20, 21] suggest a mask more than a portrait. Does the artist still want to depict and recognize himself? If that is the case, then his mode of representation is that of a negative hallucination, where what is perceived is immediately erased. There

Figure 20. *Mask* 2000.   Figure 21. *Mask* 2001.
Watercolour on paper.   Watercolour on paper.

is hardly anything left but painting the transition from being to non-being, painting the instant in which the self turns away from itself, melts away, leaving only silence behind. The last works of William Utermohlen constitute a clinical document that allows us to observe the evolution of the deterioration of the cognitive functions of a patient suffering from Alzheimer's dementia. They also show the long-term capacity of a creative process that allows the artist whose identificatory abilities are impaired to maintain a sense of self and a sense of presence in the world. We are grateful to William Utermohlen because he has succeeded in an exceptional—indeed, unique—way in depicting the reality and the pain of his experience of the disease. Through these images of pure feeling, the artist has managed to define and share with us the unspeakable suffering and sense of deterioration of a patient afflicted with dementia.

In regarding them, our whole being is moved—for a long time.

* * *

William Utermohlen was born on the 5th of December, 1933; he died on the 21st of March, 2007.

REFERENCES

Abraham, K. (1919). The applicability of psychoanalytic treatment to patients at an advanced age. In: *Selected Papers on Psychoanalysis*. London: Karnac, 1988.

Abraham, K. (1924) A short study of the development of the libido viewed in the light of mental disorders. In: *Selected Papers of Karl Abraham*. London: Hogarth Press.

Ainsworth, M., & Witting, B. (1969). Attachment and exploratory behaviour of one-year-olds in a strange situation. In: B. Foss, (Ed.), *Determinants of Infant Behavior, Vol. 4* (pp. 113–136). London: Methuen.

Alzheimer's Society (2007). *Dementia UK* [Report into the prevalence and cost of Dementia prepared by the Personal Services Research Unit (PSS-RU) at the London School of Economics and the Institute of Psychiatry at King's College London, for the Alzheimer's Society]. London.

Ames, D., Dolan, R., & Mann, A. (1990). The distinction between depression and dementia in the very old. *International Journal of Geriatric Psychiatry, 5* (3): 193–198.

Arden, M. (2002). Psychodynamic therapy. In: J. Hepple, J. Pearce, & P. Wilkinson (Eds.), *Psychological Therapies with Older People: Developing Treatments for Effective Practice*. Hove: Brunner-Routledge.

Arden, M., Garner, J., & Porter, R. (1998). Curious bedfellows: Psychoanalytic understanding and old age psychiatry. *Psychoanalytic Psychotherapy, 12:* 47–56.

Ashburner, C., Meyer, J., Cotter, A., Young, G., & Ansell, R. (2004). Seeing things differently: Evaluating psychodynamically informed group clinical supervision for general hospital nurses. *Journal of Research in Nursing, 9* (1): 38–48.

Ashburner, C., Meyer, J., Johnson, B., & Smith, C. (2004). Using action research to address loss of personhood in a continuing care setting. *Illness, Crisis and Loss, 12*: 23–37.

Auden, W. H. (1968). "Old People's Home." In: *Selected Poems*. London: Faber & Faber.

Audit Commission (1997). *The Coming of Age: Improving Care Services for Older People*. London.

Balfour, A. W. (1993). *Exploring the Experience of Dementia*. Unpublished paper, University College London.

Balfour, A. W. (1995). Account of a study aiming to explore the experience of dementia. *Psychologists' Special Interest Group in the Elderly Newsletter, 53*: 15–19.

Bell, D. (2006). Existence in time: Development or catastrophe. *Psychoanalytic Quarterly, 75* (3): 783–805.

Bender, M. (2003). *Explorations in Dementia: Theoretical and Research Studies into the Experience of Remediable and Enduring Cognitive Losses*. London: Jessica Kingsley.

Berrios, G. E. (1989). Non-cognitive symptoms and the diagnosis of dementia: Historical and clinical aspects. *British Journal of Psychiatry, 154*: 11–16.

Bick, E. (1987). Notes on infant observation in psychoanalytic observation. In: *Collected Papers of Martha Harris and Esther Bick*. Strath Tay: Clunie Press.

Biggs, S. (1994). Failed individualism and community care: An example from elder abuse. *Journal of Social Work Practice, 8* (2): 151–160.

Bion, W. R. (1961). *Experiences in Groups*. London: Tavistock.

Bion, W. R. (1962). *Learning from Experience*. London: Heinemann.

Bion, W. R. (1980). *Bion in New York and São Paulo*, ed. F. Bion. Perthshire: Clunie Press.

Birksted-Breen, D. (2003). Time and the après-coup. *International Journal of Psychoanalysis, 84*: 1501–1515.

Blanchard, M. R., Waterreus, A., & Mann, A. H. (1995). The effect of primary care nurse intervention upon older people screened as depressed. *International Journal of Geriatric Psychiatry, 10*: 289–298.

Bourestom, N., & Pastalan, L. (1981). The effects of relocation of the elderly. *The Gerontologist, 21*: 4–7.

Bowlby, J. (1969). *Attachment and Loss, Vol. 1: Attachment.* London: Hogarth Press.

Bowlby, J. (1973). *Attachment and Loss, Vol. 2: Separation, Anxiety and Anger.* London: Hogarth Press.

Britton, R. (1989) The missing link: Parental sexuality in the Oedipus complex. In: *The Oedipus Complex Today.* London: Karnac.

Brooker, D., Edwards, P., & Benson, S. (Eds.) (2004). *Dementia Care Mapping: Experiences and Insights into Practice.* London: Hawker Publications.

Bryden, C. (2005). *Dancing with Dementia: My Story of Living Positively with Dementia.* London/Philadelphia: Jessica Kingsley.

Bull, M. A. (1998). Losses in families affected by dementia: Coping strategies and service issues. *Journal of Family Studies, 4*: 187–199.

Burhouse, A. (1999). *Me, You and It: Conversations about the Significance of Joint Attention Skills from Cognitive Psychology, Child Development Research and Psychoanalysis.* Unpublished MA thesis, Psychoanalytic Observational Studies, Tavistock Clinic/University of East London.

Burns, A. (1990). Psychic phenomena in Alzheimer's disease. *British Journal of Psychiatry, 157*: 72–94.

Cabinet Office (2006). *Reaching Out: An Action Plan on Social Exclusion.* London.

Cantor, M. H. (1983). Strain among caregivers. *The Gerontologist, 23*: 597–604.

Caper, R. (1988). *Immaterial Facts: Freud's Discovery of Psychic Reality and Klein's Development of His Work.* London: Jason Aronson

Caper, R. (1999). *A Mind of One's Own: A Kleinian View of Self and Object.* London: Routledge.

Carson, J., Bartlett, H., & Croucher, P. (1991). Stress in community psychiatric nursing: A preliminary investigation. *Community Psychiatric Nursing Journal* (April).

Cattell, H., & Jolley, D. J. (1995). One hundred cases of suicide in elderly people. *British Journal of Psychiatry, 166* (4): 451–457.

Cheston, R. (1998). Psychotherapeutic work with people with dementia: A review of the literature. *British Journal of Medical Psychology, 71*: 211–231.

Cheston, R., & Bender, M. (1996). *Reframing the Non-Cognitive Symptoms of Dementia.* Unpublished paper, School of Social Sciences, Bath University.

Cheston, R., & Bender, M. (1999). Brains minds and selves: Changing conceptions of the losses involved in dementia. *British Journal of Medical Psychology, 72* (2): 203–216.

Clare, L. (2002). Developing awareness about awareness in early stage dementia: The role of psychosocial factors. *Dementia, 1*: 295–312.

Clare, L. (2003). Rehabilitation for people with dementia. In: B. A. Wilson (Ed.), *Neuropsychological Rehabilitation: Theory and Practice*. Lisse: Swets & Zeitlinger.

Clare, L. (2004). Awareness in early-stage Alzheimer's disease: A review of methods and evidence. *British Journal of Clinical Psychology, 43*: 177–196.

Clare, L., Baddeley, A., Moniz-Cook, E., & Woods, R. T. (2003). A quiet revolution. *The Psychologist, 16*: 250–254.

Clare, L., & Shakespeare, P. (2004). Negotiating the impact of forgetting: Dimensions of resistance in task-oriented conversations between people with dementia and their partners. *Dementia, 3* (2): 211–232.

Clare, L., & Woods, R. T. (2004). Cognitive training and cognitive rehabilitation in early-stage Alzheimer's Disease. *Neuropsychological Rehabilitation, 14*: 385–401.

Cohen, N. (1982). On loneliness and the ageing process. *International Journal of Psychoanalysis, 63*: 149–155.

Coltart, N. E. (1991). The analysis of an elderly patient. *International Journal of Psychoanalysis, 72*: 209.

Crisp, A. (Ed.) (2004). *Every Family in the Land: Understanding Prejudice and Discrimination against People with Mental Illness*. London: Royal Society of Medicine (available at: http://www.stigma.org/everyfamily).

Crutch, S. J., Isaacs, R., & Rossor, M. N. (2001). Some workmen can blame their tools: Artistic change in an individual with Alzheimer's disease. *Lancet, 357* (9274): 2129–2133.

Crutch, S. J., & Rossor, M. N. (2006). Artistic changes in Alzheimer's disease. *International Review of Neurobiology, 74*: 147–161.

Danermark, B., & Ekstrom, M. (1990). Relocation and health effects on the elderly: A commented research review. *Journal of Sociology and Social Welfare, 17* (1): 25–49.

Dartington, A. (1994). The significance of the outsider in families and other social groups. In: S. Box (Ed.), *Crisis at Adolescence: Object Relations Therapy with the Family*. Northvale, NJ: Jason Aronson.

Dartington, T. (2004). "Social Care and Social Death." Unpublished paper.

Davenhill, R. (1998). No truce with the furies. *Journal of Social Work Practice, 12*: 149–157.

de Beauvoir, S. (1972). *Old Age*. London: André Deutsch; Weidenfeld & Nicolson..

DOH (1997). *A New Partnership for Care in Old Age*. Cmnd. 3242. London: Stationery Office

DOH (2001a). *National Service Framework for Older People*. London: Department of Health.

DOH (2001b). *Treatment Choice in Psychological Therapies and Counselling. Evidence-based Clinical Practice Guidelines*. London: Department of Health.

DOH (2002). *Fair Access to Care Services*. London: Department of Health.

DOH (2003). *Investigation into Matters Arising from Care on Rowan Ward, Manchester Mental Health and Social Care Trust*. Commission for Health Improvement. London: Department of Health.

DOH (2004a). *Organising and Delivering Psychological Therapies*. London: Department of Health.

DOH (2004b). *Race Equality Action Plan*. London: Department of Health.

DOH (2005a). *Delivering Race Equality in Mental Health Care*. London: Department of Health.

DOH (2005b). *Securing Better Mental Health for Older Adults*. London: Department of Health.

Eluard, P. (1967). *La Vie immediate*. Paris: Gallimard.

Fabricius, J. (1991). Running on the spot or can nursing really change? *Psychoanalytic Psychotherapy, 5* (2).

Feil, N. (2003). *The Validation Breakthrough: Simple Techniques for Communication with People with Alzheimer's-type Dementia*. Baltimore, MD: Health Professions Press.

Feldman, M. (in press). The illumination of history. *International Journal of Psychoanalysis*.

Fengler, A. P., & Goodrich, N. (1979). Wives of elderly disabled men: The hidden patients. *The Gerontologist, 19*: 175–183.

Fertzinger, M. (1988). Alzheimer's disease and the mind/body problem. In: R. Mayeaux, B. Gurland, V. W. Barrett, A. H. Kutscher, L. E. Cote, & Z. H. Putter (Eds.), *Alzheimer's Disease and Related Disorders* (pp. 68–83). Springfield, IL: Charles C Thomas.

Fonagy, P., Steele, M., Moran, G., Steele, H., & Higgitt, A. (1993). Measuring the ghost in the nursery: An empirical study of the relation between parents' mental representations of childhood experiences and their infants' security of attachment. *Journal of the American Psychoanalytical Association, 41*: 957–989.

Fraiberg, S., Adelson, E., & Shapiro, V. (1975). Ghosts in the nursery: A psychoanalytic approach to the problem of impaired mother–infant relationships. *Journal of the American Academy of Child Psychiatry, 14*: 387–422.

Frampton, M. (2003). Experience assessment and management of pain in people with dementia. *Age and Ageing, 32*: 248–251.

Freud, S. (1905a). On psychotherapy. *Standard Edition, 7.*

Freud, S. (1914d). On the history of the psycho-analytic movement. *Standard Edition,* 14

Freud, S. (1917e [1915]). Mourning and melancholia. *Standard Edition, 14.*

Freud, S. (1923b). *The Ego and the Id. Standard Edition, 19.*

Freud, S. (1933a). *New Introductory Lectures on Psycho-Analysis. Standard Edition,* 22.

Freud, S. (1940 [1938]). *An Outline of Psycho-Analysis. Standard Edition, 23.*

Froggatt, A. (1988). Self awareness in early dementia. In: B. Gearing, M. Johnson, & T. Heller (Eds.), *Mental Health Problems in Old Age* (pp. 131–139). London: Wiley.

Garelick, A. (1994). Psychotherapy assessment: Theory and practice. *Psychoanalytic Psychotherapy, 8* (2): 101–116.

Garland, C. (2002). *Understanding Trauma: A Psychoanalytic Approach.* London: Karnac.

Garner, J. (1997). Dementia: An intimate death. *British Journal of Medical Psychology, 70:* 177–184.

Garner, J. (2004). Dementia. In: S. Evans & J. Garner, *Talking Over the Years: A Handbook of Dynamic Psychotherapy with Older Adults* (pp. 215–231). New York/London: Brunner-Routledge.

Gay, P. (1988). *Freud: A Life for Our Time.* London: Dent.

Gilhooly, M. L. M. (1986). Senile dementia: Factors associated with caregiver's preference for institutional care. *British Journal of Medical Psychology, 59:* 165–172.

Gillespie, L. D., Gillespie, W. J., Robertson, M. C., Lamb, S. E., Cumming, R. G., & Rowe, B. H. (2003). Interventions for preventing falls in elderly people. *Cochrane Database of Systematic Reviews, 4:* CD000340.

Graves, R. (1955). *The Greek Myths.* Harmondsworth: Penguin, 1996.

Grosclaude, M. (1987). Le dément sénile. Un sujet perdu, un sujet (re)trouvable? *Psychologie Médicale, 19* (8): 1267–1269.

Grotjahn, M. (1940). Psychoanalytic investigation of a seventy-one year old man with senile dementia. *Psychoanalytic Quarterly, 9:* 80–97.

Gubrium, J. S. (1987). Structuring and destructuring the course of illness: The Alzheimer's disease experience. *International Journal of Geriatric Psychiatry, 10:* 289–298.

Hausman, C. (1992). Dynamic psychotherapy with elderly demented patients. In: G. M. Jones & B. M. Miesen (Eds.), *Care Giving in Dementia.* London: Routledge.

Heimann, P. (1950). On counter-transference. *International Journal of Psychoanalysis, 31* (1/2): 81–84.

Hess, N. (1987). King Lear and some anxieties of old age. *British Journal of Medical Psychology*, *60*: 209–216.

Hess, N. (2004). Loneliness in old age: Klein and others. In: S. Evans & J. Garner (Eds.), *Talking over the Years: A Handbook of Dynamic Psychotherapy with Older Adults* (chap. 2). Hove: Brunner-Routledge.

Hildebrand, P. (1982). Psychotherapy with older patients. *British Journal of Medical Psychology*, *55*: 19–28.

Hildebrand, P. (1986). Dynamic psychotherapy with the elderly. In: I. Hanley & M. Gilhooly (Eds.), *Psychological Therapies for the Elderly*. London: Croom Helm.

Hill, A., & Brettle, A. (2004). *Counselling Older People: A Systematic Review*. Rugby: British Association for Counselling and Psychotherapy.

Hinshelwood, R. D. (1991). Psychodynamic formulation in assessment for psychotherapy. *British Journal of Psychotherapy*, *8* (2): 166–174.

Hinshelwood, R. D., & Skogstad, W. (2000). *Observing Organisations: Anxiety, Defence and Culture in Health Care*. London: Routledge.

Holman, C., & Jackson, S. (2001). A team education project: An evaluation of a collaborative education and practice development in a continuing care unit for older people. *Nurse Education Today*, *21*: 97–103.

Husband, H. J. (2000). Diagnostic disclosure in dementia: An opportunity for intervention? *International Journal of Geriatric Psychiatry*, *15* (6): 544–547.

Isler, A. (1996). *The Prince of West End Avenue*. London: Vintage.

Jaques, E. (1965). Death and the mid-life crisis. *International Journal of Psychoanalysis*, *46*: 502–514.

Joseph Rowntree Foundation (2004). *Black and Minority Ethnic Older People's Views on Research Findings*.

Junkers, G. (Ed.) (2006). *Is It Too Late? Key Papers on Psychoanalysis and Ageing*. London: Karnac.

King, P. (1974). Notes on the psychoanalysis of older patients: Reappraisal of the potentialities for change during the second half of life. *Journal of Analytical Psychology*, *19*: 22–37.

King, P. (1980). The life cycle as indicated by the nature of the transference in the psychoanalysis of the middle-aged and elderly. *International Journal of Psychoanalysis*, *61* (2): 153–160.

King, P. (1999) "In the end is my beginning"—T. S. Eliot. In: D. Bell (Ed.), *Psychoanalysis and Culture: A Kleinian Perspective*. London: Duckworth. Reprinted London: Karnac, 2004.

Kingman, S. (1991). The sweet smell of less stress. *The Independent on Sunday*, 5 May.

Kitwood, T. (1988). The contribution of psychology to the understanding of dementia. In: B. Gearing, M. Johnson, & T. Heller (Eds.), *Mental Health Problems in Old Age*. London: Wiley.

Kitwood, T. (1989). Brain, mind and dementia, with particular reference to Alzheimer's disease. *Ageing and Society, 10*.

Kitwood, T. (1990a). Explaining senile dementia: The limits of neuropsychological research. *Free Associations, 10*: 117–140.

Kitwood, T. (1990b). Psychotherapy and dementia. *British Psychological Society, Psychotherapy Section Newsletter, 8* (June): 40–56.

Kitwood, T. (1990c). Understanding senile dementia: A psychobiographical approach. *Free Associations, 19*: 60–76.

Kitwood, T. (1997). *Dementia Reconsidered: The Person Comes First*. Milton Keynes: Open University Press.

Kitwood, T., & Bredin, K. (1994). *Evaluating Dementia Care: The Dementia Care Mapping Method*. Bradford: Bradford University Dementia Group.

Klein, M. (1935). A contribution to the psychogenesis of manic-depressive states. In: *Love, Guilt and Reparation and Other Works 1921–1945*. London: Hogarth Press, 1975.

Klein, M. (1936). "Aspects of the Transference Situation". Unpublished paper. London: The Wellcome Library for the History and Understanding of Medicine, Melanie Klein Archive, ref. PP/KLE/C52. [In: P. Roth, & R. Rusbridger (Eds.), *Encounters with Melanie Klein: Selected Papers of Elizabeth Spillius*. New Library of Psychoanalysis. London: Routledge, in press.]

Klein, M. (1940). Mourning and its relation to melancholia. In: *Love, Guilt and Reparation and Other Works 1921–1945*. London: Hogarth Press, 1975.

Klein, M. (1946). Notes on some schizoid mechanisms. In: *Envy and Gratitude and Other Works 1946–1963*. London: Hogarth Press, 1984.

Klein, M. (1957). Envy and gratitude. In: *Envy and Gratitude and Other Works 1946–1963*. London: Hogarth Press, 1984.

Klein, M. (1963). On the sense of loneliness. In: *Envy and Gratitude and Other Works 1946–1963*. London: Hogarth Press, 1984.

LaBarge, E. (1981). Counselling patients with senile dementia of the Alzheimer type and their families. *Personnel and Guidance Journal, 60*: 139–143.

Laufer, E. (2003). The body as internal object. *Bulletin of the British Psychoanalytical Society, 36*: 5.

Lawlor, D. A., Patel, R., & Ebrahim, S. (2003). Association between falls in elderly women and chronic diseases and drug use: Cross sectional study. *British Medical Journal, 327* (7417): 712–717.

Lewis, R. (1998). The impact of marital relationship on the experience of caring for an elderly spouse with dementia. *Ageing and Society, 18*: 209–231.

Lyman, K. (1989). Bringing the social back in: A critique of the biomedicalization of dementia. *The Gerontologist, 29* (5).

Mace, N. L., & Rabins, P. V. (1985). *The 36-Hour Day*. London: Hodder & Stoughton, with Age Concern.

Main, T. F. (1968). The ailment. In: E. Barnes (Ed.), *Psychosocial Nursing: Studies from the Cassel Hospital*. London: Tavistock Publications.

Malan, D. (1978). *Towards the Validation of Dynamic Psychotherapy*. New York: Plenum Press.

Malan, D. (1979). *Individual Psychotherapy and the Science of Psychodynamics*. London: Butterworth.

Mann, A. H., Graham, N., & Ashby, D. (1984). Psychiatric illness in residential homes for the elderly: A survey in one London borough. *Age and Ageing, 13* (5): 257–265.

Martindale, B. (1989). Becoming dependent again: The fears of some elderly persons and their younger therapists. *Psychoanalytic Psychotherapy.* 4 (1): 67–75.

Martindale, B. (1998). On dying, death and eternal life. *Psychoanalytic Psychotherapy.* 12 (3): 259–270.

McEwan, I. (2005). *Saturday*. London: Jonathan Cape.

McFadyean, M. (2005). Losing our minds. *Weekend Guardian*, 20 August.

McKenzie-Smith, S. (1992). A psychoanalytical observational study of the elderly. *Free Associations, 3* (27): 355–389.

Meacher, M. (1972). *Taken for a Ride*. London: Longman.

Menzies, I. (1959). The functioning of social systems as a defence against anxiety: A report on a study of the nursing service of a general hospital. In: I. Menzies-Lyth, *Containing Anxiety in Institutions: Selected Essays, Vol. 1* (pp. 43–85). London: Free Association Books, 1988.

Menzies, I. E. P. (1960). A case study in the functioning of social systems as a defence against anxiety. *Human Relations, 13*.

Menzies, I. E. P. (1973). Action research in a long-stay hospital. In: *Containing Anxiety in Institutions: Selected Essays, Vol. 1* (revised edition, pp. 130–207), ed. I. Menzies-Lyth. London: Free Association Books, 1988.

Menzies, I. E. P. (1989). Recruitment into the London Fire Brigade. In: *The Dynamics of the Social: Selected Essays, Vol. 2* (chap. 7). London: Free Association Books.

Miessen, B. (1993). Alzheimer's disease, the phenomenon of parent fixation and Bowlby's attachment theory. *International Journal of Geriatric Psychiatry 8* (2): 147–153.

Mills, M. A., & Coleman, P. G. (1994). Nostalgic memories in dementia: A case study. *International Journal of Aging and Human Development, 38* (3): 203–219.

Milton, J. (1997). Why assess? Psychoanalytical assessment in the NHS. *Psychoanalytical Psychotherapy, 11* (2): 47–58.

Money-Kyrle, R. (1968). Cognitive development. *International Journal of Psychoanalysis, 49*: 691–698.

Money-Kyrle, R. (1971). The aim of psychoanalysis. *International Journal of Psychoanalysis, 52*: 103–106. Reprinted in: *The Collected Papers of Roger Money-Kyrle* (pp. 442–449). Perthshire: Clunie Press, 1978.

Morris, L. W., Morris, R. G., & Britton, P. G. (1988a). The relationship between marital intimacy, perceived strain and depression in spouse caregivers of dementia sufferers. *British Journal of Medical Psychology, 61*: 231–236.

Morris, L. W., Morris, R. G., & Britton, P. G. (1988b). Factors affecting the emotional wellbeing of the caregivers of dementia sufferers. *British Journal of Psychiatry, 153*: 147–156.

Murphy, M., Glaser, K., & Grundy, E. (1997). Marital status and long-term illness in Great Britain. *Journal of Marriage and the Family, 5*: 156–164.

Murray, H. A. (1943). *Thematic Apperception Test Manual.* Cambridge, MA: Harvard University Press.

National Institute for Mental Health England (2003). *Inside Outside: Improving Mental Health Services for Black and Minority Ethnic Communities in England.*

NHS Executive (1996). *NHS Psychotherapy Services in England: Review of Strategic Policy.* London: Department of Health.

NICE (2004). *Scope Guidelines for Treatment and Care of People with Dementia.* London: National Institute for Clinical Excellence.

NICE (2006). *Dementia: Supporting People with Dementia and Their Carers in Health and Social Care. NICE Clinical Guideline 42.* London: National Institute for Clinical Excellence.

Nightingale, F. (1860). *Notes on Nursing: What It Is, And What It Is Not* (2nd edition). New York: Dover Publications, 1969.

Novick, L. J. (1967). Easing the stress on moving day. *Hospitals, 4*: 64–75.

Obholzer, A. (1989). Psychoanalysis and the political process. *Psychoanalytic Psychotherapy, 4* (1): 55–66.

Obholzer, A. (2000) Preface. In: R. D. Hinshelwood & W. Skogstad (Eds.),

Observing Organisations: Anxiety, Defence and Culture in Health Care. London: Routledge.

Owen, W. (1994). "Ten Poems." In: *Wilfred Owen: The War Poems*, ed. J. Stallworthy. London: Chatto & Windus.

Parkes, C. M. (1972). *Bereavement: Studies of Grief in Adult Life.* London: Tavistock Publications.

Patalan, L. (1981). The effects of relocation of the elderly. *The Gerontologist, 21.*

Phinney, A. (2002). Fluctuating awareness and the breakdown of the illness narrative in dementia. *Dementia, 1*: 329–344.

Pincus, L. (1976). *Death and the Family: The Importance of Mourning.* London: Faber & Faber.

Pollock, G. H. (1982). On ageing and psychopathology. *International Journal of Psychoanalysis, 63*: 275–281.

Pratt, R., & Wilkinson, H. (2003). A psychosocial model of understanding the experience of receiving a diagnosis of dementia. *Dementia, 2*: 181–199.

Quinodoz, D. (1992). The psychoanalytic setting as the instrument of the container function. *International Journal of Psychoanalysis, 73*: 627–635.

Rey, H. (1994a). The psychodynamics of depression. In: *Universals of Psychoanalysis in the Treatment of Psychotic and Borderline States.* London: Free Association Books.

Rey, H. (1994b). *Universals of Psychoanalysis in the Treatment of Psychotic and Borderline States.* London: Free Association Books.

Richardson, P. H., McPherson, S., Carlyle, J., Taylor, D., Campbell, A., & Shapiro, D. (in press). A randomised trial of individual psychoanalytic psychotherapy.

Riviere, J. (1952). The unconscious fantasy of an inner world reflected in literature. In: *The Inner World of Joan Riviere: Collected Papers 1920–1958*, ed. A. Hughes. London: Karnac, 1991

Robertson, C., Warrington, J., & Eagles, J. (1993). Relocation mortality in dementia: The effects of a new hospital. *International Journal of Geriatric Psychiatry, 8* (6): 521–525.

Robertson, J., & Robertson, J. (1967–1971). *Young Children in Brief Separation.* Film Series. London/New York: Tavistock Institute of Human Relations & New York University Film Library.

Roth, A., & Fonagy, P. (Eds.) (1996). *What Works for Whom? A Critical Review of Psychotherapy Research* (2nd edition). New York: Guilford Press, 2004.

Roy, A. (1997). *The God of Small Things.* London: Flamingo.

Royal Commission on Long Term Care (1999). *With Respect to Old Age: Long Term Care—Rights and Responsibilities.* Cmnd 4192-I. London: Stationery Office.

Rustin, M. E., Rhode, M., Dubinsky, A., & Dubinsky, H. (Eds.) (1997). *Psychotic States in Children.* London: Duckworth. Reprinted London: Karnac, 2002.

Rustin, M. E., & Trowell, J. (1991). Developing the internal observer in professionals in training. *Infant Mental Health Journal, 12* (3): 233–245.

Rustin, M. J. (1989). Observing infants: Reflections on methods. In: L. Miller, M. Rustin, M. Rustin, & J. Shuttleworth, *Closely Observed Infants.* London: Duckworth.

Salzberger-Wittenberg, I. (1970). Anxieties related to loss and mourning. In: *Psychoanalytic Insight and Relationships: A Kleinian Approach.* London: Routledge & Kegan Paul.

Sandler, A. M. (1978). Problems in the psychoanalysis of an ageing narcissistic patient. *Journal of Geriatric Psychiatry, 11:* 5–36.

Schmid, A. H. (1990). Dementia, related disorders and old age: Psychodynamic factors in diagnosis and treatment. *American Journal of Psychoanalysis, 50:* 253–262.

Schore, A. N. (2001). The effects of a secure attachment relationship on right brain development, affect regulation, and infant mental health. *Infant Mental Health Journal, 22:* 7–66.

Schulz, R., & Brenner, G. (1977). Relocation of the aged: A review and theoretical analysis. *Journal of Gerontology, 32* (1): 323–333.

Schur, M. (1972). *Freud Living and Dying.* New York: International Universities Press.

Sebald, W. G. (1996). *The Emigrants.* London: Vintage.

Segal, H. (1958). Fear of death: Notes on the analysis of an old man. *International Journal of Psychoanalysis, 39:* 178–181.

Sinason, V. (1992). The man who was losing his brain. In: *Mental Handicap and the Human Condition: New Approaches from the Tavistock.* London: Free Association Books.

Steiner, J. (1997). Introduction. In: H. Segal, *Psychoanalysis, Literature and War.* London: Routledge.

Stern, J., & Lovestone, S. (2000). Therapy with the elderly: Introducing psychodynamic psychotherapy to the multidisciplinary team. *International Journal of Geriatric Psychiatry 15:* 500–505.

Strachey, J. (1934). The nature of the therapeutic action of psychoanalysis. *International Journal of Psycho-Analysis, 15:* 127–159.

Terry, P. (1997). *Counselling the Elderly and Their Carers.* London: Macmillan.

Thomas, R. S. (1995). "No Truce with the Furies." In: *Collected Later Poems: 1988–2000*. Highgreen: Bloodaxe Books, 2004.

Timmins, N. (1995). *The Five Giants: A Biography of the Welfare State*. London: HarperCollins.

Toibin, C. (1992). *The Heather Blazing*. London: Picador.

Tress, K. (2003). Looking into later life: Psychodynamic observation and old age. *Psychoanalytic Psychotherapy, 17*: 253–266.

Waddell, M. (1998). *Inside Lives: Psychoanalysis and the Growth of the Personality*. London: Duckworth. [Second edition reprinted London: Karnac, 2002.]

Walker, V. (1999). Psychotherapy with older adults: The Scottish scene. *British Confederation of Psychotherapists Newsletter* (January).

Weiner, M. B. (1988). Tuning in, tuning out: Clinical observations of interactions between patients with Alzheimer's disease and others. In: R. Mayeaux, B. Gurland, V. W. Barrett, A. H. Kutscher, L. E. Cote, & Z. H. Putter (Eds.), *Alzheimer's Disease and Related Disorders* (pp. 68–83). Springfield IL: Charles C Thomas.

Whooley, M. A., Kip, K. E., Cauley, J. A., Ensrud, K. E., Nevitt, M. C., & Browner, W. S. (1999). Depression, falls, and risk of fracture in older women: Study of Osteoporotic Fractures Research Group. *Archives of Internal Medicine, 159* (5): 484–490.

Winnicott, D. W. (1949). Hate in the countertransference. In: *Through Paediatrics to Psycho-Analysis*. London: Hogarth Press, 1978.

Winnicott, D. W. (1956). Primary maternal preoccupation. In: *Through Paediatrics to Psychoanalysis*. London: Hogarth Press, 1958.

Winnicott, D. W. (1960). The theory of the parent–infant relationship. In: *The Maturational Processes and the Facilitating Environment*. London: Hogarth Press, 1965.

Winterson, J. (1997). *Gut Symmetries*. London: Granta.

Wollheim, R. (2004). *Germs: A Memoir of Childhood*. London: Waywiser Press.

Woodham-Smith, C. (1950). *Florence Nightingale 1810–1910*. London: Constable.

Woods, P., & Ashley, J. (1995). Simulated presence therapy: Using selected memories to manage problem behaviours in Alzheimer's Disease patients. *Geriatric Nursing, 16*: 9–14.

Woods, R. (1996). Effectiveness of psychological interventions with older people. In: A. Roth & P. Fonagy (Eds.), *What Works for Whom? A Critical Review of Psychotherapy Research* (2nd edition, pp. 224–446). New York: Guildford Press, 2004.

Woods, R. T., Phibbs, E., & Steele, H. (2000). "Attachment and Care-giving in Dementia." Paper presented at the BPS PSIGE Annual Conference, Birmingham.

Wright, L. (1991). The impact of Alzheimer's disease on the marital relationship. *The Gerontologist, 31*: 224–326.

Wright, L. (1994). Alzheimer's Disease afflicted spouses who remain at home: Can human dialectics explain the findings? *Social Sciences and Medicine, 3* (8): 1037–1046.

INDEX